HOMOSEXUALITY

**Lesbians and Gay Men
in Society, History and Literature**

This is a volume
in the Arno Press collection

HOMOSEXUALITY

Lesbians and Gay Men
in Society, History and Literature

General Editor
JONATHAN KATZ

See last pages of this volume
for a complete list of titles

DESPISED & REJECTED

BY

A. T. FITZROY

ARNO PRESS

A NEW YORK TIMES COMPANY

New York — 1975

Editorial Supervision: LESLIE PARR

———◆———

Reprint Edition 1975 by Arno Press Inc.

Copyright © 1917 by C. W. Daniel, Ltd.
Reprinted by permission of C. W. Daniel, Ltd.

Reprinted from a copy in
  The University of Illinois Library

HOMOSEXUALITY: Lesbians and Gay Men in
Society, History and Literature
ISBN for complete set: 0-405-07348-8
See last pages of this volume for titles.

Manufactured in the United States of America

———◆———

Library of Congress Cataloging in Publication Data

Allatini, R
    Despised & rejected.

    (Homosexuality)
    Reprint of the ed. published by C. W. Daniel,
London.
    I. Title. II. Series.
PZ3.A418D48 [PR6001.L56]   823'.9'12   75-12314
ISBN 0-405-07389-5

DESPISED
AND
REJECTED

DESPISED & REJECTED

BY

A. T. FITZROY

LONDON : C. W. DANIEL, LTD.

Graham House, Tudor Street, E.C.4.

CAHILL AND CO., LTD., PRINTERS, LONDON AND DUBLIN.

TO YOU

WHO MADE ME UNDERSTAND

PART I.

DESPISED AND REJECTED

CHAPTER I

"WHAT I like about these small places," remarked Mrs. Blackwood as she seated herself at
one of the tea-tables in the lounge of the Amberhurst Private Hotel, "is that everybody gets to
know everybody else quite informally, and that is
such a blessing for the young people."

"Do you really think so?" queried Hester
Cawthorn. It amused her to draw the older woman
out. Mrs. Blackwood herself did not interest
Hester at all; but Mrs. Blackwood as a type—the
well-to-do, conventional, provincial type—interested
her very much indeed. She could picture Mrs.
Blackwood, queening it in her home-surroundings,
the chatty little country town of Eastwold; near
enough to London to allow Mr. Blackwood to travel
up and down every day, and far enough removed
from the metropolis to form a world to itself; a
small and very gregarious world, no doubt, in which
everybody certainly knew all about everybody else's
business, and minded it in preference to their own.

Hester was not gregarious. In the dining-room,
she sat alone at her small table, politely but firmly
declining the manageress's good-natured offer to
"find some company for her." Hester preferred
her own company, both during meals, and on her

long walks into the surrounding country. When all the hotel visitors, grouped according to their affinities, were seated upon the lawn, Hester would sit alone, reading; or armed with a masculine-looking walking-stick, and the brim of her felt hat turned down to shade her thin sombre face, would stalk off in the direction of the hills that formed a humped barrier upon the sky-line. At the end of a fortnight's stay, Mrs. Blackwood who, true to the traditions of Eastwold, had discovered the leading features of interest in the lives of everyone else in the hotel, was still no wiser about Hester.

She smiled now in answer to her question. "Why, yes, of course it's a blessing. I think the company one is in makes all the difference to one's enjoyment of a holiday—we always take ours in June, as Mr. Blackwood's partner has to have his in August." Mrs. Blackwood was as eager to impart information concerning herself and her family, as she was to elicit it from others. "Are you making a long stay, Miss Cawthorn?"

"Possibly; I don't know." Hester spoke with perfect courtesy, though her tone implied that she was quite decided as to her future plans, but wished to discourage enquiries regarding them.

"You've only been here a short while?"

"Comparatively speaking."

Mrs. Blackwood abandoned the attack for the moment, and continued: "The children love it here, and even Ottilie seems to be enjoying herself, though of course it's rather difficult for her."

"Is that the little German girl who is staying with you?"

"Yes. It's an exchange, you see. Herr Baumgartner is a business-connection of my

husband's, and Ottilie has been with us for nearly
six months, learning English. Next year, Doreen
is to go back with her to Heidelberg to study
German. She's a dear child, but her English isn't
very grand yet, though I'm glad to say that Mr.
Griggs has given her a part in the theatricals in
spite of it."

"He must be a very indulgent stage-manager."

"Oh, he's charming, I assure you. At home at
Eastwold, he's the life and soul of the place, just
as he is here; he always tries to join us, even if it's
only for a week, when we're on our summer
holiday."

At this juncture, the swing-doors leading into the
recreation-room were flung open, and the life and
soul of Eastwold, wearing velvet knee-breeches and
a tricolor waistcoat, burst into the lounge.

"Mrs. Blackwood—Miss Cawthorn—what do you
think has happened? Miss Wright has suddenly
been called away, and now there's no one to play the
incidental music for us to-night.   I wonder if
either of you two ladies——" tentatively Mr. Griggs
glanced at Hester, of whom he was very much in
awe.

She shook her head, and Mrs. Blackwood replied :
"Oh, you know I'm no good at the piano, Mr.
Griggs. Dennis has monopolised all the musical
talent there is in our family, and I'm afraid he won't
be here till too late. Can't you get on without the
music?"

"Why, the music's half the battle!" wailed
Griggs, whose neat little moustache, neat little
features, pince-nez, and hair growing rather thin
on top, accorded strangely with his dashing costume.
"It lends atmosphere—dignity.   We can't have

Marry Anto'nett guillotined without a soft musical accompaniment. It makes all the difference, you know."

"Most unfortunate, isn't it?" Mrs. Blackwood invited Hester's commiseration, " of course Doreen strums the piano a little, but she's in the play. I do wonder if Dennis——"

"You can bet your boots that Dennis won't!" A twelve-year-old schoolboy suddenly thrust his head through the swing-doors, "and anyway if he did, he'd play mouldy sort of stuff. He always does."

"Oh, Reggie," his mother reproved him, " you musn't speak like that about your brother's music. You don't understand it, that's all."

" Well, it *is* mouldy," insisted the boy, " there's no tune in it, however hard you listen for one."

Mrs. Blackwood privately endorsed this statement, but for the sake of discipline she resumed : " You're a very rude little boy! And what are you doing with that air-gun? Haven't I told you not to use it in the house?"

"I've got to have it. I'm the Mob—in the French Revolution, you know," he added for Hester's edification.

"Oh, darling," exclaimed Mrs. Blackwood, "I thought you were to be the little Dauphin."

Reggie shook his head in silence.

" *Aren't* you going to be the Dauphin?" his mother persisted. " I thought it would be such a nice part for you."

" It was a mouldy part, so I chucked it."

" Yes, but who's going to play it, if you're not?"

"Doreen.   She's got to be both the Queen's children rolled into one. *I* wasn't going to have Miss

Fayne blubbering all over me. . . . Much more
sport to be the Mob, and stick her head up on a
pike. . . . We haven't got a pike, so the air-
gun's got to do."

Griggs shook his finger archly. " Well, Master
Reggie, shall we tell them the truth about your
defalcation—good word that, eh ? You didn't mind
being the Dauphin, as long as Miss de Courcy was
playing Marry Anto'nett, did you ?"

Reggie grew pink about the ears and muttered :
" She's a sport, and anyway *she* chucked the
Queen's part, because she wanted to be Charlotte
Corday, and have the bathroom bit."

" Ssh," remonstrated Griggs, " you musn't talk
so much, or you'll spoil the effect of our performance
to-night. I don't know what we shall do about the
music, though. Don't you think there's any chance
that Dennis will be here in time ?"

Dennis's mother returned doubtfully : " You see,
I don't know exactly when he's arriving ; he didn't
say in his wire, he's rather absent-minded. I
suppose composers and people like that often are."

Hester noted that there was an undertone of pride
in her voice now, as well as deprecation ; a moment
later, the pride was unconsciously echoed by Reggie,
hovering between the swing-doors. " Dennis has
got other things to think about than remembering
to tell you if he'll be home to dinner to-morrow, or
whom he's going out with the day after ! His head's
always full of ideas, even if they do sound rotten
when they come out." Then, perhaps fearing that
he had said too much in praise of his elder brother,
Reggie added with seeming irrelevance : " Clive
won the High Jump at Westborough three years
running, and the Long Jump twice ; not bad—was

it?" Without waiting for an answer, he vanished through the door; and Griggs, after vainly scouring the drawing-room and the lawn in search of a pianist, returned to conduct the dress rehearsal.

Mrs. Blackwood sighed. " Reggie and Clive are great friends in spite of the big difference in their ages. But Clive and Dennis don't hit it off at all, though there's only a year between them."

" Opposing temperaments?" suggested Hester.

" Yes, indeed. Even as little boys they were quite different. We could never get Dennis to play with soldiers or steamers or any of the usual toys. His father used to get quite angry. He always wanted his boys to be *manly* boys. Reggie is a great favourite of his, now. He loves to take the child along whenever he goes golfing or swimming. Mr. Blackwood has been such a keen sportsman all his life, and both Clive and Reggie seem to have inherited it from him. I'm sure it adds to his enjoyment of his holiday to have Reggie here, even though it's only because they've got measles at his preparatory school. Yes, he and Mr. Blackwood are more like friends than father and son. But Dennis. . . ." Again there was in her tone that mingling of pride and concern. " Dennis has never cared at all about sport."

" More his mother's son than his father's, perhaps?"

There was a frown between Mrs. Blackwood's eyes now. She appeared to be looking straight at Hester, yet without seeing her; and a second later, at the sunlit lawn and the first tee of the hotel golf links, yet without seeing them either. Her concentrated gaze evidently beheld something that had nothing whatever to do with Hester or the lawn or

the golf links. She said in a troubled voice : " Yes
—yes, perhaps he is, I don't really know—of course
as long as he's happy—." She broke off abruptly
and fell silent. Hester watched her. So she had
reserves after all, this provincial chatterbox, despite
her readiness to discuss her own and other people's
affairs. But whatever it was that Hester imagined
to have glimpsed, was hidden away again the next
moment, beneath the flow of light conversation that
had broken out afresh. " He's been staying up in
London with a friend, Mr. Burgess, for the
Russian opera season, they're both so interested in
it. Mr. Burgess is musical too—plays the piano,
but he doesn't compose like Dennis does.   Still,
it's nice for them to have something in common,
isn't it? And now they're off on a walking tour
through Devonshire, and as we're on the Great
Western line here, Dennis promised that they would
spend the week-end with us on their way down."
She went on, " I wish they were staying longer;
I'm sure Dennis would like it here, though he
always says he hates hotels. But it's the people
who make the place, isn't it?   And I do think
they're such a nice set of people here, don't you,
Miss Cawthorn?"

Hester's " Oh, yes, I daresay they are," was
utterly impersonal and aloof, but not in the least
discouraged, Mrs. Blackwood continued : " That
Miss de Courcy, now—Antoinette—don't you think
she's charming?"

" I don't think I've noticed her. . ." Hester was
actuated by some demon of cussedness to pour cold
water on poor Mrs. Blackwood's enthusiasm.   It
was an untruth into the bargain : she had certainly
noticed Antoinette de Courcy; one could not very

well help noticing the most vivid and striking
personality in the whole hotel.

Mrs. Blackwood began again : " I believe she
comes of a very good old French family; her people
are very strict with her; I think she told Doreen
that this is the first time she has stayed away from
them—she's here with the Faynes, you know; she
and Rosabel were school-friends—Doreen is simply
devoted to Antoinette and so is Reggie."

" What about Clive?" laughed Hester.

" Oh, Clive's engaged, you see.   They may have
to wait two years till they can marry—not that Mr.
Blackwood wouldn't be quite willing to help them to
set up house now, but Clive is determined that he'll
make a position for himself before he marries. He's
always known his own mind; even as a little chap
he wanted to be an engineer, and he's stuck to it
ever since; and he's like that in his affections, too—
absolutely settled, though he's so young—just
twenty-four—but Lily knows he wouldn't change
towards her, if she had to wait ten years for him;
Reggie's like Clive; once he gets an idea into his
head nothing will move him.   They're both inclined
to be obstinate, but then if one knows how to treat
them! . . . . I can read those two like an open
book." She ended with a sigh, in which satisfaction
was blended with an indefinable regret. She was
obviously thinking again of that other son, the first-
born, whose psychology did not seem to present the
facilities of the " open book."   It was curious that
whereas she spoke of all her menfolk—of her
husband, of Clive and Reggie—with affection, with
admiration, with respect even, when she spoke of
Dennis or, as at the present moment, remained
silent about him, there was about her whole manner

something which suggested that the love she bore him was more poignant, and therefore more secret.

Presently, headed by Mr. Griggs, the other members of the theatrical company came through into the lounge. They had resumed their ordinary clothes, and flung themselves in various attitudes of weariness into the deep armchairs.

Griggs' repeated plea that they were not to spoil the effect of the play by talking about it now, was laughed down by Antoinette de Courcy, balancing her slender weight on the arm of a chair. "What does it matter? There's no one about now. Mrs. Blackwood is the mother of three of the actors, so why shouldn't she be in the know? And Miss Cawthorn won't let out any of our secrets." She smiled brilliantly across at Hester, who did not smile back, but answered shortly: "No, indeed not." Her assurance was quite superfluous, as it was impossible to imagine her condescending to take sufficient interest in anyone's secrets to lead her to betray them.

Mrs. Blackwood laughed. "Well, I can only hope that the three actors for whom I'm responsible haven't given you too much trouble, Mr. Griggs."

"Oh, how can you speak of 'trouble,' Mrs. Blackwood?" he expostulated, "it has only been a pleasure to work with them."

Mrs. Blackwood beamed upon him. "We all know you've got wonderful patience, as you need to have, I'm sure, for getting up amateur theatricals."

Griggs smiled with modest pride. "But it's well worth it, well worth it. Nothing like theatricals for making people thoroughly at home with each other. Whist-drives and picnics aren't in it! There's something about theatricals, an *esprit de corps,* as you might say."

Reggie was causing a diversion by noisily testing the spring of his air-gun. By way of rebuke, his mother with less tact than could have been desired, remarked : " I do hope all Reggie's chopping and changing didn't put you out. I think he's a naughty little boy not to have taken the part that was given him."

" Yes, and it means double work for me," declared his seventeen-year-old sister Doreen. " I've got to say all his lines as well as my own."

" And jolly glad you are to get the chance !" retorted Reggie. Doreen threw back her pretty fair head and commanded him to "shut up"; and Antoinette checked the reprimand rising to Mrs. Blackwood's lips with : " You really musn't blame Reggie, he was only following my bad example."

Here Rosabel Fayne, author of the play, broke out : " Yes, Antoinette darling, I do think it's such a pity—though of course you know best, and I'm sure you're simply wonderful as Charlotte Corday— but I did write Marie Autoinette's part on purpose for you—so sweet that you've got the same name, isn't it ? And I know I'm no good in the part . ." She paused for breath, eyes fixed adoringly on her friend's face. Rosabel's appearance was a sore trial to herself. She yearned to be tall and willowy and languorous; imperious of manner, and regal of bearing . . . . instead of which she had an angular little figure, a pointed chin, and eyes which, despite the wistfulness of their expression, were somehow reminiscent of a robin's. She was ready to lavish great floods of adoration on her friends or on characters in history or fiction. At present the said ado-

ration was equally divided between Antoinette de
Courcy and the "Unhappy Queen."

Antoinette laughed now. "You make an excellent Queen, Rosabel, and the Charlotte Corday part
was really too tempting . . ."

"It's quite unhistorical," remarked Clive Blackwood in a bored voice. He was bored with the
theatricals altogether; had only consented to play a
part, because he did not want to make himself
conspicuous by refusing; and because if you were
staying in a place like this, it behoved you, more or
less, to do as the others did. So Clive was playing
Louis XVI. with a wooden stolidity and lack of
conviction partly responsible for Antoinette's
change of rôle.

"Yes, it is gorgeously unhistorical," she agreed
with Clive, "Rosabel wasn't even certain if it was
Danton or Marat whom I had to murder in the bath,
but Ottilie managed to enlighten us, didn't you,
Ottilie?"

Ottilie, whose tartan blouse, fair basket plaits
wound round her head, and sentimental blue eyes
proclaimed her unmistakably a member of the
Fatherland, exclaimed "*Augenblick!*" and removed
her fingers from her ears. She had stuffed them in
to shut out sound, while she earnestly pondered
over the lines of her part.

"Ottilie, you ought to know your words by
now," protested Doreen.

"Och, I shall never know zem . . ." Ottilie's
voice was by nature loud, deep and gloomy, and her
present despair had added considerably to its
lugubrious quality.

"You knew them well enough just now," Doreen
strove to cheer her, but Ottilie refused to be cheered.

" *Ausgeschlossen* that I remember myself von vord vhen ze curtain up-goes . . . Only lately I exchanged ze vords. I said ' ze ' when it is ' a ' in ze text."

" But little slips like that don't matter, do they, Mr Griggs?" Doreen appealed to the stage-manager.

" Of course not, of course not," he responded genially, " as long as you give us an impression of the character, we'll be lenient about the words."

" And everybody will make allowances for you, dear," Mrs. Blackwood put in, " knowing that you're a foreigner."

" I am Madame Roland, governess of ze children of ze Qveen, and for my *Auffassung* of ze character —how do you say ' *Auffassung* ' in English, Doreen?"

" ' Conception,' " translated Antoinette, who had travelled.

" For my conception, zen, it is unbedingt necessary zat my vords shall be exact," Ottilie could not be induced to regard her part and responsibilities in any but the most serious light; and resumed her conscientious study of her lines. To Ottilie, brought up on her native Schiller and Goethe and Kleist, there was something almost sacred about the production of a historical drama, and she was grieved at the lack of seriousness with which the others approached it. Ever since she could remember, she had longed to play one of Schiller's heroines, Maria Stuart, or Joan of Arc, bidding farewell to her mountains—

" *Lebt wohl, Ihr Berge, Ihr geliebten Trifte—*" or most of all Elisabeth in " Don Carlos ". . . Yes, how she had longed to act that great scene with young Carlos, her step-son, manfully repressing his passion for her, going to his death. . . . It would have been rapturous to hear Heidmann, the romantic actor for whom she had a *"Schwärmerei,"* say to her :

. . . . *" Elisabeth, ich halte dich in meinen Armen und wanke nicht. . . ."*

But instead of all these imaginary glories, Ottilie was only playing a French governess with a German accent in an English play—a play in which historical facts had been shamelessly juggled with, and no one even cared if she did say " the " when it should be " a " . . .

As the afternoon wore on, the other hotel visitors returned from their various outings, and began to fill up the lounge. Griggs scanned them with an eagle eye, in the hope of finding amongst them a pianist capable of supplying the " atmospheric " music.

" Mrs. Greene—now I wonder if you would—no? Miss Harris—of course *you* play—no good denying it, you know, I can see it in your eyes, light of genius and all that ! What? Cut your finger . . ? Isn't that bad luck now !" Griggs mopped his forehead. " Dear, dear, whatever shall we do? All my—ah—blandishments seem to be of no avail."

Rosabel suggested dubiously : " Of course, darling Mother would play for us with pleasure—she's always so sweet—but she hasn't such an exquisitely *soulful* touch as Miss Wright had—we're spoilt, aren't we? In fact, dance-music is really Mother's strong point."

Antoinette gave a joyous laugh. " Well, why not, why not? By all means let us have the ' Merry

Widow' waltz, while Marie Antoinette is being beheaded.

"Oh, Miss Antoinette!" exclaimed Griggs in an injured voice, "you're making fun of us. This is a most serious matter."

Half amused and half impatient, Antoinette again glanced across at Hester who, this time, gave her in response a slow smile that made her pale, haggard face look strangely attractive. Antoinette flushed, shook back the short blonde cendré curls that clustered about the nape of her neck, and looked away again.

"Here's Dad!" cried Reggie, and held the door open while his father and Mr. Fayne, returning from their round of golf, passed through into the lounge. In his youth, Mr. Blackwood had been extremely handsome; with his thick iron-grey hair and ruddy complexion, he was still striking in appearance, but his features had become coarse, and he played golf nowadays for the sake of his figure as well as for the sake of the game.

"Well, you youngsters, getting ready for to-night?" Jovially Mr. Blackwood addressed the company in general. "No one's offered *me* a part, of course . . . . But if any of you had been out on the links this afternoon, you'd have seen a performance that would have rivalled your show, I can tell you." He paused, then continued impressively: "I did the eleventh hole in three—one drive clean over the lake, one iron shot on to the green, and one putt. What do you say to that, my son?"

"Pretty good," said Reggie, glowing with pleasure, despite the studied indifference of his tones. "I don't think much of the way they've cleaned your clubs, Dad, here—let me" . . . he seized the

bag, and retiring towards one of the windows, ex-
tracted the mashie and began vigorously polishing
it with emery-paper.

"That boy of mine's all right, you know . . ."
Mr. Blackwood was nearly bursting with paternal
pride; then, having slapped Clive on the back, and
pulled Doreen's plait, he turned to his wife.

"Dennis not here yet? When's he coming?"

Mrs. Blackwood became apologetic. "I don't
quite know; he didn't say definitely. I expect he'll
be here by dinner-time, though."

"The least he can do," commented her husband
in a manner suddenly devoid of joviality. "I've
no doubt he'll contrive to be late, and put everybody
out as usual, inconsiderate young beggar."

A painful flush mounted to Mrs. Blackwood's
cheeks, and Antoinette wished that she were not
witnessing this little scene.

"He doesn't mean to be inconsiderate, Daddy
dear," said Dennis's mother gently, "it's just—
that he doesn't think."

"Too much else to think about, eh, with his
theatre-going and his operas and what-not . . . .
Well, if he misses the fun to-night, he'll only have
himself to blame." Mr. Blackwood's joviality was
quite restored : "*I* wouldn't miss it for a mint o'
money; I know when I'm in for a good thing!"
He glanced approvingly at Antoinette, and she felt
by instinct that had he been better acquainted with
her, he would have winked, or dug her in the ribs.
He was that sort of elderly gentleman . . . .

Reggie, from the window, suddenly cried : " Here
they are !" and let the golf-clubs slide to the ground.

"Oh, is it really . . ?" Doreen rushed towards
the door. Antoinette reflected that the eldest son

had indeed timed his entrance effectively; and she wondered if Hester also was aware of the dramatic possibilities of the situation. Antoinette herself was always keenly aware of dramatic possibilities; in fact she lived for the apprehension of them, and for the coping with them.

As the door swung open to admit Dennis Blackwood and Crispin Burgess, Mrs. Blackwood made as if to rise from her chair, and then thought better of it. Her eyes, very bright in her flushed face, were fixed upon her son's tall figure.

"Hallo, Mother!" He came straight across the lounge to her and kissed her. The next minute, Doreen was affectionately hanging round his neck; and Mr. Griggs was exclaiming in transports of delight: "Splendid fellows to have come in time! And now they're here, let's rope 'em in, rope 'em both in—everybody's got to do something—nothing like all working together—rope 'em in, I say."

Dennis laughed in good-humoured bewilderment, and put his arm round his little sister's shoulders; but his companion, a lanky, sallow-faced youth of a gloomy and taciturn disposition, stammered: "N-noise. . . What's all the n-noise about?" He always managed to enunciate the first consonant of a word, and then had to blow hard through his front teeth, after which the remainder of the word followed with comparative ease. Doubtless this impediment in his speech accounted both for its infrequency and its terseness.

Griggs, rubbing his hands together, was still surrounding the newcomers with ecstatic pæans. "What's all the noise about, indeed? We'll soon show you. Everybody's going to help in our little entertainment to-night. *Oh,* yes. . . *You, Mr.*

Burgess," shaking a finger at the bemused Crispin, "are going to play the piano for us, Ah-ha!"

Griggs gave a triumphant chuckle, and with arms folded, stood back to view the effects of his speech.

After a prolonged interval for blowing, Crispin announced : "I d-don't d-dream of it!" and looked reproachfully at Dennis, who only laughed, and turned to exchange solemn greetings with Reggie, still ostentatiously polishing the golf-clubs.

Rosabel burst out : "Oh, Mr. Burgess, *won't* you . . . ? We've heard so much about your playing, and what we want you to do is quite easy, really. . . . Oh, dear, that sounds like an insult, doesn't it? But I didn't mean it like that. Of course I know you can play difficult things, but what I meant to say was that you needn't bother to play difficult ones for us. Just any sort of accompaniment will do, as long as there's *feeling* in it. . . . Puccini, or—or anything of that kind."

There were sounds from Crispin that might have proceeded from one in the last stages of suffocation. He was nearly purple before he managed to get out : "P-puccini—I hate P-puccini—he's obvious— ch-cheap—sugarandwater—G-r-r-r," Crispin shook himself, "no one like B-bach or B-beethoven."

Ottilie brightened at the mention of the two familiar names. "Zey are ze biggest componistors zat ze world has!"

The flexible Rosabel hastened to agree : "Yes, Beethoven is simply lovely, isn't he? Well, you play just whatever you feel in the mood for, Mr. Burgess."

Mr. Burgess shook his head. "I'm not going to p-play," then he added gloomily to Dennis : "If I'd known it was g-going to be like this, I

w-wouldn't have c-come . . ." and in an attitude
of profound dejection, sat down upon his suit-case.

"Oh, be a sport, sir, be a sport! How can you
refuse anything to such a fair petitioner?" Griggs
strove to goad Crispin's *amour propre*. But
Crispin remained entirely unmoved.

"Well, then, we shall have to ask our celebrated
composer here to oblige us. No use hiding away
there in the corner, Dennis, *I* see you "—for
Dennis, seeing that the general attention was
centred round Crispin, had profited by the occasion
to efface himself—" of course we all know you're
a shining light, but we hope you're not too proud
to shed a little of its radiance in our midst!"
Griggs beamed, delighted with his own flow of
language.

Doreen whispered : "Oh, *do,* Denny, please . ."
and Dennis, who all along had anticipated this on-
slaught upon himself, felt extremely awkward.
"I'm no good to you, Griggs. Don't think me a
surly brute, it isn't that I'm proud, or anything of
that sort, but—" he broke off. It was really very
difficult to refuse; all the more so in view of
Crispin's behaviour. He felt his mother's eyes
upon him; Doreen's. . . . But he could not play
for all these people; not just now; he could not
give them what they wanted, and they would not
want what he had to give them.

"You'll play us some of your own compositions,
I hope," Griggs went on, disregarding his refusal.
Dennis shook his head. This was exactly what he
would not do. He was in the throes of composing
an opera, his first opera. He loved it, this half-
formed work of his, with a love that was at once
passionate and tender, and intensely protective. He

felt that he wanted to protect it now. . . "I'm very sorry, Griggs, but I honestly don't know anything suitable to the occasion."

His mother said tentatively : "But you know so many pieces, darling; can't you think of any?"

"I'm afraid not, Mother dear. . . ." The thing that he was creating, for the moment obsessed him entirely; it swamped all thought of other people's music; he could only think of his own; dream of it; live in it. . . .

Griggs, in an agitated aside, whispered to Mrs. Blackwood : "Do you think he's offended because I asked Mr. Burgess before him?"

Dennis said again : "I'm sorry."

Antoinette suddenly slid down from the arm of the chair on which she had been balancing. "Your mother is just coming up the drive, Rosabel : I'm going to ask her to play for us !"

And before Dennis Blackwood's look of gratitude could reach her, Antoinette had swung through the door to waylay Mrs. Fayne.

CHAPTER II

DURING dinner, both Dennis and Crispin were given to understand that they were "in disgrace." Mr. Blackwood made frequent remarks to the effect that he was sorry he had ever allowed Dennis to take up such a nonsensical profession, if he couldn't even make himself pleasant and turn his strumming to some account when the occasion arose. He supposed it was partly due to the influence of Dennis's friends, "these new-fangled London young men," who weren't sporting enough to take part in anything that seemed beneath their dignity. And so on, *ad lib.* with variations. . . .

Dennis said nothing, and set his lips tightly, as was his way when Mr. Blackwood jarred upon his nerves more exquisitely than usual. He disliked his father, disliked the whole coarse overbearing masculinity of the man. There was between them an antagonism that was fundamental, and quite apart from the present source of grievance.

It was an uncomfortable meal. Clive and Reggie were openly ranged upon their father's side; but occasionally Doreen sent Dennis a look of unmistakable partisanship out of her soft dark eyes. Poor Mrs. Blackwood was torn between her conviction that her husband was in the right, and her fear that he was being rude to a guest. But she need not have worried on Crispin's behalf. Crispin was quite used to Mr. Blackwood's outbursts against the musical profession, having once spent a week with the family at Eastwold. He also possessed the faculty of making himself apparently deaf to

sounds which displeased him. The sound of Mr.
Blackwood's voice displeased him, so he took no
notice of it, and devoted himself exclusively to his
dinner.

The pervading gloom was only relieved by Ottilie
trying half-aloud to memorise her part, and by
Reggie and Doreen quarrelling over points in the
forthcoming play. But the quarrelling and Mr.
Blackwood's grumbling were alike carried on in
undertones, so that they might not be audible to
the occupants of the other tables. Whatever the
internal state of affairs might be, however strained
the relations between one member and another, outwardly the semblance of a cheerful and united
family-party must be preserved. To Dennis, the
pink-shaded lamp on each table seemed to hold
within its circle of light a whole complex world of
subtle affinities, subtler strains and antagonisms;
and each world seemed to be irrevocably cut off from
the rest. He began to wish that he had not come.
He was overwhelmed by the longing that always
assailed him in a large gathering of strangers,
namely to run away and hide . . . a longing that
was absurd and incongruous in conjunction with his
broad shoulders and length of limb. Perhaps his
mouth alone, curved and sensitive above the firm
chin, betrayed a nature in which such a longing,
and others equally freakish, might hold their sway.

Dinner was over at last. Pleasantly conscious of
their own importance, Doreen, Ottilie and Reggie
had left the table before the dessert was served;
Clive had reluctantly followed them; and now
Dennis and Crispin, with Mr. and Mrs. Blackwood,
were seated in the front row of chairs in the
recreation-room.

Mrs. Blackwood was saying to Dennis what a
pity it was that Reggie wouldn't play the Dauphin,
and wouldn't it have been nice if they'd had the
whole thing in French—Doreen's accent had so
wonderfully improved. . . . Someone said " Ssh,"
as the curtain rose.

Rosabel's drama should have been entitled
" Charlotte Corday " rather than " Marie Antoinette." Charlotte Corday alone did not appear to
be suffering from nervousness, nor from the usual
tendency of amateurs to get behind each other, and
cluster together as if for shelter in one corner of
the stage. She moved about with a total lack of
self-consciousness, making the others seem awkward
and lifeless by comparison. The impetus that
carried her through the play must spring entirely
from within herself, Dennis decided; for she got
little enough support from the coy and timid Marie
Antoinette, or from Marat, as played by Griggs
rather staccato and apologetically with an intermit-
tent French accent. She seemed to be giving out
passion and vitality and emotion, just because she
could not restrain them, and had to find vent for
them somehow.

" Who's the girl, Mother ?" Dennis in the
entr'acte questioned Mrs. Blackwood, who launched
into voluble descriptions of Antoinette's psychology
and parentage.

" Don't you think she's remarkable, Denny ?"

" She's inclined to over-act," Dennis returned
shortly. He was always on the defensive, even
with his mother. Perhaps with his mother most of
all, because he felt that she was most akin to him,
and might at any moment come to touch the fringe
of that secret world of his . . . world that must

remain secret even from the mother who loved him as perhaps no other woman on earth would ever love him.

Tremendous applause greeted the end of the performance. And now the actors, mingling with the audience, were being congratulated on all sides, and assured that they were " born actors " who would make their fortunes on any stage. . . . Even Ottilie came in for her meed of praise, and was told by an amiable old gentleman who evidently had no objection to perjuring his soul, that he would never have guessed that she was not English.

" *Och, was Sie nicht sagen . . .*" Ottilie, for sheer joy, relapsed into her native tongue.

But the heartiest applause and the loudest congratulations were for Antoinette. She stood in the midst of the group that surrounded her, a slim, straight figure in her short striped petticoat and fichu, laughing with childish pleasure at the compliments that were being showered upon her. She had doffed her lace cap and was shaking her thick mop of fair curls back from her flushed face. Dennis made up his mind to speak to her. He owed her a debt of gratitude for having come to his assistance with her suggestion that Mrs. Fayne should play the piano. But for the present it was impossible to get anywhere within speaking distance of Antoinette. Griggs was at her side now, sharing the compliments and honours.

"A wonderful stage-manager, Mr. Griggs, if I may say so, a *born* stage-manager. . . ."

" You should have been an actor, sir, you're quite a loss to the profession. . . ."

Griggs laid his hand upon his tricolor waistcoat, and smilingly assured the audience in general that

B

they were too kind, that he was nothing but a
humble amateur, an amateur with just a little
talent, perhaps. . . . Yes, sometimes he certainly
did feel that he had missed his vocation; still, even
stockbrokers had their uses, he supposed. . . .

And to Antoinette: "You and I must have a
special glass of lemonade together, Miss Antoinette,
just to show there's no ill-feeling, after I've been
murdered by you every day for the past week . . .
and very enjoyable too, very enjoyable indeed!"

This was greeted with shouts of laughter, but
Dennis saw that Antoinette's smile was abstracted,
and that her eyes were restlessly searching the
crowded room. Then, quite suddenly, he saw the
light go from them, and her whole figure relax its
air of tense vitality, as if the motive-power that had
kept her strung-up, had ceased to operate. Simultaneously he noticed that the dark woman with the
sullen face and ungracious manner had sauntered
out of the room.

But a minute later, Antoinette had quite recovered
herself. Someone suggested that they should end
the evening with a dance, and already she was helping Reggie and another small boy to push the
chairs back against the walls. Mrs. Fayne briskly
made for the piano, but Crispin was there before
her. Now that everyone had forgotten about
Crispin and his talent, and no one had the least
desire to listen to heavy music, he sat down and
played a Bach fugue right through. And when he
had finished it, he played another and another . . .
and he played very, very wonderfully, but what was
the use of Bach fugues to young people longing to
waltz and one-step? Oblivious of any such longing, Crispin played on and on, and out of deference

to the great artistic value of his performance, no one dared suggest that he should terminate it.

"Perhaps if we leave him alone, he'll stop . . ." sighed Reggie; so one by one the visitors trouped out of the recreation-room, trusting that the absence of an audience might bring Crispin to his senses. It did not . . . Crispin merely grunted with relief, and played on.

"Of course I knew this would happen," Dennis remarked to Antoinette in the lounge, "it's a physical impossibility to keep Crispin and a piano apart for any length of time."

She laughed, grey eyes sparkling under a thick fringe of black lashes. "And you?" she said, "you evidently do not mind being kept apart from your piano!"

"On the contrary, I want to be kept from it— to-night. I should like to say that I'm very grateful to you."

"Oh, don't mention it," she laughed again, and turned from him to Doreen, who was clamouring to be shown how to take the grease-paint off her face.

"I don't *really* want to get it off, because it's so *awfully* thrilling to have it on, but I s'pose I can't come down to breakfast like this . . ." the flapper cried excitedly.

Antoinette went upstairs with her.

Meanwhile a solitary figure crept back into the empty recreation-room, sat motionless with hands clasped and lips parted—Ottilie, rapturously listening to Bach and Beethoven and Brahms . . . revelling in the sentimental ecstasy of "Heimweh" with which the music filled her. This was as it should be : at last in this frivolous and superficial England, she had found one who understood the deep solid works of her countrymen. Inspired by her presence, and by her sympathy, no doubt, he played on and on. . . . When, eventually, he paused to light a cigarette, she addressed him in her careful English : " I sank you heartiest, Herr Crispin, zat you for me so vonderful have played."

Crispin looked round at her and blew hard. " I d-didn't even know you were here. . . ."

But Ottilie was not disheartened. She knew quite well that his brusqueness of manner was only a cloak for his true feelings. She must be patient with him, until he should have gained courage to throw off the disguise. Ottilie was in romantic mood. . . . There was no doubt that Herr Crispin did not fit into his English surroundings. But at home in her dear Heidelberg—and perhaps if Herr Crispin could be persuaded to grow a beard—— Ottilie went to bed very happy that night.

Antoinette, having superintended the removal of the grease-paint from Doreen's face, and kissed her good-night, was making her way towards her own room on the second floor. Half way down the corridor, she came face to face with Hester Cawthorn. They both stopped.

Hester's smile was half ironic, half bitter. " Tired ?"

Antoinette shook her head. She was feeling violently alive again now; strung up; ready for anything.

" I've never seen anything like the vitality of you," said Hester; and passed on.

So Antoinette, also, went to bed happy. . .

And while Ottilie was dreaming of a much-Germanised Crispin; and Doreen was deciding that she " simply must " go on the stage; and Clive was

writing a not very inspired love-letter to his Lily—
" not much time to-night, darling, because of the
rotten theatricals "—Dennis Blackwood sat at the
open window of his room, and gazed out at the dark
country and wondered if he had at last found the
answer to a riddle. . . .

But long after all the others were asleep, Mrs.
Blackwood lay awake. In her mind, she was still
turning over the jumbled happenings of the day,
her thoughts darting restlessly from one point to
another, without coherence or concentration. She
still regretted that Reggie had been so obstinate
over playing the Dauphin's part; wondered if she
were not strict enough with him; remembered having noticed that he was at least half an inch taller
than Mrs. Greene's little boy, who was three months
older; wondered if Mrs. Thompsett would have
thought that Doreen was too much made-up; wondered if Dennis would make friends with that nice
little French girl . . . wondered what it was that
made him so different from the other boys, and that
baffled all her attempts to fathom it.   Dennis—
Dennis—Dennis. . . . .

Was he happy, and if not—why not?   Why
didn't he tell her?   But as far back as she could
remember, he had clung to her and loved her, and
never told her anything. Why . . . ? Perhaps
he had nothing to tell. Perhaps she only imagined
that he wasn't happy.   Artists were sometimes
peculiar—she clutched at that—and her boy was an
artist : perhaps that accounted for it. Her reason,
working in a peculiarly narrow circle, round and
round, round and round, accepted this as the solution, and was at peace. But her instinct, less narrow, more subtle, blindly groping, refused to be

thus pacified. There must be—something. But what? What . . . ?

The snoring of her husband at her side was not conducive to the elucidation of psychological mysteries.

CHAPTER III

"COME for a walk with me—do!" The tone was half pleading, half commanding. Hester Cawthorn very slowly closed her book, and from the depths of her chair on the lawn, looked up at Antoinette's eager face. She shook her head, and Antoinette repeated under her breath "Do . . ."

Hester's sullen mouth curved into a smile. "Why should I?"

"Because I—I want you to."

"You seem to consider that an adequate reason!"

"Well—isn't it?"

The hotel visitors, grouped upon the lawn to laze away the hot after-lunch hour, were surprised at seeing Miss Cawthorn and Antoinette de Courcy stroll down the drive together. It was the first time that Miss Cawthorn had been known to set out in company.

"That child has such a way with her, she gets round everybody," murmured Mrs. Blackwood, hoping that Dennis would take notice.

Hester and Antoinette walked in silence down the length of the shady drive. Antoinette was not so sure of herself now; wondered what would be the result of her daring. It had certainly needed daring to ask Hester to come out with her. There was about Hester a nimbus of unapproachability that was recognised by everyone in the hotel, and that had aroused, firstly, curiosity and secondly, interest in Antoinette. Also, she was strangely attracted by this woman with the sombre hooded eyes and down-curved mouth that seemed to speak of much bitterness and disillusion. During her stay at Amberhurst, Antoinette had become amazingly intimate with all the hotel visitors; most of them, at one time or another, had been moved to tell her "the story of my life"; for she was a good listener, and waited with rapt eagerness for the picturesque or the dramatic note that should stamp each story with individuality. Everybody confided in her, petted her, spoilt her. Hester alone had held aloof from her, as she had held aloof from the others. But Antoinette was resolved to make herself the exception to Hester's rule.

"And now—what do you want?" Hester's question, breaking the silence, was abrupt but not discourteous.

Antoinette laughed. "To tell the truth, I don't know. 'Je ne sais pas ce que je veux, mais je le veux absolument.'"

"Well, then, believe me, you won't get it."

"How can you say that, when you don't know— when I don't even know—what it is I want?"

"I can only warn you that it's useless to expect anything from me—I've nothing to give." Hester's voice was low and beautiful, despite its occasional harshness. Antoinette thrilled at the sound of it, and at the warning that had just been flung at her. Nothing to give—why, she must have worlds to give to one who knew how to claim her gifts. Or perhaps once already she had bestowed them, bestowed them royally upon one unworthy . . . and was cautious now, distrustful of anyone attempting to approach the fortress-gates behind which was locked—herself. Antoinette would lay siege to the fortress with every weapon in her power, with daring and gentleness and subtlety, until the gates were opened to her. She felt confident of success, buoyantly happy as she strode along at Hester's side, hands thrust deep into the pockets of her jersey, the noon-day sun beating down upon her bare head.

"You'll catch sun-stroke, child."

"Not I!"

"Haven't you anything to put on your head?"

"I believe so, somewhere in my pocket," Antoinette drew out a crumpled red silk cap and swung it in her hand.

"Put it on," commanded Hester curtly. Antoinette obeyed, enjoying the sensation of being ordered about by Hester.

"Even if you do happen to be possessed of extraordinary vitality," the latter continued, "there's no need to squander it."

"Am I squandering it?" Antoinette asked innocently. She was not introspective, but she was always interested when people told her things about herself.

"Are you squandering it, indeed . . .? Rushing along a dusty road at the rate of eight miles an hour, at the hottest time of the day——"

"I'm so sorry! Is it too hot for you? Shall we go back?"

"No, I've no objection to it. But then I've not been wearing myself out with emotional acting every night this week."

"Oh, the acting . . . it was such fun! Absolute rot, of course, poor dear Rosabel hasn't the faintest notion how to write a play, but she's written half a dozen different ones about Marie Antoinette. In fact, whenever I meet her, she seems to be in the thick of writing one, and she falls upon my neck with : ' Antoinette darling, I'm writing a tragedy about *her*—it's to be something exquisite . . . six acts and nineteen scenes . . . no, don't ask me anything about it . . . the first scene is in a sort of inn and people come in and talk . . . no, I can't tell you any more, you'd think me so stupid. . . . Another time, perhaps. . . .' "

Hester was laughing outright by now; and thus encouraged, Antoinette went on : " We had an awful business with this particular masterpiece. Rosabel had left all the parts, except the Queen's, quite sketchy; so we had to invent them at rehearsals, and make them fit together as well as we could. Rosabel is never quite successful with anything she attempts. There's a certain blighted perkiness about her, that makes her rather like an early bird that hasn't caught the worm—or perhaps she's the early worm that always gets the bird . ."

" You're too brilliant, my young friend."

" Am I ? Why?"

Hester smiled inscrutably and was silent.

" Why am I too brilliant?" Antoinette was suddenly overwhelmed by the fear of disapproval. " I —I wasn't trying to be."

" No, I daresay you weren't. I was only thinking of that old proverb that was dinned into one's ears in the nursery : ' Sing before breakfast—cry before night ' !"

" Oh, do you mean that I shall—' cry before night ' ?"

Hester looked down at the eager laughing face, the boyish curls surmounted carelessly by the red cap. " You won't, at all events, cry before—tonight."

"But you think I shall eventually? Can you tell the future, then?"

"Most people's futures are written on their faces, aren't they?"

"For those who are able to read them. . . . So that's how you read mine! Well, I don't care. . ." Antoinette flung her cap into the air and caught it again. "I assure you that if I do have to 'cry before night,' I shall 'sing before breakfast' quite a lot *en attendant.*"

"I've no doubt you will," said Hester.

"I'm doing it now—simply having the time of my life."

"And in what," Hester's tone was ironical, "in what, exactly, does the 'time of your life' consist?" Then before Antoinette could answer, she covered up the question with: "Don't tell me if you don't want to—I've no wish to force confidence."

Antoinette smiled involuntarily at the notion that Hester should assume in her a reticence equal to her own. If she had told the truth, she would have answered: "I'm happy because there's so much love in the world, and because so much of it comes to me, and mostly because I'm walking beside you now. . . ."

But she only said, "It's not that I'm really doing anything extraordinary, but this is the first time I've ever stayed away from my people—would you believe it, and I'm nearly twenty-two—but Grand'- mère has quite obsolete ideas as to what a *jeune fille* should do and shouldn't do, even though she's lived over here for twenty-five years."

"Were you born in England, then?"

"Yes. And I feel quite English. The others

—Grand'mère and Mother and Father are terribly French, though. . . ." Antoinette gave a sigh, and then laughed again. "Being away is such fun, I love sitting down to breakfast in the morning with a different set of faces, don't you?"

"I never sit down with a 'set of faces' at all."

"Don't you? Not ever? Not even at home?"

Hester was silent. Antoinette tried to imagine the family-circle from which she might have sprung, and gave it up as hopeless : she could not picture Hester in relation to a mother or father, sisters or brothers. She could only see her as an individual, detached from her surroundings, lonely and alone. Her whole heart went out in sympathy to this strange woman with the fierce reserve, and the sensitiveness that lay behind her brutally direct manner; in sympathy, and something that was more than sympathy.

After a while, Hester said with quiet bitterness : "I have no home. . . ."

Impulsively Antoinette put out her hand to touch her arm. "I'm sorry—so dreadfully sorry —you must be lonely."

Hester made no movement in response, but replied coldly, "You make a mistake : I am not lonely."

Antoinette, baffled, dropped her hand and was silent. She had been tactless and deserved her rebuff; nevertheless it had hurt—rather. The conquest of Hester, impregnably immured in her fortress, was proving even more difficult than she had anticipated, and therefore ten times more desirable. Antoinette was accustomed to easy victories, victories so easy as scarcely to merit the name, and she was tired of them; but the prospect of difficulties only stimulated the fighting-instinct in her.

Hester, with an air of detached amusement, was watching her absorbed face. "I warned you, didn't I . . . ?"

Antoinette flashed out: " If you think I'm frightened of your prickliness——"

"Oh, you hot-headed little fool. . . What's all this for? If you think I'm going to make a friend or a confidante of you, you're mistaken. Real friendship is, in my experience, a treasure impossible to find, and I've no use for people who want to know my family-history, and whence I came and whither I'm going. . . . What concern of theirs can it be? No, I have no friends and I want none. You're only wasting your time with me."

"I'm not—it isn't waste!" cried Antoinette, "you're so wonderful, and ever since I've been here I've wanted to talk to you, only I never quite dared till to-day, and then I simply couldn't stop myself. . . . I noticed you the first evening I came—how could I help it? All the other people move about in lumps, three or four staying together, three or four at a table in the dining-room, three or four going out together—and only you were alone. That was remarkable to begin with."

"I shall always be alone," said Hester.

"Yes—and I know why!" Inspiration seemed suddenly to come to Antoinette. "Whereas the others want company, want to be together at any price, you only want what is really good enough for you. It's—it's as if it had to pass through fire before it could get to you."

"You're fantastic," Hester smiled, but not un-

kindly, and then, without interrupting her, she let
Antoinette have her say.

" I can understand your keeping the others out
and hating them to ask questions—you know
they're only inquisitive, and not asking because it
means a great deal to them. It means a great deal
to me, I can't tell you why, but it just does. Please
won't you let me come a little bit closer? You see,
I'm not frightened of the prickles or the fire. . . ."
Quite unconsciously she was pleading as a very
young boy might plead with his lady-love.

Hester shook her head. " Even if you do ' come
closer,' as you say, you'll only be disappointed.
Go and fall in love with that nice Blackwood boy :
it will be much more profitable than this sort of
thing."

" This sort of thing?" . . . Antoinette repeated
with a puzzled frown.

Hester looked at her sharply for a moment, then
gave a curt laugh. " Never mind. . . . Do as I
say. Stick to young Blackwood."

" To Clive?" Antoinette exclaimed contemptu-
ously. " Why, he's engaged, Doreen says, to a
girl who studies economics and won't powder her
nose."

" I didn't mean Clive, I meant the one who
arrived yesterday—Dennis. At any rate, I'm certain that he's going to fall in love with you."

Antoinette was not interested. Hester continued :
" He's quite a character-study. I should like to
hear how the affair progresses."

" Would you . . ?" cried Antoinette, overjoyed
at the idea that anything connected with herself
could be of interest to Hester. " I'd better cultivate him, then."

"I'll leave you my address," said Hester.

"Your address? But you're not going away yet, surely?"

"Going this very evening."

Antoinette stood stock-still in the middle of the road, and gasped. "Not—really?" In the case of anyone but Hester, her plans would have been known by the whole hotel for days in advance. It was but another proof of Hester's aloofness, that the time of her departure came to Antoinette as an absolute shock.

"Don't look so bewildered: it can't possibly matter to you."

"But it does—more than anything else in the world—more than ever now. When I started out with you this afternoon, I was only enormously interested in you, and I admired you—your brains, and the gorgeous way you have of choking off people you don't want. I've watched you do it— Oh, often—but you're not going to choke me off like that, because now, I—I love you. . . ." She had not intended to say those words; a few moments ago they would not have entered her mind; now she had not only said them: she meant them.

Hester looked at her gravely, without curiosity and without astonishment. "If that's the case, I've no right to choke you off. But understand once and for all that you're on a wild-goose chase. You'll find none of the hidden depths in me that you seem to expect to find."

"Whether that's true or not, I'll never expect any confidence or anything that you don't give me of your own free will. But there's nothing on earth that I wouldn't do for you, if I thought it would make you happy."

Hester said with that curious dignity that was hers : " Thank you. . . ."

They walked back then. After some time, Antoinette ventured to ask, " Where is it you're going to-night ?"

The answer was : " To Bristol—if the gods are good to me !" and Antoinette saw that Hester's dark eyes were illuminated by a gleam of light, and fixed straight ahead of her, as if in pursuance of some vision whence the light had come. Antoinette longed to know what was portended by that phrase : " If the gods are good to me . . ." wondered what was drawing her to Bristol; if she lived there; if she ever came to London; why she had been staying at Amberhurst. But all these questions remained unasked. She would prove herself worthy of Hester by showing no curiosity, by accepting as a matter of course anything that she might do.

Her offer to help Hester with her packing was declined; but she obtained permission to see her to the station.

" I may be late for dinner," Antoinette flung over her shoulder to Rosabel, as, for the second time that day, she left the hotel in Hester's company. Rosabel stared open-mouthed. . . Hester laughed. " You see, even your friend is struck by the incongruity of seeing us together !"

" It isn't incongruous really. At least I don't think it is. I'm sure I should find much more in common with you, than with Rosabel." Antoinette flushed, fearing that she had said too much; but Hester did not appear to think that she had been guilty of impertinence.

" Perhaps I'm only letting you imagine that you could. . . ." Antoinette pondered on this; then :

"No, if you were only acting, just to give me that impression, you'd be so clever that I'd have to adore you all the same. It's no earthly good trying to put me off by pretending you aren't what I know you are."

"I don't know that I am trying to put you off now. . . . I'm only trying to be honest and sincere with you, and to keep you from disappointment."

"Honest and sincere—I should just think you are! I'd follow your lead blindly through anything, and feel that I could trust you."

"Oh, child, child, don't put all that trust in me. No one but a god could be worthy of so much. It's too great a responsibility for a mere human being."

"No trust and no faith could be too great for me to give you—and—and I'll never let you feel the responsibility of me as a drag. I can look out for myself. I want to walk level with you, not hanging on."

"You shall do as you wish," said Hester.

In silence they paced the platform of the little country station. Antoinette's exaltation was shadowed now with the dread of parting from Hester. But she allowed no word of regret to pass her lips. She would be true to her assertion that she would not "hang on" to Hester. Hester's happiness, apparently, lay in going; so, with all her heart, Antoinette tried to want her to go, even though Amberhurst would seem a deserted wilderness without her. She regretted the wasted days that had gone before she had made up her mind to speak to her; the last few hours of joy had passed so swiftly; and now—and now——

Antoinette hastily shook back her curls and

smiled, as the train came in.   The door of the
compartment was slammed between them.

"Well, good-bye," said Antoinette lightly, enjoying the self-imposed necessity of acting up to
Hester, "good luck to you."

Hester leant out of the window, and, just as the
train started, bent down and kissed her.

. . . In a very agitated frame of mind, Antoinette wandered back to the hotel. What had been
the most wonderful adventure of her life was at an
end—no, she would not believe that it was at an
end, even though she had received no promise that
Hester would write to her, and had no idea when or
if she would ever see her again. The adventure
had only just begun; there must be an equally
wonderful continuation to it—some time. And in
the meantime, she would rest secure in the memory
of that last second before the train started. . . .
She could have shouted aloud with the joy of being
alive, and in love : if Hester would only allow herself to be loved, she would try to make up to her
for all the bitterness and disappointment that might
have been in her life. Antoinette was young enough
and mad enough at the moment to believe that anything was possible.

The Faynes were half-way through dinner when
she joined them at their table.

Mrs. Fayne said, "Why, you've been out with
that Miss Cawthorn nearly all day? So morose
and unsociable, I always think her."

"She looks as if she had a secret sorrow," Rosabel murmured soulfully, "did she tell you about it,
Antoinette?"

Antoinette smiled. "No, she didn't tell me
about it. . . ."

" Then whatever did you talk about, such a long time?"

" Oh—books . ." Antoinette replied at random.

Dinner was over, and most of the visitors were drinking coffee out on the lawn, glad of the breeze after the sweltering heat of the day. In couples or in groups they sauntered up and down the grounds, light dresses showing up against the sombre foliage of the trees; glowing cigarette-ends making pinpoints of fire in the darkness. Antoinette looked at the couples and at the groups and thought of one who would have walked alone amongst them. There was certainly no pathos in Hester's solitude, none of the pathos of the lonely woman of uncertain age, drifting from one hotel to another. Pathos would scarcely have appealed to Antoinette as did the compelling and magnetic dignity of Hester's voluntary isolation.

" Won't you come for a stroll?" Dennis Blackwood was beside her now, looking down upon her from his superior height.

" If you like. . . ." She accepted the cigarette he offered her, and was ironically conscious of being quite in the picture now : two and two, smoking cigarettes, just like the others.

They walked to the end of the hotel-grounds, across some adjoining fields, and stood on a bridge that spanned a branch-line of the railway.   The ridge of the hills was dim as a shadow; here and there showed the dull orange squares of cottage-windows, and on either side of the bridge, the railway-tracks stretched away into the greyness.

Antoinette did not speak.   She waited with a certain curiosity for Dennis to do so. It was he who had borne her off much as she had borne Hester off that afternoon. Decidedly, it was for him to begin. . . . . She wondered, still ironically, how his methods of attack would compare with her own. In all probability, he would try to kiss her. It " belonged " to the whole scene and setting that he should do so, but it would be a nuisance. She hoped he would be a trifle more original, so that she could give Hester an interesting description of the proceedings. . . .

The complex scale passages of the Waldstein Sonata drifted out to them on the breeze.

Dennis laughed. " That's Crispin. He's purloined the key of the recreation-room, locked himself in, and is now playing to rows of empty chairs. I bet it's the first time he's feeling happy since we arrived."

" Oh," said Antoinette, " is he so very unhappy here, then?"

Dennis shrugged his shoulders. " Well, not exactly unhappy. Just out of place. A square peg in a round hole—like so many of us . . ." he mused.

" So you, too, are a square peg?"

He looked at her intently with his clear brown eyes, that were large and curiously soft under their jutting brows. " Yes." Then, at a venture : " Like yourself . . ." and still his eyes held hers, as if seeking some response, some sign by which he might know that she knew the answer to his riddle.

She shook her head. " Oh, I'm not a square peg, I just fit in anywhere. It's fun, trying to fit into different sorts of places; it must be beastly if you can't. I'm sorry for your friend."

" He'll be all right to-morrow. We're off, you know, to Devon."

"Don't I wish I were going too!" she breathed fervently.

"Do you—do you really?" he cried. "I wish you were. You'd enjoy our long tramps, and the quaint little inn-places where we have to put up. Do you know that part of the country?"

Her answer was not to the point. "I was thinking for the moment that Bristol was in Devon—my geography is shockingly hazy."

He knew better than to comment upon her irrelevant remark. She stood with her hands on the stone parapet of the bridge, and looked out at the railway-tracks that gleamed faintly for a short distance, and then lost themselves in the mist. He had the sudden desire to stroke her head, just on top where the hair was quite smooth before it broke into the mass of short curls bunched over her ears and around the nape of her neck. He wanted gently to turn her face towards him, and to look again into her clear grey eyes, and share the dreams that must lurk in their depths. He felt by instinct that they were strange dreams, which for him, however, would hold no strangeness. Even though she had evaded his first attempt to prove the existence of a common meeting-ground, that very evasiveness showed his instinct to be correct.

She spoke then, rousing herself from her abstraction. "It seems so odd that we've never heard you play. Your mother has told me such a lot about your music—I'm really not trying to talk like Mr. Griggs—but it is odd, knowing that you're probably longing to play."

"Yes, of course I am; but I can't here."

"Because of the people?"

"Yes. I can't bear showing off; making an exhibition of myself."

"Then why not do as your friend has done: lock the door?"

Dennis laughed. "Oh, Crispin is a real child of nature. If he wants to do a thing, he just does it, regardless. I'm afraid I lack that happy faculty."

"You've got others instead, though. How I envy anyone who can compose—create—find an outlet for everything that's bubbling and frothing inside their brain."

"Your acting last night—that was a sort of safety-valve, wasn't it?"

She gave him a quick, vivid smile in acknowledgment of his understanding. "Yes, but what's the good of acting? Even if I did it properly, which I don't. There's nothing left of it to-day. You can't compare it with being able to create something really lasting. . . ." If only she could have borrowed Dennis's creative powers to-night, just for to-night, Hester should have had some wondrous tribute to their few hours together!

He said: "You needn't envy me. I haven't even started to compose properly yet. I'm still inarticulate. All that I really want to say, seems to lie beyond my reach, beyond mere terms of music; impossible to express, and impossible to set free."

"Those songs of yours, and the pieces you've published—what about them?"

"Well, they were written, as you might say, with the top layer of my brain. But how did you know of them?"

" Your mother showed them to me. She's got them with her."

He smiled tenderly. " Poor darling . . . fancy travelling my stuff around with her like that, and she doesn't even know one note from another."

" She just adores you, doesn't she?"

" Yes. I could almost wish she didn't."

" Oh—but why . . . ?"

He was silent for a moment. A train thundered under the bridge, sent up a shower of glowing red sparks, tore through the sleeping country, and, with a long-drawn shriek, vanished into a tunnel in the hills. Then the signals creaked and jerked into their places with a rattling sound; and all was still again.

" I'm so afraid of hurting her," he mused, " you see, from her point of view, I'm not very satisfactory."

" I don't see that at all," cried Antoinette, " she's awfully proud of you, and quite convinced that you're going to be famous."

" And do you imagine that it'll satisfy her even if I *am* famous—just famous? She wants something more for me than fame."

" And that is——?"

" Happiness . . ."

" Well, and why shouldn't you have happiness too? I'm not foolish enough to imagine that it comes *through* fame, but can't you have it as well as fame?"

He looked at her again. She seemed unsubstantial, wraith-like in the dim light; eyes very big in her white face; the breeze softly stirring her dull fair curls. He said, very low : " That depends . ."

Another train flew past, enveloping them for a

moment in flame-lit billows of smoke; its tail-light
was a slowly-diminishing point of red, till at last,
like some animal seeking its burrow in the ground,
it vanished into the tunnel. The earth seemed to
quiver a little after its noisy passage; the wailing
shriek of the engine was muted, by the distance, to
a sound of unbearable yearning and beauty. Somewhere a church-clock struck ten. And somewhere
in the world, there was—Hester. A sudden wave
of feeling came over Antoinette; love so intense as
to be almost pain. . . .

"Impossible to express and impossible to set
free——" In her thoughts she was unconsciously
echoing Dennis's words. Then, half-aloud: "Perhaps some day it will be set free!"

In the darkness she heard Dennis catch his breath,
but already she had moved away from the bridge,
was walking back towards the hotel. He followed
in silence; drew level with her; and noticed, as her
sleeve brushed against his, that the dew had soaked
through the thin silk of her jersey. He would not
risk destroying by the clumsy medium of speech,
the fine web of affinity that was spun between them,
and of the existence of which he was no longer in
doubt.

Antoinette reflected that the conversation had been
more interesting than she had anticipated; and after
all, he had not attempted to kiss her: she scarcely
knew whether she was relieved or disappointed. . .

The lawn was deserted now; they went straight
into the lounge, and stood blinking in the sudden
light.

Mrs. Blackwood looked up eagerly at their entrance, held out her hand to Antoinette, and telling
Reggie to bring a chair for her, drew her into the

family-circle. Dennis announced his intention of climbing through the window of the recreation-room to rout out Crispin; and Mrs. Blackwood said to Antoinette, "You've made quite a conquest of Dennis, my dear. He's not a bit a lady's man, really. I suppose he's always thinking of his work, and so he enjoys a chat with someone who *thoroughly understands* music. You must come and stay with us at Eastwold, when he comes back from Devonshire, and then you'll be able to have some nice long talks together."

"Thanks awfully, Mrs. Blackwood, I should love to come," Antoinette replied with genuine enthusiasm. She was always thrilled by the prospect of new surroundings. Besides, Hester would doubtless be amused. . . .

Doreen squeezed Antoinette's arm affectionately, and Reggie exclaimed: "Good egg! If you practise your iron-shots, and remember to keep your head down, you'll be able to play with Dad whenever I can't. He often likes a game when he comes back from the City."

Antoinette said hastily, "I'm afraid my golf will never be good enough for that, Reggie. . . ."

But Reggie responded with mingled impatience and gallantry, "You don't expect a fellow to swallow such tosh, do you?"

CHAPTER IV

A few days later, Antoinette returned to London; and old Madame de Courcy, her grandmother, was interrogating her on the subject of her stay with the Faynes. . . . Had she met many amiable young men? Had they admired her? Had she told them to come and visit her grandmother and her parents? And her friend, la petite Fayne, had she also been admired?

Antoinette answered all these questions with a comprehensive "Oui, Grand'mère. . ." Conversation with Madame de Courcy was always difficult, firstly because she was very deaf and secondly because she was of an inquisitiveness and a lack of tact and discretion, that ruled out for Antoinette all possibility of confidence or affection. She could only see her grandmother as a comic figure; sometimes as a most irritating one; never by any chance as one to be loved or reverenced. Grand'mère frequently indulged in fits of hysteria, in which at the top of her voice, she would set forth the failings and shortcomings of three generations of the family, with a special notice for the particular offence of which each individual, whether dead or alive, had been guilty towards herself. The performance would usually be started by some quite irrelevant trifle—some slight breach of etiquette or imagined lack of consideration for her years and dignity. Part I would be purely personal and insulting; but Part II, transcending the limits of the personal, would be wider in range, epic and panoramic; while Part III was crudely effective through sheer noise

and smashing of furniture, or whatever chanced to
be most handy. But Madame de Courcy possessed
the remarkable faculty of being able, without the
slightest transition or modulation, to switch off her
hysterics, if a change of front seemed desirable.
Thus at one moment, with tears streaming down
her face, she could rave fortissimo because Antoinette had omitted to say good morning to her, or
because her son-in-law René of Grenoble had once
passed out of the dining-room in front of her . . .
and then when she had succeeded in working up
everyone else to a similar pitch of excitement, she
could on the instant turn round and smile, in
dulcet tones demand of Antoinette the assurance
that she " *aimait bien sa petite grand'mère*," and
resume the conversation where it had previously
been abandoned. The audience—if audience there
happened to be, and there usually did—was invariably staggered no less by the suddenness of the
change than by the actual recital of the Family
Saga.

She was a marvellous old lady, despite her
seventy years; and her fierce dark eyebrows met
above her patrician nose, and the hairs upon her
upper lip were many. She had a wonderful
memory—for grievances. And she needed to have,
as her family was very extensive and scattered
about in all portions of the globe; and only by
reciting the tale of their manifold iniquities could
she draw them together in her mind's eye. . . .
At least, so though Antoinette, who from childhood
upwards had listened to Grand'mère's outbursts,
first in fear and trembling, and later on in pure
artistic appreciation of a spectacular performance.

Grand'mère's chief hobbies and interests in life

were births, deaths, marriages and operations; but especially marriages, the arrangement, furtherance and consequences of same. She combined the notion that a young girl should be brought up in darkest ignorance of the facts of life, with a fondness for discussing them publicly in intimate detail, and with a Rabelaisian virility of language. She had married off her six daughters, with more or less success, to gentlemen in suitable positions residing in France, Italy and Spain. But when Anatole, her darling only son, had come to England for business-reasons, she had accompanied him and his young wife, and lived with them ever since. Anatole de Courcy was a wholesale dealer in coffee, and a fairly astute man of business. In appearance he was lean, dark, rather yellow in the face, with projecting front teeth and a ragged moustache that he was in the habit of gnawing. He was the only one of her children whom Madame de Courcy had spoilt, and still manifested all the most objectionable characteristics of the nursery favourite. He was both obstinate and petty, and prone to outbursts of temper, not unlike his mother's. Sometimes, indeed, mother and son would scream at each other for hours together, the duet only terminating when one of the vocalists fell dumb through exhaustion.

On these occasions, Henriette de Courcy, who had long ago learnt the futility of interfering between her husband and her mother-in-law, would with a sweeping gesture of her beautiful hand, beckon Antoinette out of the room. " Come, my child, we are not needed here. . . ." which was obvious : Anatole and his mother, both weeping tears of rage, and hurling the bitterest taunts and

recriminations at each other, were supremely
happy. . . . But Henriette could never let the
slightest occasion for theatricality pass unnoticed.
In her youth she had studied elocution, and had
even had dreams of going on the stage, dreams
which she had been obliged to relinquish when her
parents married her to Anatole de Courcy. Anatole
was rich; Henriette was poor, and one of a great
many sisters. . . . But she never allowed
either herself or her environment to forget that but
for her marriage, she might have become one of the
leading *tragédiennes* of France. Her whole
bearing, her gestures, the flowing draperies she
affected, were all reminiscent of the great actress
who, in her own opinion, had been sacrificed to
matrimony with a coffee-dealer. Perhaps the
constant habit of the theatrical pose accounted for
the fact that Antoinette never felt any real warmth
of affection existing between herself and her
mother. There was always at the back of her
mind the suspicion that Henriette's magnificent
gestures, and deep thrilling inflections expressive
of maternal passion, were really no more than
gestures and inflections, practised, perfectly
finished, but with nothing genuine behind them.
Henriette was perpetually voicing lofty sentiments
upon the true development of the soul, and had
even been known, in the presence of her family, to
extol free love and the beauties thereof. Needless
to say Anatole and old Madame de Courcy did their
best to counteract her evil influence upon her
daughter. But Antoinette felt that they need not
have troubled : here again she could not rid herself
of the conviction that her mother was not sincere,
and that her vaunted broad-mindedness would turn

into the righteous indignation of the conventional *bourgeoise,* if ever it were put to the test.

The house in Cadogan Gardens was hideously furnished; the rooms, spacious and gloomy, were crammed with dreadful ornaments and pictures that were either family heirlooms or had been Anatole's wedding presents from his numerous sisters. Many small tables in the drawing-room were laden with photographs of the six sisters with their respective husbands and offspring; a most alarming exhibition, thought Antoinette, as neither her aunts nor her cousins were remarkable for their beauty. On the contrary. However, the plain young cousins made up in virtue what they so manifestly lacked in looks; witness the embroidered mats and doyleys and cushion-covers that had been worked as birthday or Xmas presents for Madame de Courcy, and testified to many hours of patient toil on the part of her grandchildren. Antoinette's handiwork alone was not represented in this orgy of cross-stitch and crochet. Antoinette could do neither cross-stitch nor crochet, wherefore her grandmother argued that there must be something radically wrong with her.

As long as she had been too young and helpless to protest against the outrage, she had always been made to recite on Madame de Courcy's birthday. On one occasion she had been heavily coached by her mother in a long speech from " Athalie," and Madame de Courcy, who was not interested in the classics, and too deaf to understand much anyway, began to chatter in the middle of the recitation. Antoinette stopped dead. Her mother signed to her to continue. Grand'mère went on chatting. . . . Antoinette fumed, shifting from one leg

on to the other.   " Go on, *chérie,*" whispered
Henriette.   " I'll go on when that horrid old
woman stops talking!" cried Antoinette, loud
enough to be heard by the deafest of grandmothers.
     . . . . In the course of the scene which ensued,
Grand'mère hurled a book at her young grand-
daughter's head.   It missed its mark and fell to
the ground; Antoinette, obeying the histrionic
instinct inherited from her mother, picked it up
and with icy politeness handed it back : " I think
you have dropped something.   .   .   ."
Since that day, Madame de Courcy had realised
that Antoinette was somehow different from her
other grandchildren, and that she had " a difficult
little character."   " *Tant pis,*" she was wont to
reflect, " we will have to marry her young. . . ."
But so far Antoinette had refused to accept her
grandmother's   sovereign   cure   for   an   unusual
temperament.   Grand'mère could not understand
it.   .Why,   she herself had manœuvred several
meetings with suitable people, and the girl went
out in that disgraceful free-and-easy English way
with quite a lot of young men—by dint of some
picturesque perversion of the truth, Antoinette had
succeeded in obtaining a certain amount of liberty
—but   hitherto   nothing   had   come   either   of
Grand'mère's   efforts   or   of   Antoinette's   gadding
about.   And it was not that Grand'mère was not
vigilant, or that she failed in her duty towards her
Anatole's only child : no man could take Antoinette
out to tea, or write or telephone to her, without
Madame de Courcy enquiring into his financial
position, and, after the second or third meeting had
taken place : " *Eh bien, ma petite,* he has not yet
spoken to you of marriage?"

When Antoinette, after many discussions, had
finally been allowed to go to Amberhurst,
Grand'mère had propounded the theory that she
had been invited because the Faynes knew of some
rich young man who would be staying there at the
same time, and that they were doubtless trying to
bring about a match between him and Antoinette.
Henriette languidly reminded her mother-in-law
that the Faynes had a daughter of their own; but
Madame de Courcy, who was wonderfully imaginative where her favourite topic of matrimony was
concerned, argued that even if Miss Fayne *did* get
engaged to the " *parti*," the " *parti* " might be
struck by the charms of Miss Fayne's friend, and
remember that he also possessed a friend, rich and
suitable like himself, who would wish to be introduced to the friend of his friend's *fiancée*. . . .

Hence Grand'mère's flood of questions on
Antoinette's return.

As the family sat down to dinner that night, the
old lady greeted her son as usual with : " *Eh bien,
mon fils, comment vont les affaires ?*" And he,
also as usual, replied impatiently : " *Mal, mal . . .*"
for he was a confirmed pessimist. This short
duologue took place between mother and son every
evening. Having performed the ritual, Grand'mère
continued to question Antoinette with an air of
false benignity that was intended to put her at her
ease, and draw forth her artless confidence.

" Tell me the names of the young men you have
met. Do they live in London ? Was there not
one amongst them who pleased you more than the
others ?"

Very demurely, with dark lashes sweeping her
white cheeks, Antoinette launched forth into

descriptions of Mr. Griggs and Clive Blackwood.
She drew a particularly beautiful imaginary
portrait of Griggs, and Grand'mère pricked up her
ears.

"He lives in the country, that one? He has
estates? He has asked you to visit his family?"

Antoinette immediately robbed Mr. Griggs of
his vast country estates, by saying that alas, owing
to the innate nobility of his character, he had
renounced them in favour of a consumptive younger
brother. . . . Grand'mère lost interest, until
it struck her that the consumptive brother might
die, and Griggs thus recover possession of the
estates. Antoinette did not think it likely: the
brother wasn't as consumptive as all that. . . .

"You waste your time with the wrong people,"
her father declared irritably, "people who can be
of no use to you."

"She lacks the commercial instinct," Henriette
spoke very slowly and beautifully, and putting up
her lorgnon, surveyed Antoinette through it.
"C'est bien ma fille. . . ."

Anatole banged his fist upon the table. "It is
the nonsense you put into her head, that makes
her so difficult."

Henriette smiled her best smile of martyrdom
and patient endurance.

. . . And Antoinette was glad that this wasn't
all: that this hideous house and this family-party
with its bickerings and discussions, did not repre-
sent the sum-total of her universe; glad that she
had given a more or less fictitious account of her
stay, and that she could keep to herself everything
that had really mattered. This sense of having a
secret which the others could not guess, made her

c

feel wonderfully secure, invulnerable, almost : as
if no irritation or annoyance could touch her, while
she wrapped herself around with her memories of
Hester.

On the plea of fatigue after her journey, she
soon escaped upstairs to her room; smiled at the
tablecloth that had been embroidered by her cousin
Marguerite from Lyons, and that Grand'mère had
placed in Antoinette's room, hoping it might
exercise a beneficent influence upon her character.
Antoinette laughed happily; went to bed, and was
soon fast asleep, dreaming of Hester.

It was a long time since she had been as happy
and as excited as she was now. Her schooldays had
held occasional periods of a similar excitement, but
the three years since she had left boarding-school,
had been conspicuously barren, compared with what
had gone before. When she was thirteen, there had
been the melancholy-eyed young teacher of literature
whom she had adored; a dreamy unpopular woman,
who had been made to suffer horribly in the innumerable little ways in which schoolgirls can torment
their victims. Antoinette had been seized with a
kind of holy wrath, and desire to avenge and protect; she had flamed out against the whole class,
almost wishing that they would turn and rend her,
so that she might have the pleasure of sacrificing
herself for her idol. . . . The idol very soon
learnt to return the adoration of the fervent and
hot-tempered worshipper; and simultaneously
Antoinette began to lose interest. She had only
enjoyed her rôle, as long as Miss Prescot had taken
no notice of her : had been apparently unaware of
the flutter and throb of excitement caused by her

mere presence in the class-room, or her casual good-night kiss at bed-time. When Miss Prescot had come to single her out from the other girls and to linger fondly over that good-night kiss, Antoinette had had quite a fit of repulsion. She only enjoyed an up-hill battle; even at that age, the easy conquest had bored her. Also, she hated being touched, except in cases where her own feelings were aroused. She shook off the girls who sought to walk with their arms through hers, or to stroke her funny boyish head of hair; she would run away from them, revelling in the fun of the chase, yet dreading capture. . . . the fear in her eyes contradicted by the laughing curves of her mouth; the eyes of a nun, indeed, and the mouth of a voluptuary.

And then, some time later, there was the Russian girl, Natasha.

This time, Antoinette's passion was not killed by easy reciprocity, but kept alive by a thousand subtle tortures, rekindled by a single look or gesture, whenever Natasha imagined that it showed signs of waning. Her beauty was her strongest weapon, and at seventeen she used it with a refinement of cruelty that would have done credit to a woman twice her years. Antoinette was fascinated by her long sleepy eyes, that were green as jade, and as hard; by the heavy black hair growing low down upon her forehead; by her indolent graceful body, and the coldly indifferent manner that seemed to express the disdain in which she held her schoolfellows and her teachers alike. She had many slaves and admirers in the school, but none so ardent, so abandoned in her devotion, as Antoinette. Therefore, seeing that this was the case, Natasha ignored

her completely; avoided her on purpose when she
knew that the younger girl was hovering about the
stairs on the chance of being allowed to say good-
night to her; ridiculed her adoration in front of the
others; paraded ostentatiously with her favourites
before Antoinette's jealous eyes.   And then, as she
did not wish to forfeit altogether the entertaining
spectacle of Antoinette's passion, she would suddenly
and unexpectedly be nice to her, making amends
in five minutes for all the ill-treatment of the
previous weeks.   Antoinette forgave her gladly and
generously, but the moment she imagined that her
troubles were at an end, Natasha would with equal
suddenness withdraw her favour, and treat her as
badly as ever.   .   .   .

Antoinette suffered greatly at the time, but when
her passion had worn itself out, she began to look
forward with new zest to being grown up.   If
already this world of women and girls, narrow
though it was, could contain for her such a wealth
of thrills and excitement, how much more wonderful
must be that other world, the world beyond school,
the world of men.   So far, she was inclined to feel
contemptuous of the world of men, as represented
by the elderly masters who took some of the classes
at the fashionable boarding-school, and by the
coarse-looking schoolboys who grinned at the girls
when they passed each other on their daily walks.
But she knew that when she was grown-up, everything would be different.   Antoinette, counting the
months, the years—fifteen, sixteen, seventeen—
indulging in occasional passing flickers of feeling
for this girl or that mistress; Antoinette, young,
eager and glowing with an exuberant vitality, could
scarcely await her eighteenth birthday, and the

meeting with the lover who, she knew, awaited her
. . . . a lover to whom she could give all the passion
of her soul, and whose touch would thrill her even
more potently than had the touch of those women
she had adored.

But when at last she was released from school,
the grown-up world of men proved singularly disappointing; totally devoid of that stimulus for which
she craved.   The wonderful lover of her imagination
had certainly not yet appeared upon the scene.   In
the meantime, various supers tried to play the part,
but with no success as far as she was concerned.
She let them kiss her, because she hoped that thus
she might find what she sought; but those that did
not arouse active repulsion in her, merely bored
her, left her with a sense of staleness and dissatis-
faction.   She began to fear that she would never be
capable of feeling anything for anybody again.   And
now Hester had proved her fears to be groundless.
. . .   Gladly, gratefully Antoinette welcomed her
advent, and the rush of emotion which she had
called forth; turned with relief from her fruitless
search in the world of masculinity, to give herself
up to whole-hearted worship of this proud silent
woman, who had had the power to arouse her from
her temporary lethargy.   And in so doing,
Antoinette was free from the least taint of morbidity;
unaware that there was aught of unusual about her
attitude—Hester herself had perceived this—she
merely felt that she was coming into her own again,
and was healthy-minded and joyous in her unques-
tioning obedience to the dictates of her inmost
nature.

Hester wrote, giving her address at Bristol;

nothing more. Antoinette turned the scrawled half-sheet over and over in the hope of finding some other message, but in vain. She had to rest content with having the address, and hence, obviously, the permission to write to Hester. . . . She wrote by return a very long letter that was amusing as well as ardent, for she remembered that she had on occasions been able to arouse Hester's caustic sense of humour. And fervently she hoped that by-and-by Hester would come to reveal herself in writing more intimately than she was ever likely to do in speech.

The strain of waiting for Hester's answer was almost unbearable; at last it came : a brief acknow-ledgment of the receipt of Antoinette's letter, and the date of her departure from Bristol. . . .

Hereupon Antoinette wrote despairingly : " Won't you for once write me a *real* letter?" And Hester wrote back : " I never write what you call *real* letters. . . ."

After the first disappointment, Antoinette was conscious of renewed stimulation. Hester was unlike anyone she had ever met. What must be the life-history, every clue to which was guarded from the merest chance of revelation by pen and paper? Antoinette determined that one day she would break through Hester's reserve. In the meantime she continued to batter it with letters into which she put all the warmth and passion that were in her.

About the time she received Hester's second note, a letter came from Dennis Blackwood in Devonshire. Without a formal mode of address, it started straight away with a request for permission to write to her, and then rambled on for many pages in a particularly charming style, giving vivid bits of description of the places where he and Crispin were staying, and telling her little humorous incidents of the day's tramp. Antoinette said that certainly he might write to her, if he pleased; but she did not write to him at any length, because her one-sided correspondence with Hester was absorbing all her spare time and interest. But apparently her letter was cordial enough to call forth an answer by return.

Soon Dennis was writing to her every other day, then every day, then twice a day. . . . Regretfully she compared his long and truly delightful letters with Hester's curt scrappy communications. It seemed such a waste not to be in love with Dennis. His veritable avalanche of letters undoubtedly pleased and flattered her, but did not cause one fraction of the palpitating excitement that she felt at the mere sight of Hester's writing on an envelope.

But her grandmother's agitation alone would have made it worth Antoinette's while to keep up the correspondence. Grand'mère had naturally demanded full details concerning the young man who wrote to her grand-daughter with such improper frequency. And Antoinette, more demure and " jeune fille " than ever, had modestly said that he was a great artist. . . .

" *Hein, hein,* an artist? That does not please me at all. He has doubtless not a farthing, and you know very well that *la vie de bohème* is nothing for you," with a warning glance at Henriette, from whom Antoinette was assumed to have inherited all her immoral tendencies.

Antoinette continued gleefully to foster in her grandmother's mind the vision of Dennis as an impecunious artist with short nails and long hair, who would encourage her to dance upon tables, drink champagne for breakfast, associate with people who posed for " *L'ensemble* "—even if she did not actually pose for " *L'ensemble* " herself — and generally behave in a manner incompatible with Cadogan Gardens and the dignity of the de Courcys.

CHAPTER V

June 29th, 1914.

" . . . WE'RE putting up to-night in rooms above a pastry-cook's shop . . . wonderful rooms. I know you'd love them. I've been taking for your benefit an inventory of the sitting-room furniture. There are yellow faded family-photographs on the walls, and wedding-groups with bridesmaids wearing hats with quills all pointing the same way. There's a dusty wooden shelf with mugs that are all Presents from the Seaside, or else symbols of the Jubilee, the Coronation or other events of national unimportance. There's a red plush anchor with shells round it; there's a cardboard model of a ship under a glass bell; there's a slippery horsehair sofa, upon which Crispin is now reclining, fast alseep. And chiefly, there is a piano with a green silk front and a yellow keyboard so short that I find myself clawing the air if I venture too far away from the central C. There's such a funny foreign look about the way the houses here grow in a square round the market-place. They are painted all different colours, too; there's a bright blue one just opposite, with a tiny salmon pink one, half its height, leaning confidingly up against it; ours is a modest saffron yellow, with red bars under the window-ledges. There's a pump in the middle of the market-square, and around it the most delightful mixed assorted collection of dogs doze in the sun. I'm going to fetch one of them in to talk to me when I've finished this letter. We

don't quite know if he's meant to be a bull-dog or a
spaniel, but he's long and slobbery and brindled
and adorable, and he's going to lie across my lap,
while I whisper absurdities into his long soft ears.

I can't get rid of the impression that this is a
little foreign town. Between the houses are narrow
passages that are spanned by tiny stone archways,
dazzling white against an Italian blue sky; and
from each archway flutter boldly the coloured
banners of somebody's washing. And the hotel,
painted brownish pink and built round a triangular
court planted with shrubbery, is just such as you
might find in a small place in Switzerland.

No, I think I've got it now : it's not a foreign
place, in fact it isn't a real place at all . . . It's
just a toy village that you're allowed to take out
of the nursery cupboard and play with, when you've
been good.

Please won't you come and play with my toy
village with me? I'll be awfully nice about it, and
even let you work the pump and hang up the washing when I'm tired of doing it myself.

No, it isn't a toy village either : it's just a
dream-place. I knew that, the instant we came in
sight of it this afternoon. We'd been walking over
the moors to the accompaniment of a tearing wind
that swept magnificently up and down the scale,
as it drove great lumpy golden clouds over the edge
of the horizon, and roared in our ears and muttered
in the hedgerows. And then suddenly the white
road began to dip down and down into a hollow in
which lay this handful of coloured roofs. And the
sound of the wind became softer and softer, as if
whoever was conducting the orchestra, had hushed
all the brass-instruments. And by the time we

reached the village-street, after a last faint murmur there was no sound at all, only the most wonderful thick sunny silence you've ever listened to. And I want you here in my dream-place. You belong in it. I may tell you that, mayn't I? Besides, you know. Of course you know . . . don't you? "

July 5th.

. . . " You want my village for keeps? I'm afraid you can't have it, because if I packed it in my suit-case to bring home to you, the water from the pump might get loose and make my collars damp. I'm sorry! I'm sending you a nice fat tin of cream instead, which will no doubt upset your grandmother—morally, of course. She must be a delightful old lady, according to your descriptions, and I look forward to making her acquaintance on my return. . . . We're staying in quite a different sort of village this time; it has an old-world trian-gular village-green, planted with giant oak-trees, and enclosed on two sides by dear little thatched cottages with trim little gardens; and it has an ivy-clad church and the usual combination of Post Office and all-sorts shop, in which you may revel in the complex odour of boots, cheese, liquorice, soap, sawdust, biscuits, Fry's chocolate and warm humanity. And best of all, this village of ours boasts an absolutely authentic Idiot, Vicar, Oldest Inhabitant, Lady of the Manor and Village Belle— I expect she'll lose some of our socks, as she hap-pens to be the laundress in private life—and they all come on and speak in character when the strings are pulled. Unfortunately, the Wicked Squire is lacking from the set; he must have been mislaid. But I hear they've got a Squire of sorts some miles

away, and for the sake of tradition let us hope that
his morals are infamous and his jowl unshaven and
blue.

We had a long tramp to get here from Chagford,
and at every farm we encountered on the way, we
halted so that Crispin might still his insatiable
appetite for bread and cheese and beer. And while
he sat and gorged in state in the parlour with the
best antimacassars and the coloured prints of the
Royal Family, I prowled round the farm-buildings,
and had much speech with velvet-eyed calves, and
watch-dogs straining at their chains, and sleepy
kittens, and ducks sailing proudly on the pond in
the orchard. I loved all their quacking and purring
and barking and lowing, and the excited flutter in
the poultry-yard and the rich deep sounds from the
pig-sty. And oh, the farm-smell of earth and damp
straw and clover and animals and hay. . . .

The fields are brown and red and green, and
brown again; and scattered in the hollows, or
perched on the hillsides are villages—mere clusters
of whitewashed and pinkwashed cottages—gleaming
in the sun. But even the tiniest cluster has its
battered grey church-spire. The smoke from the
gorse-fires floats in heavy blue clouds above the
Tors, and I do so badly want someone to share it
all with me . . . ! Crispin? Yes, he's a dear
good sort and I like being with him. He's so restful because he takes me so for granted; doesn't ask
questions; and there's never the least strain between us. I believe Crispin is really wedded, heart
and soul, to his Bechstein grand at home. Whilst
I—Oh, I don't know. Perhaps some day I'll be
able to tell you. . . .

I'm afraid we shall have to push on very quickly

from this perfect spot, as Crispin has succeeded in getting us into trouble. We've got no piano here, and he was told on enquiring that the only one in the neighbourhood is up at the Manor. I had to restrain him forcibly from marching straight in and taking possession of the instrument. I put it to him that it couldn't be done—no, not even if he pretended to be the piano-tuner. . . . So very morosely, he gave way, and consoled himself by borrowing the key of the church from the vicar, and playing the organ. That was all very nice, of course, but Crispin, from force of habit, locked himself in; and that afternoon there was to be a christening . . . and he didn't take the slightest notice when they came and hammered on the church-door; merely thundered away, louder than ever, on his wheezy old organ. The christening procession had to wait outside, with the baby catching cold, till Crispin got hungry, and came out to have his tea. . . . Of course they might have entered by another door, but that spoils my story. . . .

I'm writing you such a lot of nonsense; you don't mind, do you? If you only realised how difficult it is to stop writing to you! I want to go on and on and on, and tell you things—but they are just the things you know already. . . . You seem very near to me to-night. Perhaps you were thinking about me just a little, and have come here in a dream. I believe you're beside me now, only if I turn to look you'll vanish. . . ."

July 7th.

" . . . It's nice of you to ask about my opera. I haven't worked at it much lately. I've been so lazy and happy, just walking and dreaming and eating and sleeping, and writing to you. But as regards the opera—do you remember Andersen's fairy-tale, ' Karen and the Red Shoes '? A friend of mine, Neil Barnaby, has turned it into a three-act play, and I'm writing the music for it. It's the first time I've attempted anything quite so big. We want to have it put on with an entirely modern impressionistic setting—perhaps next opera-season at Covent Garden. Perhaps. . . . To-night I can almost believe that it will be so, and that the work that is nearest and dearest to my heart will actually be played before hundreds and hundreds of people. Perhaps they'll acclaim it, go mad over it, as I've seen them go mad, and gone mad myself over the Russian Opera. And I know I shall have a ridiculous desire to cry, and there won't be an ounce of conceit in me, because after all it's just my child they'll be making the fuss about—not me. And I'm glad that it should be like that, for I hate being taken notice of, and always want to run away and hide. But the child is different. The child, I think, is going to be strong. And I love it so. . . . And all the pleasure that my music may bring to the people who listen to it, won't nearly equal some of the top-moments of joy I've had in creating it. Yes, to-night I can believe that the opera will be a success ; to-night I can believe even more than that ; to-night I can believe—anything, Antoinette.

When I was at school, I was terrified of my musical gift ; I hated it, and did my utmost to suppress it, because I thought it was that which made me different from the other boys. I loathed being ' different ' ; it made me feel so alone, so I played hard games with the others, and tried to make friends with the others, and tried to forget that there was something inside my brain that turned everything I felt and experienced into music, which clamoured to be released, and which I refused to release, because I knew that if I did so, it would widen still more the gulf between me and the others. I built barrier upon barrier to shut in the fragments of music that sang in my ears all day and all night; I was powerless to keep them from entering, but at least I would give them no chance to escape. I wouldn't take music-lessons at school; that would have been too dangerous; old Harper, the piano-master, was a pretty shrewd person, and might have spotted me. I resented having this thing to hide, and envied my brother Clive and the other boys, for not having to wage this perpetual war against part of their own selves. There were times when I did long so badly just to give in. . . . And if I did that, I could never again keep up the pretence of being like the others. Somehow, that pretence seemed the all-important thing : there was safety in it.

When I was sixteen, a Jewish boy called Eric Rubenstein came to Westborough. He was clever as they're made, but ugly and undersized, and appallingly sensitive; he had a rotten time of it. Everything about him seemed to lay him open to being ragged—his looks, his name (they called him Little-by-Little ' for short ') and the way his people kissed him before the whole school, and brought him pineapples and grapes when they came down to see him. He used, for some unfathomable reason, to follow me around with his great intelligent eyes, that were like the eyes of a dog that expects to be kicked; but I didn't even try to befriend him. You see, I realised that young Eric was likely to be dangerous too : he played the violin, and he played it like an artist. . . .

He fagged for a great loutish Sixth Form chap called Burnley, who did his best to make Eric's life a misery. I was in Burnley's study one Saturday afternoon, and he and some of his pals were banging away on the piano. Someone suggested that the Jew-boy, who was toasting muffins by the fire, should play his violin. . . . The Jew-boy refused, and I was glad that he had refused to play to them. Then I saw that Burnley was looking at him with a very evil gleam in his heavy eyes. The next instant the storm broke. ' What—you won't ? Is there any law in your benighted religion to prevent you playing the fiddle on Saturdays ? '

Eric blazed out : ' My religion's as good as yours ! ' and then relapsed into his usual attitude of defence.

' Oh, no, it isn't, Ikey,' Burnley grinned, ' don't make any mistake about that ; you're a Jew, that's what you are, a dirty Jew . . . ugh ! '

They went on badgering him about his religion and about his father, who was supposed to have kept a fried-fish shop before he got rich. And they threatened him with lickings, and with red-hot pokers down his back if he wouldn't play. . . . I daresay most of it was bluff, but he must have had memories of previous tortures, for he turned absolutely white, and tried to hide his funk under a rather sickening smile.

He kept on looking to me for help, but I just sat there, with the palms of my hands getting hot and sticky, and didn't move. They forced him finally by threat of sheer physical violence, and I felt that

it was indecent that he should play before those
boys who didn't really want to hear his music, and
only wanted to make a mock of him; and indecent
that I should be listening. But I had to stop and
listen. I hadn't interfered to protect him, but I
couldn't leave him quite alone while he played. . . .
And then I realised that Eric wasn't really giving
himself in his music; he seemed to be withholding
himself from expression. I was terribly afraid that
as he went on he'd overstep the borders of his reserve, but he didn't. His playing was correct and
polished; and absolutely soulless.

When he had finished, I was unthinkingly
whistling the Russian song he'd played; and he
looked up and came across to me, seeing that the
others were all busy round the piano. ' Yes, of
course that's how it ought to have been played, but
I couldn't do it like that—could I—for them.' I
had to take care not to let him guess how heartily I
agreed with him, so I said off-handedly : ' I don't
see why not ! '

' Oh, yes, you do,' he persisted, ' you *know*. . . .
You must have a wonderful ear to be able to whistle
it straight off like that. Don't you love Wieniawski ?
I do. . . .' He was no longer the cringeing little
Fourth Form fag addressing a senior boy; he was
speaking as man to man, or as one artist to another.
But I had to shut him up; told him I didn't ' know,'
and hadn't any ear at all, and hated Wieniawski
and all other kinds of music, and advised him to
stow his cheek. . . . Oh, I could talk the verna-
cular right enough ! He just gave me one look,
half reproachful and half apologetic; then he
blurted out, under cover of the song that the others
were bawling in chorus : ' I—I suppose you thought

me an utter worm just now—I know I am, but it makes me sick—pain does—even the idea of it—and being helpless and knowing that it isn't going to stop—and it comes over you in waves each a bit more ghastly than the last. It isn't what they do, though that's bad enough sometimes. . . It's what they might do . . . and you know exactly what it would feel like, and you lie awake at night and think about it, and wait——'

It was all too horrible for words. I longed to shut him up again, but I saw that he'd reached the limits of his endurance, and simply had to talk. . . . He went on to tell me about his people at home. ' My father thinks I'm ever so happy here, and popular, and good at games and all that—he's so absurdly proud of me, you see—so in the holidays I have to keep it up—fib about cricket matches I'm supposed to have played in, and invent stories of practical jokes in which I figure as the hero instead of the victim . . . and he drinks it all in, and loves it, and I can't bear to let him know.'

He said that, when I suggested that he should get his parents to take him away from Westborough. Plucky, wasn't it? And heartbreaking. He was such a kid. . . . I had an insane desire to be nice to him, to make up for what the others were doing to him. But after that one outburst, I avoided him more than ever. With his subtle Jewish instinct he'd discovered well enough that I *was* different from the others; but he never again attempted to speak to me about music, although he must have known all along. I was grateful to him for that; the barriers I had built were getting weaker and weaker; and I had the almost superstitious conviction that they would only stand firm as

long as I didn't tell anybody about myself, or let
them give me the sympathy and understanding I
craved for. I dared not let myself get fond of Eric,
or I might have been swept away to heaven knows
what headlong flights of—' differentness.' So the
desire to be nice to him had to be fought down as
well. . . .

And then one day—it was the half-term holiday,
and pouring with rain. I went up to the practice-
room at the top of the house to fetch something I'd
been sent for—and the piano was open—and no one
was about—and I thought I'd just see if I could
remember one of the absurd pieces Clive and I had
been taught by our nursery-governess.

I don't know how it happened : I had started by
picking out ' The Merry Peasant,' but a while
after, without realising what I was doing, I was
finding chords that began to release, bit by bit,
some of the music that was imprisoned inside my
head, and that seemed to be spurring me on,
impatient of my clumsy fingers that groped so
slowly for the magic formula that would set it
free. . . .

Later on, I was out on the Downs, running away
from what I knew I should never be able to escape,
now that I had let *it* escape me. . . . given the
thing that was in my mind a separate existence, by
putting it outside myself. It was just that—putting
it outside myself—that had swept me right over my
own barriers. I knew then that come what might,
I'd got to be musician, even if it did mean being
different and being lonely. I knew I'd got to suffer,
and by suffering—create. I determined that the
one person who should share that knowledge with

me, should be Eric. I looked forward to being able
to be decent to him at last. . . .

I wandered about for hours in the wind and rain,
and when I got back, there was a little knot of
boys whispering in the hall. 'I say, have you
heard?' 'No, what?' 'About the Jew-boy—
appendicitis—awful agony, the Matron says,
quickest case she's ever heard of—*scream*—you
should have heard him, fair blood-curdling, I can
tell you.' 'It's awfully quiet now; his people have
come. . . . Will they take him—take *it*—
away. . . .?'

That was the end of Eric, who dreaded the idea of
pain.

. . . . After that, I didn't make any attempt
to crawl back behind my barriers; they weren't
strong enough anyway to stand against the flood-
tide that had broken out. Everything that I felt
about Eric would set itself to weird horrible music
that drummed unceasingly in my ears, and demanded expression, and I was dead tired of choking
it back. So I had to let myself become a musician.
But I put up an awfully hard fight against it. It's
queer to think of it now. . . .

I don't know how it is that I can talk to you like
this. I've never told anyone else about Eric, and
I know I couldn't do it so easily if you were really
here. But being miles away from you, there's
nothing to frighten me into shutting myself up,
nothing to destroy my conviction that you *do*
understand.

Good-night, dear. I've enjoyed talking to
you. . . ."

July 12th.

" We're zig-zagging about the country in the most
amazing style. And I wish I could collect all the
things I've loved most, and bring them back to
you. There's the early-morning smell—such a
foreign smell, too—of pines, and fresh-cut grass,
and stone walls and burning wood. And there are
the evenings when the scent of the earth and the
trees after the day's heat is so strong and sweet and
poignant that it hurts you; and there's a glamour
over the whole world; and the lights begin to show
in the cottage windows; and a great golden moon
swims up over the hard black edge of the moor. . .
Yesterday we found a river, gleaming silver in the
depths of a forest—such a river. . . . It rushed
onward at a tearing rate, hurling itself down over
great moss-grown boulders, working itself into a
white frenzy of foam as it fretted its way between
them, and swirled around the outstanding tree-roots.
And, oh, the colours of the water—crystal and gold
where the sun touched it, clear amber and brown
and green where it was flecked by the shadow of
the branches. You've never heard such a wonderful
orchestra of bird-voices : the low clear note of the
blackbird as soloist, and all the warbling, trilling,
chirping and whistling that went to make a har-
monious accompaniment, together with the sooth-
ing monotone of the bees, and the hurry, hurry,
hurry of the river—but what's the good of trying to
tell you about it in words? Perhaps I'll put it into
music for you some day. There's such a lot to be
done ' some day,' isn't there? When I get back,
you must come to Covent Garden with me. And
there'll be concerts, too. It's a regular feast of

good music in London this season. We're taking
the train to Exeter to-morrow, and I may be coming
straight home from there, unless Crispin lures me
on into Cornwall. I'm too sleepy and drunk with
the air to make up my mind definitely to-night.
But I'll let you know to-morrow.

Good-night. . . ."

CHAPTER VI

ANTOINETTE smiled tenderly over those letters; he must be a queer person, Dennis Blackwood, to write to her like that, after having only spoken to her once. She liked his letters from an artistic point of view, and the bulk of them gave her a feeling of warmth and contentment; but once read, she put them aside; did not pore over them as she pored over Hester's, striving to read between the lines, and to put into the words meanings which did not exist. Hester at a distance was most unsatisfactory, so much so, that it sometimes cost Antoinette a real effort to conjure up the image of her personality. She ventured to express the hope that she might soon be allowed to see Hester again; and to her infinite surprise, Hester replied that she was at Birmingham now, and that if Antoinette thought it worth while, she might come and spend a day with her there.

Antoinette trembled with joy on receiving that letter. It lay beside the one in which Dennis had told her about Eric Rubenstein, and Grand'mère peered inquisitively over the silver coffee-pot. But Antoinette cared naught for Grand'mère that morning : she was going to see Hester, and Dennis was evidently in love with her, and the world was altogether an excellent place; gratefully Antoinette accepted the gifts that fate was showering upon her —gratefully as a flower opens its petals to the sun.

Some days later, by dint of a series of lies and precautions, she set out for Birmingham. She could not tell the family where she was going. They knew nothing about Hester, and had they done so, would doubtless have deemed the two hours' journey to see her, crazy and an unnecessary expense. She had stated that she was spending the day at Rosabel's in Hampstead; and Rosabel, good soul, had been sworn to secrecy.

What would the day give her? Antoinette wondered, as the train bore her northwards, her excitement growing and growing with every beat of the wheels. In what circumstances and in what state of mind would she find Hester? She was entirely in the dark, her imagination free to illuminate it with the most fantastic of pictures. It was fantastic enough in itself that she should be tearing across England just to spend a day with Hester. Just one day—that was the joy of it! One magic day standing out in high relief from the monotonous flat background of days all alike; one day to look back upon, robbed from the calendar. . . . Would Hester be as unapproachable as ever, or would she at last overcome her fierce reserve, and of her own free will admit Antoinette to her confidence? Antoinette's heart beat faster, as she pictured this eventuality. She stood up in the corridor, too restless to sit down, feverish with anticipation. . . .

Then the train swung into the station, and Antoinette saw Hester on the platform; and suddenly all the fever and excitement that had been worked up to such a pitch died down, so that it required no special effort to greet Hester with nonchalant calm. It was as if her pulses had become tired of beating and hammering merely in anticipation, and had ceased to do so, now that anticipation was about to merge into realisation.

"It was nice of you to come," smiled Hester.

"It was nice of you to let me," responded Antoinette.

They made their way through the crowd and out into the street.

"You'll lunch with me at my lodgings, won't you?" said Hester.

"Thanks very much."

After that they walked in silence. Obviously Hester waited for her to open conversation, but their unsatisfactory correspondence had established no link of intimacy between them, and Antoinette was at a loss, not knowing where or how to begin. Hester stopped in front of a boarding-house in a rather dingy side-street, and Antoinette followed her in through a dark and stuffy hall that smelt of roast mutton, and thence into a drawing-room with cheap lace curtains and bamboo tables ornamented with dusty ferns.

"We can stop here for the present," said Hester; "everybody seems to be out."

Antoinette glanced at the pretentious knick-knacks on the mantelpiece, the dirty crinkled paper round the flower-pots, the gaudily-framed pictures. . . . a third-rate boarding-house was about the last place in the world, in which she would have expected to find Hester. Her sense of the fitness of things was outraged.

"Do you—do you live here?" she began at last tentatively.

"For the moment, yes."

"But. . . . do you like it?"

Hester shrugged her shoulders. "If you can't be where you want to be, this place is as good as any other. And I'm not a millionaire, you know."

All the same, Antoinette reflected, millionaire or not, surely it was possible to live in surroundings less actively repellent than these! Apparently Hester carried her habitual detachment even to the lengths of being quite oblivious of their sordidness.

She hunted in her mind for a suitable topic of conversation. "What was Bristol like?" But almost before the words were out of her mouth, she realised that she had infringed that unwritten law which decreed that she should display no curiosity with regard to Hester's private affairs.

She was prepared for the inevitable cold and evasive reply, when Hester said : "Bristol? Oh, good enough while it lasted. But what are two weeks in a year, compared with the fifty bad ones?"

"Are they always bad—the odd fifty?"

"More or less. He's married, you see. His wife's in an asylum; and things are difficult on account of his position; he's a schoolmaster. . . . The good times just have to be snatched."

Antoinette felt stunned—and then disappointed. Hester had revealed to her the secret of her life, but she had expected so much more drama from the actual moment of revelation. And the secret itself struck her as very commonplace; it seemed as if Hester, by taking Antoinette into her confidence, had forfeited some of her mysterious charm. . . . Antoinette tried in vain to fathom the reason why her burning love for Hester should be thus transformed into a feeling of faint repulsion—repulsion, no, that was absurd. What she felt was jealousy, perhaps; jealousy of the man to whom Hester gave all there was to be given, so that she had nothing left over for Antoinette. . . . It was not that, either. She had always dimly suspected the existence of such a man, and assuming that Hester's happiness lay with him, she had been generous enough not to be jealous. And now that his existence was no longer a hypothesis but a certainty, she was less inclined than ever to be jealous—but she knew it was from indifference rather than from generosity.

Hester was saying: "As you know, I never discuss my life with anyone, but I thought I had better tell you just the bare facts, as you've been foolish enough to honour me with a certain amount of your affection." Her great eyes gazed straight into Antoinette's with the old look, which only three weeks ago had stirred in her such depths of feeling. But now she could only flush and avert her eyes from Hester's, so that Hester might not see that all the affection she had ever had for her was dead. Also, she had a shrinking fear that Hester would come to elaborate the "bare facts." It struck Antoinette as indecent that Hester should do so now, when she lacked the tenderness with which she would once have received such confidence. . . . So she talked feverishly and brilliantly, and was all the while full of a pitiful amazement, because Hester's appreciative laugh, that could so wonderfully transform her sullen face was powerless to rekindle the dead emotion. Antoinette was relieved when they sat down to lunch with the other inhabitants of the boarding-house at the one long table in the dining-room. She was getting tired of the strain. . . . And by the end of the day she was more tired of it still, tired of pretending to Hester, pretending to herself. And evidently she had not pretended so very well after all, because Hester said as she walked with her to the station :

" You're disappointed—but remember, I warned you. . . ."

" Oh, I'm *not*!" cried Antoinette, in a last attempt to delude herself even more than Hester.

But Hester only smiled and shook her head. " It's no use, my child, I know you are, as I knew you would be. People who pour out such great floods of feeling as you do are bound to suffer from disillusionment. Especially if they come up against people like me."

" How d'you mean—people like you?" stammered Antoinette.

Hester laughed harshly. " I suppose I'm deceptive. Oh, you're not the first person I've deceived—involuntarily, of course, because I've always warned them as I warned you. Imaginative people of your type are drawn to me because, apparently, I give the impression of having more in me than I have. That's all. It's not a tragedy. But I don't think we'll see each other again, you and I."

" Not. . . . ?"

" Better not. And by the time you get home you'll realise if you haven't done so already, that you don't want to either."

 . . . . The world would be a terribly dreary place, now that there was no one left in it to love. Even if Hester had been cruel to her, it would have been easier to bear, than just discovering that she no longer cared for Hester. The greatest cruelty on her part could not have killed the love that Antoinette had had for her only three weeks ago, only yesterday. . . . But Hester had been kind; kinder than ever before; and it was not her kindness that was to blame. Nor was it the mere fact of having found her in the wrong setting. Again, only yesterday, Antoinette's adoration would have been proof against such trivialities—would have deepened at the thought of Hester in that depressing environment.

It was not Hester's fault. Antoinette knew that; Hester was unchanged. It was only she who had lost the power of endowing her with a charm that she had never possessed. The queer impetus that had made her love Hester had suddenly become paralysed, just as her pulses had ceased to hammer, the moment she arrived at the station.

But if the whole of that brief magical passion had been but a fever of Antoinette's own imagination, a temporary madness, and if her present state of mind heralded her return to sanity, then with all her soul she longed to become mad again, so that she might go on loving. . . .

Her wonderful day was over, and it had not held one single moment upon which it would be good to look back. She was returning empty-handed. And she would have to rouse herself into giving the family a chatty and fictitious description of how she had spent the day with Rosabel.

In the midst of her desolation, it gave her a little comfort to remember that Dennis's promised letter from Exeter would be awaiting her at home. She hoped it would be one of his specially nice ones. She was in a mood to appreciate it to-night. . . .

But that night there was no letter from Dennis; neither the next night; nor the one after.

CHAPTER VII

" AND what now?" queried Dennis Blackwood, as
they got out of the train, and stood upon the drip-
ping wet platform at Crannack.

" P-put up here for the night, and p-push on to-
morrow," Crispin responded. Dennis agreed that
it was the only thing to be done.

They had left Exeter that afternoon, Dennis
having agreed to Crispin's suggestion that they
might sample the Cornish coast. Dennis was in
no hurry to return to London. There was a dream-
like quality about all his days just now, days
shared with his dream-companion, Antoinette. And
perhaps at the back of his mind lurked an indefinable fear of the moment when he must exchange
dreams for reality. If he went on to Cornwall,
there would be more days, and more, of hard walking and healthy sleep, and all the haphazard fun
of eccentric stoppages at eccentric places—and
above all, the dream-companionship would be prolonged. . . .

From Exeter, they had intended taking the train
down to Penzance, and thence starting to explore
the Land's End district; but it had got late while
they visited the Cathedral at Exeter, and on arriving at the station they found that they had missed
the Cornish express, and had to be content with a
very slow train that stopped at all stations, and
finally stopped altogether at Crannack, the centre
of the mining-district. They were informed that
they could get no connection to Penzance the same
night.

" Dismal-looking hole, isn't it?" remarked Dennis, as they trudged up the High Street, through the rain, in search of lodgings. Crispin grunted assent, and turned up his coat-collar. He detested the wet. They took rooms at the first Commercial Hotel they reached; and had a belated supper in a dingy and badly-lighted dining-room. When they had finished, Dennis declared : " I'm going out for some air, rain or no rain," but Crispin preferred to remain in the stuffy little smoking-room with a book and a pipe.

Dennis resolved that before settling down to write to Antoinette, he would have a look round the place. It seemed unprepossessing enough, especially when contrasted with the clean cheerful Devonshire villages which they had just left. Crannack was neither clean nor cheerful; yet for Dennis there was a certain fascination about the way its little twisted streets ran steeply upwards from the docks, as if trying to scramble away from the perpetual harbour-noises; the rasping of chains, hooting of steam-sirens, rattling of coal-trucks. But the few upward-winding streets which Dennis explored attained to nothing more romantic or beautiful than a tin-roofed Methodist Chapel or Temperance Hotel. And as if in mockery of, or in opposition to, these hideous symbols of virtue, a great multitude of public-houses and drinking-saloons clustered about the centre of the town and straggled all along the wharf. From behind the blurred windows came the sound of drunken laughter and voices raised in discussion; voices raucous and yet mournful, that reminded Dennis of the screeching of sea-gulls. He strolled across the market-place, where the gas-flares over the stalls

spluttered and wavered in the rain-laden wind, and
cast fantastic lights and shadows—evil lights and
shadows—upon the grimy faces of the men who
hung about in groups, seemingly aimless, as if
waiting to take their turn in the overcrowded
drinking-saloons.   Whenever any of the swing-
doors were pushed open, giving a glimpse of sanded
floor and iridescent bottles, and some figure reeled
out, or was pushed out into the night air, his place
was immediately filled by one of the waiting crowd.
Dennis moved away from the noise and glare, and
up a quiet side-street.   The wet soft wind was in
his face, bringing with it a faint tang of the sea.
He walked on, while behind him the lights of the
town became dimmer and more dim, and the sounds
more and more muffled; and at last the monotonous
outlines of the houses on either side of the narrow
street merged into irregular humped shadows, that
represented tumbledown barns and deserted cottages, and then fell away altogether.   The wind
blew harder now, and Dennis guessed that he must
be in open country.   The darkness was thick and
moist; tangible almost.   But further up the road,
a red glow of light beckoned, that was neither the
light of a public-house, nor yet the flare above a
market-stall.   It was the unmistakable glow of a
blacksmith's forge, that was luring him on through
the darkness; and Dennis pressed forward, for
there was something subtly attractive to him in
these sudden alternations of blackest shadows and
glaring light.

The door of the smithy stood wide open.   Dennis,
rather dazzled, sat down upon a ramshackle fence
on the opposite side of the road.   Two swarthy-
faced men stood facing the forge, and a third, a

muscular-looking giant was holding by the bridle
a great cart-horse, that impatiently pawed the
ground and shook back its mane.

A youth was at work at the anvil.   He was
stripped to the waist, and in the leaping light of
the flames, his body seemed white and slender.
Dennis reflected that it was a most effective picture : in the midst of the clammy surrounding
darkness, this great square of blazing heat and
light ; crimson glow illuminating the men's dark
faces, the glossy coat of the horse, and the boy's
black head ; and showing every ripple of the muscles
under the fine skin, as he raised his arms to hammer the red-hot iron into shape.   The three men
watched him attentively, talking in their Cornish
dialect that was almost incomprehensible to Dennis
across the road.

He caught snatches.   "Coomin' on fine, that be."

" What d' I tell ee, la-ad ?   Slowly does ut—
slowly."

" Ee doan't want fur tu use all that strength—
thur, I knew it'd 'appen . . . ." as the boy
brought down the hammer with a smashing blow
upon the horseshoe, and a piece of the red-hot iron
flew off and, before he had time to avoid it, landed
upon his foot.   He dropped the hammer and broke
into a picturesque flow of bad language ; but to
Dennis's surprise, his speech bore no trace of Cornish dialect, but every trace of the accent that is
manufactured at Oxford. . . .

" All right, you needn't crow over me, Tre-
mayne !   I tell you, that shoe would have been every
bit as good as one of yours, if I hadn't smashed it.
Holy saints and martyrs, the touch of red-hot iron
on the flesh is damnable, simply damnable.   I wish

D

my mother were here to ' kiss the place and make it well ' . . . ."

There was a burst of gruff laughter from the blacksmith and the man holding the horse, but the third, a round-shouldered little man with weak, kindly eyes, spoke with some concern. " And what'll yer fa-ather be sayin', Mr. Alan, if us let ee go knockin' yerself tu bits like this?"

" My father, Jenkins, would send down another army of chaperons and guardians to look after me, or would censure you most heartily for allowing me to play with the nasty fire. . . . Have any of you got a spare handkerchief? I want to tie up my foot and hobble home."

Several more or less grimy rags were produced simultaneously, and Dennis came forward across the road. " Here, take mine. Are you badly hurt?"

" Oh, dear me, no, I'm not badly hurt. It's fun, dropping pieces of red-hot metal upon portions of one's anatomy. Especially if one isn't accustomed to it."

" A fresh emotion, at any rate," Dennis smiled.

Alan looked up at him quickly from where he sat on the ground, nursing his foot. " I say, where do you come from? What are you? We don't get any tourists here. You're not another new inspector, sent down by my benighted parent, are you?"

" Inspector?" Dennis repeated blankly, " inspector of what?"

" Of coal-mines, of course. In this God-forsaken place we think of nothing but coal. We live in it, count in it, breathe it—lots of them die of it. Jenkins here has nearly lost his sight through it.

. . . No one comes to Crannack who isn't some-how or other connected with coal."

" I assure you solemnly, then, that I haven't the least connection with it, and that I know nothing whatever about coal, barring the strictly domestic variety that appears in the family grate."

" Thank God at least for that! Well, if it isn't coal that has brought you here, what is it?"

" A train that refused to carry us on to Pen-zance, as we desired, and apparently preferred to deposit us here. We're staying over night and going on to-morrow morning."

" I thought as much. It was too good to be true. No one stops at Crannack longer than they can help. Where are you putting up?"

Dennis told him, and he replied : " That's not far from my digs. Are you going back there now? If so, we may as well walk together, and you can support my fainting footsteps if necessary. I say—will you?"

There was so much boyish eagerness in the tone, that Dennis laughed. " Of course I will. Come along."

Alan put on his coat, bade good-night to the three men, and he and Dennis set off together down the dark road. At the bottom of the hill, the clus-tered lights of the town twinkled sleepily.

" It doesn't look so bad at night," remarked Alan, " but in the daytime—Lord, the ugliness and the filth of it! And the ugliness and the filth of the people, too. Not that it's their fault, poor devils. The material is good enough in itself—it's the use that's being made of it."

" But," said Dennis, " whatever are *you* doing

here, in this place that you hate, and among these
people to whom you don't belong?"

Impatiently Alan replied : " My father sent me
here to study mining-engineering after I left Oxford. He owns several more or less prosperous coal-
mines up in Lancashire, and he's having this one
developed as a speculation. He wants me to take
over the management of it. So I'm supposed to be
learning the ropes—seeing how the thing's done—
or how the maximum of profit can be ground out of
the minimum of expenditure ; financial expenditure
of course ; not expenditure of human life."

" But I thought that everything in mortal power
had been done to reduce the liability of accidents in
mines ; is the expenditure of life really so great ?"

" Greater than it need be. Oh, we have sanitary
inspectors nosing around, and plastering up the
Government regulations, and finding everything to
their satisfaction—but all the same, every lump of
coal that is burnt is soaked in blood, human blood.
. . ." The boy was talking with a curious vehemence and excitement—vehemence and excitement
that seemed to have been long pent-up. " Sometimes we have quicksand, and sometimes we have
floods, and sometimes we have fire-damp and ex-
plosions, and sometimes we have all the lot. . . .
You can see the results : you've only to look at
the blind and the cripples and the consumptive
wrecks in the streets. It's in the pits that they've
lost their sight and their limbs and their health,
grubbing in the dark, in the foul air, so that capitalists like my father may grow sleek."

" That's socialist-talk, isn't it ?"

" Not only talk ; I'm going to *do*. . . ."

" What can you do—what is there to be done about it ?"

" That's what I'm trying to find out; and the only way to find out is to do what I'm doing now.

" Well . . . .?" Dennis looked at the boy limping along at his side; saw his face, white and dim, in the darkness, the clean line of the jaw and throat. It might have been the face of a young knight, Dennis thought; a young knight ardent and fearless, setting out to combat evils as old as the world. . . .

Alan replied : " I'm living with the people and among them and beside them. My father thinks I'm safely wrapped in cotton-wool, and that sometimes the head-engineer takes me round the mine in state, with very clean hands, while the miners touch their caps to me and say ' Yes, sir,' when out of my graciousness I put the asinine questions that show I'm taking an intelligent interest in my father's property. . . . But I've worked in the mine day by day myself, I tell you, and come out as grimy and ready for drink as the rest. It's no use standing at the top of the shaft and wondering —I must get at things from the inside—discover exactly where these Labour conditions of ours are wrong, and how to improve them."

" You've got your work cut out! Forgive me for saying so, but you seem so young to be attempting so much."

Alan grinned and swung his arms a little. " I'll give all the youth and nerves and strength that are in me, if by giving them I can achieve my ends."

" I think you will achieve them," murmured Dennis. He was suddenly lost in admiration of the earnestness, the virility and the steadfastness of purpose on the part of one who still seemed—he could not help coming back to it—such a child.

"Don't you ever let yourself play?" he asked.

Alan laughed. "Oh, Lord, yes. I go down to the harbour and mess about with the old boats, old iron and rusty cranes. And I watch the kids digging up winkles out of the mud at low tide. And I sit on barrels and let the seamen tell me their yarns, specially concocted on the spur of the moment for landlubbers like myself. That was playtime just now, up at the smithy. . . . Well, you saw how that ended!"

He was limping badly now. Dennis put an arm through his as they crossed the glaring market-place, and once again found themselves in the darkness of a side-street, rising steeply from the wharf-side. Alan led the way into one of the houses, lit a candle-end which he found on a shelf in the hall and painfully climbed the wooden stairs to his room. Dennis followed. The light from the guttering candle wavered and flickered in the draught from under the front door, and cast grotesque, elongated shadows of the two men upon the opposite wall. Dennis had time to reflect that here indeed he had stumbled into a strange adventure, but he was in no mind to withdraw from it. Alan lit the candles in his room. It was small and bare, but the walls were covered with pen-and-ink sketches and caricatures nailed up with drawing-pins.

"Are those yours?" asked Dennis, and Alan replied : "Yes; that's how I keep myself from going crazy with depression."

"They're good, by Jove," said Dennis; the drawings, indeed, some of them only half-finished, were exceptionally strong. "Living in the wilds doesn't seem to have spoilt your technique."

Alan looked pleased. "Greatest effect in the fewest possible lines—that's what I tried to get."

"And that's what you have got, no doubt of it. I must look at the drawings closer later on, but let me see to your foot first. One puts oil on a burn, doesn't one? Have you got any?"

The landlord eventually produced a doubtful-looking compound in a bottle; and Dennis removed his handkerchief from Alan's foot, and began to bandage it afresh. As he did so, a quick spasm of pain passed across the boy's face, and Dennis thought again with an odd pang of tenderness, how absurdly young he looked, and how his mother must love to stroke back the dark hair from his forehead. There was a photograph of her on the mantelpiece—a tired-looking woman with dull eyes and long slender hands. The father, from his portrait, was evidently thick-set, with side-whiskers and a self-assertive expression. A queer couple, they seemed, to have bred this finely-strung creature with the tanned face, sensitive level brows, and great black eyes that burned with a smouldering fire.

"Thanks awfully," said Alan, as Dennis finished his task; you've been a god-send to me to-night. I was getting pretty near the end of my tether—I do sometimes, you know. It's the loneliness, and being so completely cut off from everything down here. It's been refreshing to talk to an absolute stranger who doesn't understand any of the technicalities appertaining to this beastly mining-village.

Dennis smiled. "You're right. I know nothing

whatever about mining, and not much about any
trade or profession outside my own. You make me
feel fearfully narrow and selfish.''

" Rot! What is your line?''

" Music.''

" Music? Oh, good. . . . I've not heard any
music for over six months. Sometimes I'm positively hungry for it—any sort of music—even a
barrel-organ. . . . If anyone played one of those
tango-tunes that were all the rage in London before
I came down here, I believe I'd weep!''

" Poor kid,'' said Dennis.

Alan went on : " Do you come from London?''

" Near enough to be there as often as I want to.''

" Oh, lucky beggar! To think of being in London now—theatres—dancing—art-shows. They've
got the Russian Ballet on too, haven't they?''

" Yes, and the opera. Chaliapine is just beyond
all powers of description. I heard him in ' Boris '
before I left.''

Alan groaned. '' We're buried alive here. Not
the humblest and shoddiest of touring-companies
comes to alleviate our boredom—we haven't as much
as a picture-palace. The only diversions our people
get are drink and women, women and drink. If it
were ' Woman, wine and song,' it wouldn't be so
bad ; but there's no ' song ' about the people's lives
in Crannack, and in all the other places like it,
that are dead to all beauty, and are mere sores on
the face of the earth. . . . And you come from London—I look at you positively with awe—and you're
going back there, when is it? To-morrow?''

" We're going to Penzance to-morrow.''

" Oh, what'll you do at Penzance?'' Alan exclaimed impatiently, '' it's an awful hole, not much

better than this—and without even me in it, as a redeeming feature. . . ."

" I am going to be shown the beauties of the Cornish coast, not to hunt for social reformers tossing red-hot horse-shoes in blacksmiths' shops! And anyway," Dennis added in a lower voice, " I shouldn't find one like you. I shouldn't find anything half as good. . . ."

Alan glanced up with a quick flush of pleasure. " You've liked meeting me, then. . . . Ah, but you can't have liked it half as much as I've liked meeting you. Think of it—after all this time and among these people, suddenly to come across another human being from the world I've almost forgotten!"

Dennis said half-aloud : " Consider the even greater wonder of meeting someone from a world that one didn't know really existed—that one had scarcely dared to dream into existence."

Alan cried eagerly : " Then you'll stop on here for a bit, won't you? Give a poor starving wretch a chance! I want to hear you talk about London with the London voice; I want to be able to talk about ideas instead of machinery; and I want to hear your music—do you play the piano? I haven't got one . . . . but I believe there's one up at the Sunday-school. You will stop, won't you?"

It would be cruel to refuse Alan's request. In spite of the magnitude of the task which the boy had set himself, and although he was engrossed in it heart and soul, he was still young enough to want his play-time, genuine play-time; not the play-time of which, ironically he had told Dennis. . . . He was asking for his play-time now, but Dennis knew that he must not yield; must tear himself away

from a danger doubly dangerous, because, far from
wishing to avoid it, he longed to succumb to it.

He said, with an effort to play for safety : " I
can't tell you off-hand. I must consult my pal, and
see what he says. . . ." He could not quite bring
himself to make his refusal absolutely definite just
yet. . . . " But our train doesn't leave till eleven
in the morning, so perhaps if your foot's well
enough, you'll come round and see what we're
doing." He had quite decided that he must go, but
at least by this arrangement, he would see Alan
again before he left. " Ask for Dennis Blackwood,
if you turn up."

" I'll turn up all right," said Alan.

Dennis walked back to rejoin Crispin. He felt
oddly stimulated, oddly excited. And all night
long his heart throbbed to a new and strange music ;
and his brain found utterance for that music that
was as virile and splendid as the one who had inspired it.

It was not the music that he had promised to
Antoinette. He did not write to Antoinette that
night, nor the next night, nor the night after. . . .

.   .   .   .

Alan came round to the hotel early next morning,
and burst into Dennis's room.

" Well, what have you decided? Where's your
pal? I'll murder him, if he doesn't agree to your
stopping."

Dennis was kneeling on the floor, packing his
bag ; and he spoke without looking up. " You
needn't murder him, Alan : but I'm not going to
stop."

The boy said after a moment's silence : " Why
. . . .?" Then hotly, almost pitifully he began to

plead : " When I've only just found you—and when I needed you most. . . . Why must you go? Why?"

Dennis picked up a roll of manuscript-music. " This will tell you why, Alan, if you can understand it. I wrote it out for you this morning. It will tell you all that I mustn't tell you in words, or —or "—he clenched his hands desperately and continued : " You can play it to yourself, boy, on the piano at the Sunday-school, after I'm gone. . . ."

The secret terror that had beset him ever since he was a boy, was upon him, urging him to flight ; secret terror, unavowed, unshared, upon which even in thought he had scarcely allowed himself to dwell . . . . terror that nevertheless had been part and parcel of his being, since the first dawn of adolescence.

Different from the others, even in his schooldays ; different, not only by reason of his music. It was not his music alone that he had striven to keep out, when he had avoided Eric Rubenstein. . . . He must be for ever an outcast amongst men, shunned by them, despised and mocked by them. He was maddened by fear and horror and loathing of himself.

Abnormal—perverted—against nature—he could hear the epithets that would be hurled against him, and that he would deserve. Yes, but what had nature been about, in giving him the soul of a woman in the body of a man?

And beyond all powers of reasoning ; beyond the fear, and the horror, and the loathing, the thought of Alan reasserted itself, and the blinding pain that had been inflicted at parting from him.

The train pounded onwards—westwards—Dennis cared little enough whither it bore him. He knew only that it carried him away from that which all his life long he had sought, and from which he now must flee, in order that it might not become shameful.

Shameful—strange that such a word might ever be applied to love such as his for Alan; love that had grown up in one night of happiness, and that every instinct bade him welcome with glad lips and eyes and heart . . . love that was so strong that it would not die even under the torture that was in store.

CHAPTER VIII

" . . . . It will be such a nice surprise for Dennis," mused Mrs. Blackwood, as she stamped the letter inviting Antoinette de Courcy to spend the following week-end at Eastwold. "If I tell Mrs. Ryan she's a great friend of Doreen's, and staying in the house, she can't possibly object to our bringing her along to the dance." Mrs. Blackwood reflected further that in the event of Mrs. Ryan's proving averse from the prospect of having yet another to add to her list of girls, she must be propitiated by the offer of the loan of lemonade-glasses or fish-forks. Perhaps even, if necessary, Susan, her inestimable parlour-maid, might be thrown in as a make-weight. One was always neighbourly about these little things in Eastwold.

It was Mrs. Blackwood's "At Home" that afternoon; she expected Mrs. Ryan and her daughters; and no doubt they could come to some satisfactory arrangement, whereby Antoinette's invitation to the fancy dress ball could be secured. But she would not send off the letter to Antoinette until she had made quite sure. Mrs. Ryan, as the wife of the richest stockbroker in Eastwold, was considered a very important personage; and her dance was undoubtedly a fitting climax to the season of 1914, and one not to be lightly trifled with. . . . To-day was July 16th, the dance was on the 24th. Dennis would be back by then. In her last letter, Mrs. Blackwood had asked him to make a point of being back, but of course she had not said why. . . She was well pleased with her little scheme, as she

waited in the pretty sun-flooded drawingroom for
her guests to arrive. The chintz furniture-covers
that had just come back from the cleaner's gave
the room a bright and cheerful appearance; there
were flowers out of the garden in all the vases; and
the piano was heavily laden with silver-framed
photographs of the four children at various ages and
stages of development. The French windows stood
wide open, and the shouts of the tennis players were
clearly audible in the still air. Doreen and Ottilie,
and their partners, Tom Sanderson and Hugh
Clavering, were trying to finish a sett before tea.
Mrs. Blackwood could hear Doreen's pretty laugh;
and Tom's noisy exhortation to Ottilie to " run for
her life "; and Hugh's praise of Doreen's neat
strokes; and Ottilie's punctilious counting, as
vigorously she served into the net. " Lof-fifteen—
lof-zirty—lof-forty—Ach, such a camel *ist noch
nicht dagewesen!*"

Mrs. Blackwood wondered if it wouldn't be
possible to get up a tennis tournament while
Antoinette was staying with them. They could
have it on the Saturday after the dance; then there
would be Clive and Lily to play; Antoinette and
Dennis; one of the Ryan girls and Tom Sanderson;
Doreen and Hugh—Doreen and the doctor's handsome son from next door always seemed to pair off
together automatically, so why thwart the designs
of nature? The 25th—Reggie would be home from
school by then; perhaps he could be bribed to pick
up the balls, if it was a very hot day; she wondered
how many socks and handkerchiefs would have been
lost in the wash again this term, and if he had
already grown out of those coloured shirts she had
bought him last holidays. . . .

Her reflections were cut short by the entrance of
Mrs. Ryan with her daughters Millie and Amy.
They were followed by Miss Simpkins, a funny little
old maid, wearing stout boots and a multitude of
charms and bangles, with which she continually
fidgeted.

Mrs. Blackwood shook hands with her guests.
"This is nice of you, Mrs. Ryan. And you've
brought the girls, too. Doreen and Ottilie will be
here directly—they're just finishing a game. Dear
Miss Simpkins, how are you? You've had a very
long way to come."

"Oh, not so very long," chirped the little
spinster. "I met Mrs. Ryan, and she gave me a
lift in her carriage. Wasn't it *kind* of her?"

"Very kind," assented Mrs. Blackwood.

"Not at all," Mrs. Ryan pronounced with
dignity, "if one happens to be fortunately placed
oneself, one naturally likes to do what one can for
others." She had very white hair, a very red face,
and very thick black brows; a combination that
was awe-inspiring rather than pleasing; and she
wore an obviously expensive, but quite unsuitable
hat which, by means of a high bandeau, was prevented from entertaining any definite relations with
her head. Her elder daughter, Millie, was pretty
in an insignificant way, with yellow hair and a
good complexion, but she had a slightly strained
expression that made her look older than her age.
She wore a coat and skirt of light grey cloth, and
an unbecoming straw hat with a feather. Amy was
nineteen and a fluffier edition of her sister. She
spoke with a lisp, and wore a costume cut like
Millie's, only in pale blue, and the same kind of hat

with a wreath of daisies round it, instead of a feather.

"I expect you are all getting very excited about the dance," Mrs. Blackwood began, "I'm sure my young people are."

"We won't ask you what they're wearing," said Millie, "the costumes are all to be surprises. It adds to the fun."

"Oh, certainly," Mrs. Blackwood agreed. "And it was so thoughtful of you to make the fancy dress optional for the men. Of course, my boys don't mind a bit, but I know some who hate putting on fancy dress—they think it makes them look ridiculous."

"It'th a pity," lisped Amy, "becauthe it'th tho much prettier if everybody ith drethed up, ithn't it? I mean—for the thpirit of the thing."

"My dear, it's hard enough to get sufficient men, as it is. . . ." Millie, rather bitterly, voiced the preponderating sentiment of a community in which there were never enough men to go round.

"I'm sure *you* never suffer from lack of partners, Millie," her mother interposed, and Millie quickly took her cue.

"No—no, of course not; I'm always all right."

"Tho am I!" giggled Amy.

"So I should think," said Mrs. Ryan proudly, "after having seen the programme you brought home from the last subscription dance at the Town Hall. It was scrawled all over with ' T.S.'—that's Tom Sanderson, you know. . . . he's been most attentive ever since; drops in quite informally at all hours of the day. And," with an arch glance at her younger daughter, "I think it's easy to tell the reason why!"

"That was my dance-programme you saw, Mamma. . . ." Millie had listened to the foregoing with a gradually stiffening face.

"Was it, my dear?" Mrs. Ryan laughed indulgently, "well, you really can't expect me to remember all your conquests apart, can you, now?" Millie looked sullen and her mother continued: "I met Tom yesterday and told him we were coming here this afternoon, and he said he might be calling in too."

"Yes, he's playing tennis with the girls now. . . ." said Mrs. Blackwood, making her point.

Mrs. Ryan's face dropped; then she recovered herself with a swift counter-attack. "Of course we're delighted that you are allowing Doreen to come to the dance, Mrs. Blackwood, even though she's not really 'out' yet. But don't you think it's rather a pity to let her pretend to be grown-up before her time?"

Little Miss Simpkins sighed sentimentally. "Yes, a young girl's bloom is her chief charm, isn't it? Her freshness. . . ."

"Oh, I don't know that it's so very much before her time," Mrs. Blackwood smiled, "she's seventeen and a half. . . . and putting her hair up, too, for the first time, in honour of your dance."

Mrs. Ryan thought that this was an honour with which she could easily have dispensed; it was most undesirable that a child like Doreen should enjoy the same privileges as girls who really had a right to them. Doreen was quite unnecessarily pretty, and it wasn't fair on the other girls that she, at her age, should already absorb a quantity of the male attention, that should have been directed towards her elders and betters. . . . But before Mrs. Ryan could say anything more, the tennis-players came in from the garden, all very flushed, and Ottilie still inclined to be argumentative with herself about the badness of her playing.

"Well, young people, have you had a nice game?" Mrs. Blackwood beamed upon the quartette.

"Splendid!" cried Hugh Clavering, looking at Doreen, "hot work, though, when you've got to live up to a partner like mine."

Doreen blushed and murmured : "Oh, Hugh. ." as she shook hands with the Ryans.

"Not nearly such hot work as dancing these days," remarked Tom Sanderson, gulping down his tea. He was a nice, fresh-faced boy of twenty-two; reputed to be the best rider in the county; and endowed with a divine gift for saying the wrong thing, and appearing utterly oblivious of having done so.

"Do you really find dancing such hard work, Tom?" queried Mrs. Ryan with some acerbity.

"Yes, rather, don't you?" retorted the ingenuous youth; "takes it out of you, you know, luggin' your partner round and round, especially if you can't get into each other's stride."

"Well, I trust you won't find much difficulty with your partners on the 24th. . . ."

"The 24th—why, I'd almost forgotten. Going to be great sport, what? Weather looks settled, too. You'll be able to use the garden for sitting-out."

Amy nodded vigorously. "Yeth, all decorated with fairy-lighth and Chinethe lanternth and thingth."

Mrs. Ryan turned to her hostess. "Dennis is sure to be here for the dance, isn't he? One likes to know how many to count on, even though, as I say, when you've got to beyond fifty, another half dozen or so doesn't make any difference."

"Oh, yes, Dennis will be back," replied Mrs. Blackwood, "but you can't count on him as a dancing-man, you know."

"Non-starter, eh?" said Tom with his mouth full.

"Oh, Denny likes different things to what we do," Doreen was always ready to rise in defence of her favourite brother, "he prefers getting up early in the morning and going for long walks by himself, to dancing or playing tennis."

"I thpothe that'th when he geth hith inthpirathionth—early in the morning," suggested Amy.

"How wonderful the artistic temperament is. . ." sighed Miss Simpkins, "don't you sometimes feel quite *overawed,* Mrs. Blackwood, to think that you've got such a clever composer for your own son?"

"I must admit that the dear boy doesn't try to make his family feel small beside him," Mrs. Blackwood laughed, "he's most modest about his work."

"A charming young fellow," concurred Mrs. Ryan, "but it's a pity he's not a dancer. Perhaps we can persuade him to play us some of his compositions, though, while the band has supper."

Remembering Amberhurst, Mrs. Blackwood thought this extremely unlikely; but passed the matter over in silence, and suggested that as Doreen would be having a friend to stay with her next week—

But before the words were out of her mouth, and

before she had time to dangle Susan and the cutlery in front of Mrs. Ryan's eyes, the door opened to admit Mr. Griggs.

He was greeted on all sides by shouts of welcome, to which he replied, beaming and rubbing his hands : " Really, this is too much—I am overwhelmed—so much kindness. . . . I expected I should find a large gathering here, all chatting about the dance next Friday, and I'm not disappointed !"

" Of course we're relying on you, as one of our best dancers, to make things go," said Mrs. Ryan graciously.

Griggs sat down beside Amy, who was looking very animated. " You can trust me for that, Mrs. Ryan."

" You'll come early, won't you?" pleaded Amy, " it thayth nine o'clock on the invitathionth, but it'th nithe to thart booking up before the danthe really beginth, tho we athk all our thpethial friendth to come at ten to nine."

" Ten to nine it shall be, Miss Amy," cried Griggs, " or I might come at half past eight and be mistaken for a waiter or part of the orchestra !"

" But the waiters and the orchestra won't be in fancy dress, as I hope *you* will be, Mr. Griggs," said Mrs. Ryan, very benign.

" Your hopes are not unfounded, Mrs. Ryan. . . Of course I shall be in fancy dress, I'm not one of your ' optional ' shirkers. I wouldn't dream of missing such an opportunity to—ah—improve my noble features. I'm coming as——"

" Don't tell, don't tell," Amy broke in excitedly, " let it be a thurprithe."

" Very well, Miss Amy, I will be mute as the grave. . . . What about starting the advance-

booking right away? Let me see, have I got any
paper in my pocket? No? Well, what's a cuff
for? May I claim the honour of the first lancers,
Miss Millie?"

". . . . Such a dear girl," Mrs. Blackwood
started for the second time, " Doreen is so fond of
her."

" It's her first dance in England, isn't it?"
responded Mrs. Ryan, thinking she meant Ottilie;
" well, I hope she'll be favourably impressed."

" Could she be otherwise, Mrs. Ryan. . . .?"
Griggs' voice vibrated with emotion.

" Ach, I shall remain sitting all ze night," said
Ottilie in accents of gloom.

Tom chuckled irrepressibly. " How will you
manage that?"

Ottilie repeated with conviction : " I shall remain
sitting—I know it ganz gewiss."

" She means she'll be a wallflower," translated
Doreen, and Griggs cried : " We Britishers aren't
the people to let a fascinating foreign lady be a
wallflower for long. When Miss Ottilie returns to
the Fatherland, she'll be able to tell them so, won't
she?. . . . And now, Miss Simpkins, what may I
have the pleasure of booking with you?"

Miss Simpkins blushed and giggled. " Why,
Mr. Griggs, I shan't be there—what do you
imagine? An old woman like me. . . ."

" Oh, Miss *Simpkins*. . . ." with gallant indignation.

" It's just a boy-and-girl affair, Mr. Griggs,"
put in Mrs. Ryan, and thought it just as well to
make no mention of the fact that some of the parents
of the "boys and girls" were being invited to
watch their progeny disporting themselves, and

perhaps to have a quiet game of Bridge.   The
cosmogony of Eastwold fell naturally into two
groups; elderly married people, and young people
to be married.   There was no room in the scheme
for Miss Simpkins and her like, who did not come
under either of these headings. . . .

For the third time, Mrs. Blackwood came forward
with her request, and this time Mrs. Ryan was left
under no illusion as to its nature. " Another girl,
and a very good dancer, you say? We shall be
delighted. . . ."   For the sake of her prestige, she
had to pretend that this was the case.   " Any friend
of Doreen's is welcome, and I'm sure *my* girls won't
mind sitting out a dance now and then, if it's to
give a visitor a chance."

" Oh, you needn't fear that Miss de Courcy will
be a drug upon the market," exclaimed Griggs with
less tact than enthusiasm, " there'll be no difficulty
in getting partners for *her*!"

Mrs. Ryan said that she was glad to hear it, and
inwardly boiling with annoyance, turned to Mrs.
Blackwood to exact her full toll of fish-knives,
lemonade-glasses, Susan, and whatever else Mrs.
Blackwood had to offer her.

The invitation to Antoinette was sent that night;
and Antoinette, receiving it next morning, was
conscious of a reawakened interest in life. It had
indeed been depressingly dull and flat, ever since
Hester had ceased to fill her thoughts, and there had
been no word from Dennis. His sudden silence was
strange to the verge of uncanniness.   That last
letter of his had not given the slightest indication
of the silence that was to follow it; the conversation
—his letters were really more like very intimate
conversations, than like written epistles—was to

have been continued the next day. And it had not been continued. It was as if someone, in the middle of a sentence, had been struck dumb.

And now his mother had invited her to Eastwold —asked her to bring a fancy dress for the dance— *good!* It would be great fun to see Dennis Blackwood again, and dance with him—she assumed that he would be there—and to solve the mystery of his extraordinary behaviour. She decided to go as a Bacchante; and Grand'mère raised her hands and her voice in horror at the unmaidenly abandonment of a costume that would assuredly frighten away all the prospective " partis " her hostess intended her to meet at the dance. . . .

Henriette, who secretly shared Madame de Courcy's opinion of the costume, but did not like to say so, talked in a large, vague manner about not cramping a young soul's development; and Grand'mère, with one of her not infrequent lapses into coarseness, replied that it wasn't Antoinette's soul which the prospective " partis " would be thinking of.

Anatole, for the sake of keeping up his parental authority, remarked that he didn't care for his daughter going to stay with people he did not know. But Antoinette paid no heed to any of them. She set out once more with a light heart, brimful of high spirits, and ready for anything in the shape of an adventure, which the gods might see fit to offer her.

She was met at the station by Doreen and Reggie; and was greeted by the former with affectionate enthusiasm, and by the latter with becoming restraint. Doreen explained volubly that Reggie had come down from his preparatory school that morning; that Clive was expected by a later train

from London; that Dennis hadn't turned up at all
—wasn't it a shame?—and that she hoped Antoinette
wouldn't mind having tea in the nursery—they
always had it in the nursery to please Nanna, on
Reggie's first day home from school. . . .

Antoinette replied that she would love to have tea
in the nursery, but secretly regretted that Dennis
had not arrived. It looked as if her anticipations
were doomed to disappointment after all.

They walked through the little town, and up a
steep sunny road, bordered on either side by neat
villa residences with neat carriage-drives and neat
gardens planted with neat shrubbery and flower-
beds.   Further on, there were larger houses,
separated from each other by wider spaces of
garden, houses built in imitation of the old-fashioned
cottage-style, with gabled roofs and rough white
walls with black beams running across them. These
houses represented the imaginative flights of Tom
Sanderson's father, the architect; and the one which
bore upon its gate the words "The Hermitage,"
was the home of the Blackwoods.

Mrs. Blackwood's welcome was hearty enough,
but Antoinette thought that she seemed worried and
restless, and that beneath her continuous light
chatter, some real trouble or disturbance lay concealed.   Doreen conducted her to the spare bedroom
with its little wooden balcony and wide view of the
Downs.   Appreciatively Antoinette took in the
details of the room; the bright flowered wall-paper;
the names of the books on the revolving stand—
"Wild Kitty," by L. T. Meade; "What Katy Did
at School"; . . . one or two Hentys; "Alice in
Wonderland," of course . . . . a room, reflected
Antoinette, in which to feel very girlish and happy.

Half an hour later, a large party was enjoying nursery tea, presided over by the old nurse who had brought up all the four Blackwood children. The long table was richly spread with home-made cakes and jams; Nanna sat at the head of it, with Reggie and Clive on either side of her; Lily Hallard, Clive's fiancée, was between him and Doreen; and Antoinette was between Ottilie and Reggie. Mrs. Blackwood had said that she would not join the nursery party, as she had already had tea, and was busy. She would see them all later on. . . .

Nanna brooded fondly upon their faces, occasionally admonishing her favourite with : " Now, Master Reggie, my lamb, remember you're not at school : it's butter *and* jam in the holidays. . . ."

Reggie responded : " Good job !" but the reminder was superfluous, in view of the thickly-buttered and jam-smeared slice of bread that he was conveying to his lips during conversation as well as in the intervals. He and Clive were at present engaged in trying to disguise from each other their pleasure at seeing each other again; and their talk was conducted with the careful indifference worthy of the traditions of Westborough and all the other Westboroughs in the United Kingdom.

Reggie said : " Some of our fellows did rifle-practice this term."

Clive said : " Daresay we could fix up a target in the garden."

Reggie said : " Daresay we could."

After a pause, Clive re-opened : " Your last term at the prep. school, isn't it ?"

Reggie nodded with his mouth full.

" Like to have that old bat of mine to take to Westborough ?"

" The one you made a century with in the house-match against St. Winstan's—ra-ther!" for one instant Reggie defied tradition by showing enthusiasm; then quickly he retrieved himself : " Daresay I could do with it. . . ."

Antoinette decided that she did not like Clive's fiancée.   She had an aggressive personality, a shiny complexion, large hands and untidy dark hair.   Doreen had previously explained that all these were outward and visible signs of " brains." Lily went up to town daily to a School of Economics, and usually came back in the evening by the same train as Clive and Mr. Blackwood, and the other male denizens of Eastwold, whom business and the excellent train service took to London for the day, and restored to their families at night.

" I had to cut a class this afternoon," Lily was grumbling, " all because of that beastly dance to-night.   I do think dancing's rot !"

Clive agreed with her, but Doreen protested. " How can you say so?   I think dancing's simply ripping—at least, I've only been to parties and the dancing-class. . . . but real grown-up dances, like this one, must be—Oh, just perfect !"   Doreen's eyes were very bright, her lips tremulously parted. She was thinking of Hugh Clavering from next door.   He had engaged her for the supper-dance, and for ever so many other dances besides, and he was so strong and fair and sunny, with his golden hair and laughing grey eyes.

The whole atmosphere of the house appealed to Antoinette, typically English atmosphere different enough from that of her own foreign home—the old nurse at the head of the table; the schoolboy just home for the holidays; Doreen's excitement over her first dance. . . . But she did wish that Dennis were here : she wondered how he fitted into the picture.

Ottilie, for the hundredth time that week, was expressing the conviction that she would " remain sitting."

" And when my dancers see I cannot dance in ze English vay, zey vill bow zemselves and leave me."

" They can't do that," Antoinette consoled her. " In England, once a man is engaged to a girl for a dance, he's got to stick to her for better or for worse. He can't just plant her there and run away, if he doesn't like her."

" Not ?" queried Ottilie doubtfully.

" Of course not."

" *Verrückt* . . . ." muttered Ottilie.

" It's different in Germany," Antoinette went on, " I've been to dances there myself, so I know. A man introduces himself to a girl, whirls her twice round the room, and throws her back again into the arms of her chaperone where she waits for her next partner. But here it's one dance, one partner. You can't give bits of the same dance to different men."

Ottilie looked puzzled. " And to supper ? In Heidelberg sometimes sree and four dancers have me to supper engaged."

" In Eastwold, Ottilie," Clive spoke with authority from his end of the table, " you will have one supper-partner, and one only."

" And lucky if you get him. . . ." muttered Reggie. Ottilie as a type did not appeal to him.

" Don't be rude, Reg," cried Doreen, but he continued irrepressibly : " Ottilie's going as ' Britannia '. . . . what a rag !"

"Well, and I'm going as a Dresden Shepherdess—there's nothing funny about that, stupid," Doreen was staunch in her defence of her friend.

"What a nice idea," said Antoinette, "a compliment to each other's nationality. It's like foreign potentates wearing the uniform of which ever country they're visiting—oh, Reggie, dear, have you swallowed a plum-stone?" For Reggie, in the simultaneous appreciation of her remark, and an extra large mouthful of bread and jam, was slowly but surely choking himself into an apoplectic fit.

.   .   .   .

Mrs. Blackwood had not had tea ; neither did she want any. She sat alone in the drawing-room, as she had done for the greater part of the afternoon, hoping against hope, and wondering and wondering if the next train would bring Dennis, or the next. She had had no definite word to say that he was coming; still, he knew that she expected him to-day. . . . she was used to his indefiniteness in the matter of letters or telegrams. . . . perhaps he wanted to surprise her. . . . He was sure to come, knowing that she expected him. She had to cling to the certainty of his coming, to stave off as long as possible her inevitable disappointment if he did not come.

But when at last Dennis himself stood in the opening of the French window, just for one second she wondered if it were really he, or if all her wishing had conjured up an image that would vanish. . . .

"My dear, dear boy," her arms were round him now, "so you've come in time after all. What a fright you gave me. I'd promised Mrs. Ryan that you were coming, and it would have been so awkward if you hadn't turned up."

He repeated in a dazed kind of way : " In time for what?   Turned up—where?"   And she saw that his face was drawn, and that his eyes were full of an unutterable weariness.

"Mrs. Ryan's dance, of course, dear."   She was making a pitiful attempt to ignore the things that she saw, " it's to-night—I wrote to you; didn't you get my letter?"

He shook his head.   " No—or perhaps I did, and —and forgot.   I don't know. . . ."

They looked at each other; he battling with the longing to go to her, and hide his head on her breast, and tell her everything; and she, struggling against this strange terror of something unknown, not understood, that had befallen her son.

" It's a fancy dress dance. . . ." she faltered with stiff lips.

He almost smiled.   A fancy dress dance—well, why not? Since the whole of his life henceforth must be a masquerade, a travesty to disguise every impulse, thought and feeling; to make them appear not different from other people's impulses, thoughts and feelings. . . .

The dread in his mother's heart, shadowy and shapeless, tightened its grip.   What had been done to him?   What shuddering depths of unhappiness had brought that look to his face?   But all her love for him could not give her sight where she was blind.   Was there nothing with which she could heal him?   She clutched at a faint hope.   " I've got a surprise for you, dear.   I've asked Miss de Courcy down for the dance—she's here already—in

the nursery with the others.   Won't you go up to
them?"

He heard himself saying : " Oh, good. . . ."
and walked away, because he could no longer bear
to feel his mother's troubled, searching gaze upon
him.   He would go up to the nursery, and to the
dance, and pretend that he had come back on purpose
for it, and pretend that he was glad to see
Antoinette—

Antoinette. . . .   If at least he had been spared
—that.

The shouts of the party in the nursery fell upon
his ears, as he went upstairs. . . .

CHAPTER IX

DENNIS, Clive and the three girls motored over to
the dance, and sent the car back for Mr. and Mrs.
Blackwood, who were to come on later. It was a
very silent drive; Doreen tremulous with anticipation; Ottilie despondent as usual. The symbolism
of her costume was powerless to disguise her true
Teutonic instincts—no sooner was she arrayed in
helmet and shield, than Britannia immediately saw
herself as Brunhilde, and this despite the Union
Jack swathed around her buxom figure.

Antoinette was feverishly excited by that queer
restraint that had characterised Dennis's manner
ever since his first appearance in the nursery that
evening. If it was acting, she reflected, it was phe-
nomenally bad acting—too tense and white-lipped;
altogether overdone. But he had kept it up all
through dinner, and he was keeping it up now,
though they sat opposite each other in the car, their
knees almost touching. He was not looking at her,
but out of the window, and the moonlight showed
up the strained set expression of his face. What
lay behind it all, she wondered. When that elaborate restraint was broken down, as undoubtedly it
would be during the evening, what would she find?

Dinner had been an awkward meal. Mr. Blackwood had insisted on telling Antoinette stories that
made Mrs. Blackwood say reproachfully: " Oh,
Daddy *dear* . . . ." and that left Antoinette in
doubt as to whether it were better to incur her
hostess's displeasure by laughing at them, or that
of her host by pretending not to understand
them. . . .

When they had almost reached their destination, Ottilie broke the silence by saying to Dennis : " Your friend who so excellent piano plays—comes he also to ze ball?"

" I'm afraid not, Ottilie. I left him up in town this morning. Wild horses wouldn't drag Crispin to a dance, you know."

" Schade . . . ." sighed Ottilie, regretting the wasted opportunities which her costume, and Crispin's appreciation of Wagner might have offered.

When Doreen introduced Antoinette to Mrs. Ryan, that lady favoured the bacchante with a glance not unlike the one with which Grand'mère had surveyed her. Antoinette argued from this that she was looking her best, and prepared to enjoy herself. Her clinging draperies of warm reds and browns and purples, and the vine-leaves in her hair, made her look distinctive enough among the crowd of pierrettes, fairy-queens, peasants and columbines who clustered around the doorway of the drawing-room, booking up their programmes.

" I am delighted to welcome you here—Millie— Amy, this is Doreen's friend, Miss de Courcy ; will you see that she gets some partners?"

Amy, Queen of Hearts, with a golden paper crown upon a head of hair that had been vigorously treated with curling-irons, rushed up to Antoinette. " Tho glad to meet you—let me introduthe Mr. Thanderthon," presenting a very chubby Arab, " we've jutht been out in the garden to thee if everthing ith all right, we've had flagth put on the theat in the arbour, tho we than't thpoil our dretheth. . . ."

Tom having booked his dance with Antoinette, she was handed on to Millie, who wore a composite " national " costume, of which the main ingredients were Dutch sabots, a black velvet bodice, a red gypsy head-dress with coins attached to it, and two straggly little yellow plaits reaching just to her shoulders. She introduced to Antoinette several men whose programmes were already full, and turned to speak to Mr. Griggs, resplendent in a hired " Charles II " costume, several sizes too large, and a very luxuriant wig. The moment he espied Antoinette, he hurried to her side, his would-be majestic gait somewhat impeded by his sword, to which he was not yet accustomed. " Miss Antoinette, I am charmed—charmed—to meet you again. The memory of Charlotte Corday still lingers in my heart, I assure you, and though this time we meet in a different guise, I trust we shall be as good friends as ever. . . . May I have the pleasure of the second waltz ?" suddenly reverting to the business on hand.

Antoinette accorded him the pleasure of the second waltz, and he continued raptly to gaze at her. " That's a very pretty dress you have on—worthy of its wearer, if I may say so. There's what you might call a laissay-allay about it——"

" Mr. Griggs," interrupted the voice of Mrs. Ryan, " would you mind seeing that Miss Holt has a supper-partner ? I think she's in the garden now —dressed as a Draught Board, you know," she added in a confidential undertone, " we always have difficulty with her, and her people will be so offended if they see her sitting out."

" She shall have a partner, if I have to bring her one by the scruff of his neck," vowed the gallant Griggs, and made for the iron stairs that led down into the garden.

" Oh, and—Mr. Griggs !" his hostess recalled

E

him, " you will see they don't lift the girls off their
feet in the third figure of the lancers, won't you?"

" Your commands shall be obeyed, dear lady,"
declared Griggs, and promptly fell down the stairs.

In the meantime Clive had dutifully booked two
dances with Antoinette. Handsome in his sullen,
black-browed way, he looked very effective as an
Indian Chief. Lily had come as a Squaw to match
him, but as she disdained the use of external aids
to nature, her complexion retained its blameless
European hue.

The first waltz had already been played, Antoinette had been whirled round by a perspiring
Neptune, and her programme was nearly full, before Dennis made any attempt to approach her.

" Have you anything left for me?" His tone
was carefully conventional. She gave him a quick
amused look, but as there was no answering twinkle
in his eye, assumed that he was not yet prepared
to throw off the restraint that was a more effectual
disguise than any of the fancy dresses could hope
to be. Undoubtedly he was working up to a scene,
and had quite definite notions as to how the scene
should be played. It was far from her to complain.
She appreciated the histrionic instinct wherever she
encountered it; and she was quite capable of giving
him all the support that he needed.

She answered demurely : " Yes, I think I have
one or two dances to spare."

" May I see?"—he scanned her programme—
" I'm not a dancer, but perhaps you'll sit out the
lancers with me?"

" I shall be delighted," murmured Antoinette.

Mrs. Ryan tapped Dennis's arm with the end of

her ostrich feather fan. "Naughty boy, not to
have come in fancy dress."

He smiled. "I didn't know in time, Mrs.
Ryan."

"Didn't you? What a pity. Of course you were
on a walking tour. Cornwall or somewhere like
that, wasn't it? Did you have a pleasant time?"

"Very pleasant, thanks."

"I'm glad . . . . but I thought your mother had
written to tell you it was a *fancy dress* dance?"

"I think her letter must have been lost," he
lied piously.

"Or perhaps it was you who lost it . . . . well,
well, we must make allowances for these great composers, I suppose. Tell me if there's anyone you'd
like to be introduced to, won't you? You know
you're quite at home here."

Released from Mrs. Ryan's expressions of un-
wonted amiability, Dennis wandered down into the
garden. The trees were hung with Chinese lanterns; the paths picked out with coloured fairy-
lights; on the lawn, deck-chairs awaited the couples
who, between the dances, would sit there and whisper under the sighing trees. For him the whole
scene was imbued with that feeling of horror and
oppression which characterizes a nightmare; if he
cried out, his voice would not be heard; if he attempted to run away, his limbs would refuse to
obey him. . . . Some volition other than his own,
was compelling him to act and speak as he was
doing, while part of himself was being tortured,
beating against prison bars . . . . crying out for
help, for understanding to a world that would
neither help nor understand, but condemn him to
eternal suppression, eternal loneliness. This night-

mare-sense had overlain the whole of the last dreadful fortnight since he had left Crannack.   Passively he had let Crispin drag him round the Cornish coast.   He had not wanted to come home just yet, and Crispin at least was restful, because he asked no questions . . . . no questions, even, concerning a vivid-looking brown boy, who had burst into the little hotel at Crannack, and asked to see Mr. Blackwood, and left again a few minutes later with all the light gone out of his eyes. . . .   And Mrs. Blackwood's letter, mentioning the dance, lay with some of her other letters in the pocket of Dennis's tweed suit; he had read them; but the names, the dates, the local gossip she retailed, had conveyed absolutely nothing to him.   It was only by chance that he had returned to-day, returned because he was tired of perpetually striving to banish from his mind a companion who asked so much, and to whom he longed to give so much, and to whom he might give—nothing.

At home, at least there would not be those long hours of silent, hard walking, dangerous hours when he had felt that he must take the next train back to Crannack. . . .   He could only keep away, by resolutely shutting Alan out of his thoughts, admitting him but for rare seconds, precious seconds, when the danger of returning to him was minimised by the absence of such things as railway-connections.   Even his imagination must be forbidden too much free play. . . .   And all the while, he felt that he was being cruel to the boy in thus keeping him out; pleaded with him in the nights when he lay sleepless and through the days when, unheeding, he tramped along the beautiful Cornish roads : "Don't you understand that I can't?   That I daren't? That it isn't because I don't love you enough . . . .?"

Very tiring, this eternal struggle: . . . He had imagined that it might be easier at home. And at home there had been Antoinette. . . . She fitted into the nightmare well enough; he might have expected that she would be in the very centre of it. But so far he had betrayed nothing; he had done the correct thing, asked her for a dance . . . . and heaven alone knew what he would say to her, when it was his turn to claim her for Number 6!

Voices reached him where he sat in the shadow of a clump of trees.

" That's all right—I think we're safe now. Griggs has been dogging me all the evening with a Draught Board, he can't get rid of her at any price." It was Neptune who spoke, and his companion, arrayed as Father Christmas, responded: " Yes, for the Lord's sake, let's get a quiet smoke. Griggs is the very dickens. . . . Always trying to introduce me to Little Bo-peep. I don't know if there are two of her, or if I've been introduced twice over, or if I'm seeing double, but I don't like either of them."

" Awful rot, these fancy dress hops," mused Neptune. Father Christmas gloomily assented. " My sisters rigged me up like this—there was no getting out of it."

" Whatever am I to do with this beastly trident thing? Every time I forget it somewhere on purpose, some silly ass brings it after me and says: ' I think you've lost this.' "

" Oh, just drop it here, and the crowd who call themselves Harvesters can use it as a hay-fork. I wish to goodness I could leave this ghastly beard behind too. . . . ."

They strolled off into the more secluded portions of the garden, grotesque figures moving across the background of Dennis's nightmare.

" Denny darling, I'm having a simply lovely time —even lovelier than I knew it was going to be!" Doreen's voice now. . . . . The dainty little Dresden Shepherdess tripped across the lawn to where her brother sat smoking, " it's such a pity you don't dance, dear old thing, you do miss a lot."

" Do I, Kid?" He smiled up at her radiant face.

She breathed " Yes . . . ." and young Hugh, a slim and golden-haired Black Knight from " Ivanhoe," came and joined them.

" Doreen and I both agree that it's top-hole, being grown-up."

" Yes, but I'm only pretending just for to-night," replied Doreen, " I shan't be really grown-up till I come back from Heidelberg next year."

" It's rotten luck, your having to go there," said Hugh.

" I know, but you see, I must. I'm the exchange for Ottilie. She says that girls of seventeen can go to grown-up dances over there, but being grown-up in Germany isn't the same as being grown-up here, is it?"

" The insularity of your views is something appalling, my child," teased Dennis.

Doreen pouted. " Well, it's not the same, is it?" she appealed to Hugh.

" Rather not!" he concurred, his eyes resting tenderly on her; then he said to Dennis : " You and I are in luck to-night—I've got half the dances on the programme with Doreen, and you're out of it altogether. The other poor chaps are having an awful thin time, trying to remember whom they're engaged to. There are so many duplicates—half a dozen Ophelias, four Red Riding Hoods, innumerable Snow Queens, and two Queens of Sheba—I thought there'd be murder there : did you see them glare at each other when they first met ?"

" I suppose each thought the other was a distorted figment of her own imagination, and was properly resentful on discovering that she wasn't," said Dennis.

Hugh gave his hearty, boyish laugh, and Doreen said, " I think Antoinette's costume is one of the prettiest, don't you, Denny?"

" And even that's been duplicated three times over," Hugh broke in, " rotten imitations, I grant you. As Amy says, ' they're all drethed in thkinth ' . . . . I've booked dances with all of them—got 'em down on my programme as ' Tigerskin,' ' Bunny-skin ' and ' Hearthrug,' to be able to tell the difference."

" And ' Hearthrug's ' father is in the fur trade," Doreen giggled delightedly. " I heard Daddy say that she was a very bad advertisement . . . ."

" Ah well, I daresay there wasn't enough tigerskin to go round," mused Dennis, " let us not be uncharitable."

" Let's go across to the arbour, Doreen," suggested the Black Knight, " I'll carry you, because you'll get your shoes damp."

Doreen argued that as she had been standing on the grass all this time, her shoes were already as damp as they were ever likely to be; but Hugh, with a gallant show of mastery, picked her up in his arms and carried her across the lawn. The figure of the Black Knight and the light blur of Doreen's dress receded from Dennis's vision, as the sound of their mingled voices faded from his hearing.

He reflected quite dispassionately that it was odd that he should still be able to talk to the others as if he were one of them; odd that they should not divine the gulf that yawned between himself and them. But it was a strain. . . . He became conscious afterwards of how great the strain had been. He was alone again now, and could relax, grant himself a few moments' respite from effort. Wearily he wondered when and how the next demand would be made upon him. He could hear voices not far off.

" Shall we stay here for a little while, Miss Millie?"

" Yes, I should like to, Mr. Griggs . I'm sure you deserve a rest after all your hard work."

" Everything that I do in your service, is pleasure, Miss Millie."

" Oh, Mr. Griggs. . . ."

A very cross Little Boy Blue here interrupted the budding tête-à-tête. " I say, Griggs, can you tell me whom I'm dancing the next with? I can't read what I've got on my programme." He presented the crumpled programme to Charles II, who rallied him in debonair fashion. " Now—now—now, what's all this? Someone's always in trouble and coming to me for help. Can't say I admire your caligraphy, old chap—are these the lady's initials?" He deciphered slowly : " ' Goggle—eyes—and—flat—feet——' "

Little Boy Blue snatched away the programme : " Not there, man, not there—here !"

" Oh, *here* . . . . why, that's Miss Baumgartner, surely—Britannia—or is it the Queen of
Sheba?"

" I didn't know we'd got the next one together
too," Little Boy Blue stared reproachfully at his
partner.

" We haven't," retorted she coldly, " I'm engaged to Neptune."

" And Neptune's dancing with Dolly Dickson,
the other Queen of Sheba—I just saw them go in,"
said Millie.

" If two people *will* come as the same thing——"
began Little Boy Blue with resentment.

" I should have thought it was easy enough to
tell us apart," said the Queen of Sheba haughtily,
" her costume's home-made and mine came from
Clarkson's."

" Yes, that was what the other one said too . . ."
murmured Little Boy Blue, and evaporated into the
shrubbery. Griggs palmed off the Queen of Sheba
on to an unsuspecting Highwayman, who had come
out to have a peaceful cigarette. Then he sank
back into his chair and mopped his manly forehead.

" Poor Mr. Griggs," cooed Millie, " how tired
you must be."

" Oh, Miss Millie, I would willingly incur far
greater fatigues if only to hear you say ' poor Mr.
Griggs ' in just that tone. . . ." He put his hand
to where the hilt of his sword should have been,
but finding that he had mislaid the sword, arrested
the gesture half-way. " I love that costume you're
wearing. National, isn't it?"

" Yes, national."

The voices became inaudible for a space, then—

" I don't know very many of the steps—there are
such different ways of doing it, aren't there? But
perhaps if you'll teach me. . . ."

" It will be a labour of love, Miss Millie."

. . . . Retreating footsteps and silence. Then
the music, faintly audible, struck up again; but
instead of the accustomed beat of waltz or two-step,
came the less familiar, haunting rhythm of a
tango.

*" If anyone played one of those tango-tunes that
were all the rage in London before I came down
here, I believe I'd weep. . . ."*

Piercing through the stupor which, for the moment had numbed pain, came memory, keen and
poignant as a rapier-thrust. Alan was before him
again, looking up into his face with eager, burning
eyes.

" You can stay with me a minute, boy," Dennis
whispered to him, " there's nobody looking. . . .
Would you like to be dancing the tango in there?
I could easily introduce you to Mrs. Ryan—she'd
think you a delightful acquisition. . . . How we
could have laughed over all this together, you and
I. . . . Are you eating your heart out in loneliness, Alan, as I am—as I am? You must go now
—I—the others are coming. . . ."

Obediently the vision faded.

The dancers were straggling out into the garden
again, grouping themselves upon the lawn. Griggs
picked up the trident from the ground. " What
have we here? Anybody claim this valuable
article? Is it yours, Madam?" offering it to the
home-made Queen of Sheba, who paused, wondering
perhaps if she could not use the weapon upon her
rival from Clarkson's.

" No, it's not mine; it's yours, isn't it, Neptune?"

" I've been trying to lose it all the evening," he groaned, " can't you raffle it or use it as a toothpick or a toasting-fork? I don't care what you do with the damn thing!"

Mrs. Ryan's opulent aigrette appeared upon the balcony.

" Not catching cold, any of you, I hope?" . . . . and in answer to the chorus of : " Oh, no, Mrs. Ryan. . . ." " It's lovely out here. . . ." " The garden looks ripping. . . ." " It's such a perfect evening . . . ." the hostess nodded benignly. " That's right. I like to see you all enjoying yourselves—Oh, what is it, Susan?" She turned to Mrs. Blackwood's faithful retainer who had been lent to her for the occasion, and who had come out on to the balcony to speak to her.

" Please, M'm, it's the freezing-salt," Susan announced in sepulchral tones.

" Well, what about it?"

" It's got into the strawberry ice, M'm."

" Dear me, how very careless. What can we do?"

" We can't do anything, M'm, the ices 'll just have to taste salt, only I thought I'd better tell you."

Susan withdrew and there was a burst of laughter from the group on the lawn.

" Never mind, Mrs. Ryan, they'll be cold even if they are salt," cried Tom Sanderson.

" Some people like them better that way—more piquant," from Hugh.

" Yeth, quite a novelty, ithn't it?" from Amy.

" Yes, rather . . . ." from the chorus.

Mrs. Ryan was very distressed. " You're dear,

sweet children to take it like that, still there are
plenty of other good things for you, so you won't
starve. . . . Now, have you all got your partners
for the lancers?"

Dennis waited till the group on the lawn had re-
assorted itself and paired off into different combina-
tions of incongruity; then, as the last couple disappeared into the house, he went across to fetch his
partner.

Father Christmas, with whom she had just been
dancing, was taking his leave of her, and as Dennis
appeared at the foot of the steps, his father, together
with Mr. Ryan and Dr. Clavering, came out on to
the balcony.

"Here's Romeo come to fetch his Juliet," Mr.
Blackwood jovially apostrophised his son, "lucky
young dog—I wish I were your age!" with an appreciative glance at Antoinette.

"Yes, that's all very well—all very well when
you're young"—Mr. Ryan was a stout little red-
faced man with a wheezy voice—"but I can't understand this preference for sitting about in the damp,
with next to nothing on. It would kill me!"

The doctor smiled and Mr. Blackwood guffawed.
"It wouldn't kill me, but then perhaps I've got a
stronger constitution, eh, Doctor?" He threw out
his chest and positively winked at Antoinette.

"You needn't boast," snapped Mr. Ryan, "your
gout is as bad as mine any day, isn't it, Clavering?"

"There's not a pin to choose between you," declared the doctor, a twinkle in his humorous grey
eyes. He was clean-shaven and soldierly in appearance; a very pleasant type to look upon. Young
Hugh could be glad if he resembled his father in
twenty years' time.

Mr. Blackwood began again : " That boy of yours, Doctor, and my little girl . . . . hitting it off very well, eh ? Haven't seen the young rascals all the evening. . . ."

" One is only young once," smiled Clavering.

" . . . . Trio of dear old gentlemen," murmured Dennis, as he and Antoinette walked across the lawn. The " trio of dear old gentlemen," after a little more facetious banter, and digging of each other in the ribs, returned to their game of cards.

In silence they entered the arbour. Dennis swept aside the flags with which the seats were draped. " I don't like the patriotic decorations in conjunction with your costume."

She laughed with easy response to his mood. " Isn't it rather a waste of Amy's forethought ?"

He did not answer, and she wondered, not without a trace of impatience, when at last he was going to throw aside his pose. Antoinette herself was feverishly strung-up ; every nerve in her craving the relief of some violent scene, some violent emotion. The whole dance, dull enough in itself from her point of view, was but a preliminary, an accompaniment, a working-up to this moment.

Still he sat silent ; and at last, unable any longer to bear the strain, she took the initiative. " You have quite a genius for making dramatic entrances, just in the nick of time, when everybody has given you up for lost. Your arrival at Amberhurst was good enough, but to-day was more effective still."

He said : " Amberhurst—yes, I remember. They were hoping I'd play for the theatricals, and I wouldn't. It's a pity that anticlimax seems inevitably to succeed what you call my dramatic entrances."

" You shouldn't let it, then !" she cried, " surely it's in your power to prevent it."

" Not always."

She became aware then, of the utter weariness of his tone, the weariness of his deep-set brown eyes. It seemed incredible that this was the man who had written her those wonderful letters. Where was the promised continuation of the long, intimate talks that had been started in them? Where was his anticipated delight at seeing her again? Had he ever really told her about himself and Eric Rubenstein? Taken for granted her understanding of all his moods? Said to her : " I want you here beside me in my dream-place . . ."

Well, she was beside him now, and there was nothing wrong with the place—stars twinkling in a pale blueish sky, wind rustling faintly in the trees, and swaying the Chinese lanterns to and fro—but he made no attempt to break the oppressive silence, or in any way to shatter that impalpable barrier which seemed to have arisen between them. Curiously, critically almost, she watched him, as she leant back in her corner of the arbour, and smoked her cigarette.

. . . . And to him also the silence was becoming oppressive. He had not found, in talking to the other figures in the nightmare, the same appalling difficulty as he found in trying to talk to Antoinette. The soft light of the lantern, swinging from the roof of the arbour, fell upon the slim, lithe curves of her body ; on the white throat and shoulders above the wine-coloured draperies ; on the flushed face and hair tumbled to a riotous mass of curls. The face and hair and body of a bacchante, indeed.

He was fully aware of her decorative value ; admitted it at every point; but of the appeal which she might once have made to his senses, nothing remained. Alan, with his virile personality, had blotted out for Dennis the fainter magic of Antoinette, so that he could no longer perceive it— or if he did perceive it, then but dimly, remotely, as something not felt at all, but just seen through a misty glass. He had wondered once—it seemed a very long time ago, now—if Antoinette were not the one girl in a thousand, in a million, with whom he could find happiness and rest from the ceaseless internal wars of his own nature. And while he had still been doubting, wondering, playing with the idea, writing letters to a girl of his dreams, Alan had come . . . .

Yet he knew that he owed her some explanation; that she expected one of him. But what was he to tell her? What could he tell her? The truth . . . .? He suddenly felt a mad desire to tell her the truth. Groping back to his first impression of her at Amberhurst, he was still convinced that she would understand. She too, or so it had seemed to him, was different from other girls, just as he— And it would be just a little less lonely, if he could tell her . . . .

The strains of the " Chocolate Soldier " lancers floated out to them with bursts of clapping and laughter between the figures. Antoinette sat listening with concentrated attention to the music. The fourth figure was nearly over now; soon the dancers would come swarming into the garden, encroaching upon their solitude, which might have been such a thing of wonder . . . and had merely been a thing of emptiness. She resented the waste of the good moment, of the good setting—of herself. . . .

Dennis seemed suddenly to awaken from his
stupor. He said, " I'm sorry—about anticlimaxes,
but believe me, they're not my fault. They happen
—just happen—like everything else in this world
that's crazy and cussed and without rhyme and reason. I——"

But already the dancers were pouring down the
stairs into the garden, and the voice of Britannia,
deep and lugubrious, uprose upon the still night
air. She was addressing a Pierrot, whom Griggs
had jockeyed into asking her for the supper-dance,
not knowing that Little Boy Blue, in self-defence
against the joint Queens of Sheba, had previously
engaged her for it. " Ach, no, I cannot. I have
got von man already, and zey say I must not have
more zan von . . . ." as regretfully she refused
the second offer. " Ach, to zis England shall I
never myself accustom . . . ."

" Poor Ottilie," murmured Dennis, " it's a hard
life." He was secretly relieved at the diversion
that had checked the confession on his lips. After
all, it would have been a great mistake to tell her—
he must have been crazy even to have contemplated
it. He must guard against these incalculable impulses in future. For the present he was safe,
thanks to Ottilie.

" They might have let her have her Pierrot as
well—what would it have hurt?"

But Antoinette made no answer. She was possessed by a dull fury, her nerves strained to snap-
ping-point.

He had cheated her of a sensation.

PART II

CHAPTER I

But Ottilie had no occasion "herself to zis England to accustom"; neither was Doreen obliged to put to the test her assertion that being grown-up in Germany wasn't the same as being grown-up in Eastwold. A European war intervened in time to prevent a further exchange of daughters between Herr Baumgartner and Mr. Blackwood. Ottilie, wailing bitterly, was bundled off post-haste and with considerable difficulty, to her native land. Mr. Blackwood was taking her as far as Dover, and the rest of the family saw her off at Eastwold station; where she kissed them all, including Reggie, much to the latter's disgust. And they put her into the train, together with the brand-new English hold-all, of which she was so proud, and the large canvas bag on which were embroidered in red cotton the words: " *Gluückliche Reise* ". . . . And up till the last, she craned her head, surmounted by its absurd little straw hat, out of the window, and assured the Blackwoods repeatedly that she loved them, and loved England; and enjoined Doreen to " Greet me Mr. Griggs—greet me all dear friends. . . ." Then, as the train began to move out of the station : "Ach, zis vor. . . . *Jammerschadø!*" The rest was smothered by the noise of the engine. . . . . Doreen cried all the way home, and Reggie was compelled to remind her with some severity that Ottilie was a German—the term " Hun " in these early days of the war had not yet become incorporated in the language, or he would certainly have used it. Ottilie was a German, and hence,

obviously, a spy; Reggie expressed the devout hope
that he had said nothing in her presence that might
lead to giving information to the enemy; and tried
to obliterate the shame of her parting embrace by
assiduous rifle-practice in the garden.

And young Hugh Clavering, looking very elated,
climbed over the wall into the Blackwoods' garden
that afternoon, and told Doreen how awfully, awfully
glad he was that she couldn't go to Heidelberg now,
even if she wanted to. . . . but he might be there
himself, with any luck—Heidelberg would do just as
well as Berlin, he wasn't particular—yes, of course
he'd enlisted; was going straight into camp; fine
sport. . . . and he'd bring her a German helmet
for Christmas.

And Doreen said how awfully, awfully proud of
him she was, and she did hope he wouldn't get hurt,
and yes, of course she'd write to him, and would
he send her a photograph of himself in uniform?

And Griggs and Tom Sanderson and Clive Blackwood, and all the clowns, pierrots, highwaymen and
the rest of the motley crew from the fancy dress
dance, had likewise enlisted; and of each one of
them it was proudly claimed by his family that he
was the first man in Eastwold—the first man in the
county to have done so.   Be this as it may, Eastwold made gallant response to the call of King and
Country.   Clive applied for a commission in the
Royal Engineers; Tom gravitated naturally towards
a cavalry regiment; Griggs appeared in the modest
uniform of a private, and bore himself with that
ingratiating charm of manner that had distinguished
his impersonation both of Marat and Charles II.

" Only a simple Tommy—but ready to do his bit

with the best of 'em. We'll show Fritz the stuff
Old England is made of!"

So, with a great deal of excitement, and
metaphorical clanking of spurs, and generally with
the sensation of taking part in a picturesque
pageant, the manhood of Eastwold, very pleased
with itself, left the sunny, sleepy little town for the
various camps and headquarters, where it was to be
instructed in the art of " showing Fritz the stuff old
England was made of ". . . .

" And what is Dennis going to do?" Mrs. Ryan
at last voiced the question which had agitated the
whole of Eastwold ever since the outbreak of war.
Dennis's mother replied that for the present she
didn't know that he was going to do anything, and
rather hastily changed the subject. Eastwold, with
a tolerance and forbearance which later it was to
lose, assumed that Dennis, being an artist, and
hence possessing a certain right to be " peculiar,"
would take longer than the others to realise his duty
towards his King, country and family. But inspired
by the example of his brother Clive and the rest of
Eastwold, he would no doubt soon long to feel his
hand upon the hilt of his sword, as did every true-
born Briton in times like these. . . .

Little Miss Simpkins ventured to suggest that
the Blackwoods, in giving one of their sons to the
army, were adequately fulfilling the dictates of
patriotism.

" We women of England must give *all* our sons,"
returned Mrs. Ryan who had no sons to give; and
reiterated the ominous catch-phrase that had just
been coined : " in times like these. . . ."

The war had run the course of four horror-stricken
months, and still the Blackwoods' eldest son had

made no move towards the recruiting office. Nor
had he any intention of doing so. The thought of
war inspired in him none of those feelings with
which convention decreed that every true Briton
should be inspired—in times like these. He had no
desire to feel his hand upon the hilt of his sword;
no desire to help to bring the "day of victory"
nearer. The whole thing was damnable and stupid,
and cruel; and so was all the talk and the bombast
with which everyone strove to gloss over the fact
that it was damnable, and stupid, and cruel . . . .
pretended that it was a noble thing, a glorious game,
a game which every Englishman should be proud to
be playing.

"A little blood-letting won't do the nation any
harm." Often and often Dennis had heard that
phrase upon his father's lips, as comfortably Mr.
Blackwood smoked his after-dinner cigar, and fixed
his son with a baleful eye. Dennis at all events
would not give himself up to become part of the
machinery of nations trying to prove which could
stand the most blood-letting; machinery that organised the murder of individuals by individuals
who had no personal quarrel with each other. And
greater even than his repugnance to the "great war
game" as a whole; greater even than his revolt
against the senselessness of it, and the pity of it;
greater than any personal physical fear of death or
wounds was his fear of being sent out to inflict death
or wounds on others . . . . deliberately to maim
and shatter the bodies of men as young as himself,
the bodies of men as young as Alan.

He would not enlist. And Eastwold might do its
worst. . . . Eastwold was, in fact, already growing
restive.

Mrs. Ryan took him to task one day when she met him in the town. She had just come out of the grocer's shop, where she had been complaining because the price of bacon had gone up again; and the grocer had replied that in times like these. . . . She was therefore considerably ruffled when she met Dennis outside. After a preliminary exchange of hostilities, and a meaning glance at his civilian clothes, she said : "Well, I should like to know where the war would be if everyone thought like that !"

"Presumably there would be no war at all," he returned gently.

"Nonsense ! The Germans would have been here long ago."

"Not if *everyone* thought like that."

"The Germans would never think like that, even if the English did—and I'm thankful to say they don't. It's the Germans who wanted the war."

"And now the English want it every bit as much as they do."

"Well, now they've started it, we've got to go on with it—we didn't want war."

"I daresay they think and say exactly the same, only the other way round. . . ." Dennis walked away, weary of the argument. He would have been wearier still, if he could have foreseen the countless times he was to repeat that argument with different people, in different places, with variations and amplifications. These were still the early days of the war, and the crusade against pacifism was not so strenuous as it became later on.

But Mrs. Ryan reported that conversation to Mrs. Clavering who reported it back to Mrs. Blackwood; and Mrs. Blackwood, half uneasily, told Dennis that it had been reported. "Of course Mrs. Ryan thinks you ought to go, Denny."

"Everybody does, Mother," he smiled at her.

"And—shall you. . . .?"

"Do you think I ought to, Mother?"

She was troubled by the direct question. "I suppose every man ought to go, but it's difficult to want them to. I suppose one can't help being selfish. . . . Daddy thinks you ought to go, Dennis."

He ignored this, being already acquainted with his father's views on the subject. "And you Mother?" he persisted.

"I know it's very wrong of me," she murmured, as if apologising to the wrathful spirits of her husband and Mrs. Ryan and the rest of the community; apologising for being a mother first, and a "woman of England" afterwards.

Dennis laughed, and took her in his arms. "You dear. . . ."

She returned his kiss, but repeated : "Mind you, I know it's wrong."

"Wrong that you should want me not to go out and kill people whose mothers love them every bit as much as you love me?"

She was silent, disconcerted by a point of view unfamiliar to Eastwold.

"Or do you think that because they're Germans, they love their sons less?" he teased her, and she pretended to be indignant.

"You're trying to make fun of me, and to muddle me, and I—I'm sure you ought to go, really. . . ."

"That's all right," laughed Dennis.

But all the same, life at "The Hermitage" was far from ideal just now. Mr. Blackwood reading

the paper aloud to his family every morning, dwelt
with reproachful emphasis upon those portions
detailing the atrocities committed by the German
soldiery in Belgium—as if to make Dennis responsible for them. "Inhuman brutes—savages—
devils! No Englishman should rest till the last
one of them has been wiped off the face of the
earth."

"And I suppose no mention is made of the
atrocities our Russian allies have probably committed in Germany," said Dennis, "don't you see
that once the 'dogs of war' are loose, there's bound
to be that sort of thing all round? For the baser
elements of all nations alike? Debauch and
beastliness on the part of people sent mad by blood-
lust?"

Mr. Blackwood turned purple. "Your views are
disgraceful, sir. Why, to hear you, anyone would
think you were pro-Hun."

"I'm not pro-Hun any more than I'm pro-
British. I'm not pro-anything that's driving
millions of innocent people to slaughter and be
slaughtered by each other. I'm for the first people
who've got the courage to put down their arms and
end the whole thing."

"You say that because you don't want to fight
yourself. Must I own that a son of mine is a
coward and a shirker?"

"That's as you please. . . ."

Mr. Blackwood turned to vent his fury upon his
wife. "This is your doing—you always did bring
him up to be a spoilt namby-pamby!"

Between Mr. Blackwood's spluttering rage, and
Clive's cold contempt for Dennis, and her own secret
relief at the attitude which he had taken up, Mrs.

Blackwood had no easy time.   The house was
divided against itself.   Doreen had as yet not
declared herself openly on one side or the other.
She was sincerely convinced that every man ought
to go, but she was half inclined to think that an
exception might be made in Dennis's favour.   It
was different somehow, for Dennis, though she had
not the faintest idea why. . . .

But Reggie, taking no heed of any psychological
subtleties, wrote from Westborough, saying that he
jolly well hoped Dennis would have joined up by
Christmas, and that he ought to be jolly well
ashamed of himself if he didn't, and that he—
Reggie—jolly well hoped that the war would last
long enough to allow him to enlist.

About the middle of December, Dennis realised
that he could no longer stand the strain of guerilla
warfare in the home-circle, and decided to go to
London for a while.   No doubt the strain upon his
mother, too, would be lessened, once his own
irritating presence was removed from the house.
Mrs. Blackwood approved his decision; told him to
be sure and write if he wanted anything; and hoped
he would often run down for the week-end.

Then, very tentatively, she said : " Will you see
anything of Antoinette when you're in London?"

He answered without looking at her : " I daresay
I shall."

" I'll give you her address."

He smiled.   " I know it, thanks."

It was the first time that they had mentioned
Antoinette since she had stayed with them for the
dance.   Mrs. Blackwood still did not know why
nothing had come of that little scheme of hers.   It
seemed just to have fallen flat, . . . Dennis had

been in such a queer mood when he came back from
Cornwall. . . . Perhaps Antoinette had been
capricious or unkind to him; he was so absurdly
sensitive. Of course she had never ventured to ask
him about it. But perhaps if they met again in
London——

Dennis certainly went to London with his
mother's blessing. . . .

He was very glad of the £150 a year which had
been left to him and his sister and brothers by Mrs.
Blackwood's father, and that enabled him to live as
he pleased. He made a little money out of the sale
of his compositions, but not sufficient to keep himself entirely; and he would have hated to be
dependent upon his father.

He took a room in Tavistock Square, and went
the next day to see his friend Neil Barnaby.

Barnaby was sitting at a writing-table littered
with papers when Dennis entered. He looked up
at him with a casual "Hallo?" and a funny,
twisted smile that seemed confined to one corner of
his mouth only.

"Hallo?" responded Dennis.

Barnaby put down his pen, and swung round in
his revolving chair. "It's six months, or there-
abouts, since I saw you here last. Shall we pass
over the intervening time in silence, or do you wish
to make statement of it in detail?"

"Oh, pass it over in decent silence, I think,"
laughed Dennis, "the best of you is, Barnaby, that
after six months' separation, one can take up the
threads of intercourse as easily as if they'd been
dropped yesterday."

Barnaby grunted. "Nevertheless you might
have had the decency to report upon the progress of

your opera, considering that the libretto is mine. Have you finished it yet?"

Barnaby, in his time, had tried his hand at nearly all branches of literature; had perpetrated plays, a novel or two, an occasional set of verses and newspaper articles. But he retained a special fondness for the fairy-tale of "Karen and the Red Shoes," which he had turned into a play for which Dennis was writing the music.

He answered Barnaby: "No, it isn't finished. I haven't been able to do any work at home of late. That's partly why I've come up here for a bit."

"Can't work at home, eh?" Barnaby fixed him with a critical glance. "What is it—white feathers?"

Dennis nodded. "More or less."

"H'm," reflected Barnaby, "I at least am immune from that delicate sort of attention."

Dennis glanced quickly away from the crutches that lay beside his friend's chair. He was conscious of almost physical pain whenever Barnaby made allusion to his deformity; fine massive head sunk between rounded shoulders; one leg shorter than the other . . . .

Dennis said: "Supposing you hadn't been immune—that way?"

"You mean, if my physical disabilities hadn't been so blatantly apparent to the naked eye? In that case, my dear Dennis, I should be doing exactly what you're doing now—or rather, what you're not doing."

"You think I'm right in refusing to go, then?"

"If only they'd all refuse. . . ." The concentrated fierceness of despair was in Barnaby's voice.

"'Then,'" Dennis parodied Mrs. Ryan, "'where would the war be?'"

"Nowhere! That's the obvious answer to that riddle."

"I know it's the answer. I've given it myself over and over again."

Barnaby continued impatiently: "The brute stupidity of the thing. . . . and all the waste of art and intellect! Don't give in, Dennis. Don't let white feathers and the opinion of your next-door neighbours drive you into it. Get on with your opera. That's the 'bit' for you to do, and a 'bit' which only you *can* do. . . . Let's at least preserve art from the general wreckage."

"I doubt if the old ladies at home would agree with you," said Dennis, "they'd say that art, too, must be sacrificed 'in times like these.'"

"The Vandals. . . . I'd rather be a Hun than a Vandal any day! If the old ladies at home get too much for you, for heaven's sake don't bring the conflict of your opinions to me. I'm not interested in psychology at present: I'm doing free-lance journalism just now, for which it isn't necessary. And keep in mind that it's better to write music that will live, than to help to fill the world with things that look like me—and worse. . . ."

But Dennis had no need of Barnaby's reminder. The sight of the wounded in the streets was enough; and the thought of the wounded in the hospitals, being tended and mended, so that they might be sent out again, and broken again. . . . And already one saw those who could not be sent out again: armless, legless, blind; wreckage that could not be utilised either on the field of battle, or on any other.

He plunged into his work, taking it up where he

had left it before he went to Devonshire. But the
horror that was all around and about him, got into
his music and became part of it. The ideas that came
to him, found expression in harmonies that had an
ominous and sinister beauty. He knew that they
had beauty, despite the horror with which they were
impregnated. He never lost his critical faculty
where his work was concerned, nor yet a certain
detached surprise with regard to it. Sometimes he
wondered from what strange sub-region of consciousness issued these visions—yes, that was the
right word—visions of sound, audible to himself
alone, and that he had the power to translate and
transmit to others. And sometimes he was afraid
of this music of his, that sprang from he knew not
whence, and over the going and coming of which,
he had no control. He was afraid now. . . . The
clamour in those submerged regions of his brain
was so great and so complex that it obsessed his
every thought; waking or sleeping he heard the
tortured dissonances and weird scurrying arpeggios,
that left him no peace until he had found the right
form of expression for them.

. . . . Music such as might have been heard in
a nightmare. . . . music horrible and unreal, that
in itself constituted a nightmare from which there
was no escape. Like Karen, the girl in the
fairy-tale who was compelled to dance on and on
in the red shoes which she had so ardently desired
—on and on past the loves with whom she would
fain have lingered—so was Dennis compelled to
listen without respite to this nightmare-music, that
was like an evil spell upon him.

As a child, some haunting phrase of music,
suddenly remembered; or the sound of a coach-

horn heard in the stillness of the night, had had
this power to fill him with helpless terror. He had
stuffed his fingers into his ears, hidden his head
under the bedclothes, but still the sound had
pursued him. . . . He was equally helpless now,
equally terrified; lonely, too; a loneliness that could
be banished neither by talks with Barnaby, nor by
the long musical evenings he spent at Crispin's
flat.

. . . . And the little khaki-clad processions
marched gallantly through the streets; shopboys
and bank-clerks and grocers' assistants, weedy and
pasty-faced, with a smile on their lips, and a joke
to be tossed at the girls they passed on the pave-
ments. . . . Arms swinging, caps set rakishly upon
their heads. . . . a bit of swank and a ·bit of
curiosity and a great deal of heroism. And here
and there for Dennis some face would stand out,
upon which there was neither swank, nor curiosity,
nor heroism; only wonder, dazed wonder; or a
stupefied kind of patience. . . And he would long to
drag that man out of the marching ranks, to ask
him what madness possessed him, or what ideal
inspired him, that he must thus go out and offer up
his all to the Juggernaut of war. . . . And the
answer would always have been the same: he didn't
really know; but everybody was in it, and he
supposed that a fellow ought to do his bit.

And sometimes, Dennis caught sight of some face,
some figure that remotely recalled Alan's.   And
the pain that had never quite ceased, only lain
temporarily dormant, awoke anew: pain, and a new
panic-fear. . . . Supposing Alan were to be in one
of those marching processions! He had probably
joined up by now, and with his democratic ideas,

he would have gone in the ranks. Alan was the
type that could not be held back, that would be
eager and impatient to go. Dennis was certain of
it. . . . He would be crazily brave on the battlefield; would storm trenches in the face of enormous
odds. . . . And he would not return. People like
Alan did not return. He would lie out there with
his body torn and shattered; piteous unseeing eyes
open to the pitiless heavens. Dennis turned sick
as his fancy painted for him the things that might
befall Alan; things that had perhaps already befallen
him.

Consciously and unconsciously, Dennis scanned
the faces of those who marched past him, his heart
throbbing hotly at the discovery of every fugitive
resemblance of look or feature. Soon he hunted
for Alan not only amongst the passing soldiers, but
amongst the crowds thronging the streets, pouring
out of restaurants and tea-shops, waiting outside
theatres. . . . lived for the momentary thrill of
encountering that chance resemblance.

. . . . Deeper and deeper into the crazy depths
of the nightmare—nightmare set to his own horrible
music, and filled with strange faces, figures, voices;
and, almost like a futurist picture, with bits of
streets, buildings, bridges, where he had caught a
glimpse of this one, and that. . . . There was
danger in his present mood, as there had been
danger that night at Crannack. . . . Deeper and
deeper into the nightmare, sinking in it, drowning
in it. . . .

With a last remnant of sanity, and obeying a wild
impulse to fling out a hand for safety while yet
there was time, he rang up Antoinette, and asked if
he could come and see her next day.

CHAPTER II

OF the astonishment which his sudden appearance caused her, Antoinette betrayed no sign when she received Dennis in the particularly hideous drawing-room of the house in Cadogan Gardens. The resentment which she had felt against him at the dance, had long ago died down, leaving only an insatiable curiosity with regard to the cause which could have engendered in him that queer dazed mood. The way he had seemed to clutch at her at Amberhurst—and then his letters—and then the sudden silence—the anti climax of the dance—and now his re appearance after nearly six months—he was really rather an extraordinary person! Antoinette felt distinctly " intrigued," and hoped that this time her anticipation of dramatic developments would be justified.

He began without preliminaries : " I'm not going to apologise for not having communicated with you before. There were reasons—I'll explain some time, and I'm sure you'll understand. But for the present, may I just pretend that I'm still talking to you on the bridge at Amberhurst and that there's been nothing in between ?"

" Certainly," she smiled, suppressing her curiosity regarding the " in between," and noticing that he also suppressed all mention of his letters to her. " Pretend anything you like, and keep the apologies for Grand'mère. She likes them—thrives on them, in fact."

Dennis laughed. " Is she at home ?"

F

" No, but she will be soon, don't fret. You shall be introduced to her."

" Won't she be shocked at your receiving the visit of a gentleman not in khaki?"

" She'll be shocked at my receiving the visit of a gentleman in anything at all," sighed Antoinette, " so it really doesn't make much difference."

She had flung herself back upon the stiff and unresponsive sofa, one arm stretched along the side, in a posture that seemed literally to crave the yielding softness of cushioned divans. But there were no cushioned divans in the house of the de Courcys; and to Dennis it seemed that Antoinette with her short mass of hair and supple boyish figure, was absurdly incongruous with her surroundings.

" You can contradict as much as you please," he said, " but you *are* a square peg in a round hole."

" Oh, I should just think so—here!" she assented quickly.

" Is it very bad?"

" Sometimes."

" Spiked railings, and ' Please don't touch,' and plenty of witches and dragons to see that the rules are enforced—poor little enchanted princess, I'm so sorry . . . ."

She thought she caught a faint echo of something that had been in his letters, and that had been lacking that night at the dance. Eagerly she responded to it : " Sometimes the witches and dragons can be put to sleep with fairy-tales, and the enchanted princess comes and dances outside the spiked railings."

" Will she dance with me, I wonder "—Dennis began, then burst out laughing. " Metaphorically,

of course. I wouldn't dream of really inflicting on
you a sample of my terpsichorean art."

" No, I remember you were kind enough to spare
me at the fancy dress ball. . . ." She could not
resist getting in this little thrust, and wondered
how he would parry it. He did not parry it;
merely left it alone; and she went on : " How are
they all down at Eastwold? Very full of good
works?"

" Very! The Ryans, needless to say, have
started a sewing-class—two sewing-classes, one for
the matrons and one for the maidens of the neighbourhood. Mother and Doreen attend them, and
Lily is at the local V.A.D. hospital. She hopes in
time to appear in a khaki uniform, with initials on
her shoulders, and a strap under her chin. . . .
There was some talk of Millie Ryan's taking up
nursing too, but that project was knocked on the
head, I believe, when her esteemed mother discovered that there were only Tommies at the hospital and not officers !"

Antoinette laughed, and then sighed. " Yes, it's
all very well, ... personally, I haven't as much
as knitted a muffler. It's an awful confession to
make, but I loathe the idea of nursing (even officers !), my sewing is beyond description, and I don't
feel drawn towards scrubbing floors in a hospital."

" Go on," said Dennis.

She leant forward, clasping her hands around her
knee, and shook back her rebellious hair. " If I
took up any of those things, it wouldn't be because
I believed it was my sacred duty to my country to
do them : it would only be so that when people start
with the inevitable : ' And what sort of war-work
are *you* doing?' I could fling them my mufflers or

my dish-washing or my entirely superfluous sec-
retaryship as a sop. And that's not quite good
enough, is it?"

"Not nearly good enough," smiled Dennis. He
was discovering, somewhat to his surprise, that he
was really very glad to see Antoinette again. He
must have forgotten her peculiar exuberant charm
during the time that he had not seen her; but he
was fully aware of it now—and glad that he was
aware . . . .

"So you're a rebel too, Antoinette."

She flashed out: "Yes, I won't make button-
holes just because Mrs. So-and-so thinks I ought
to! One must do war-work from genuine patriotism or not at all."

"And you haven't any genuine patriotism?"

She shrugged her shoulders. "I believe I had
—once; only I've seen and heard so much of the
artificial kind, that it's been spoilt for me."

She fell silent, brows slightly contracted. He
was more and more convinced that she fitted into
her environment as little as he did into his, and that
somewhere they would find a common meeting-
ground, he and she. . . .

He glanced from her to the photographs of the
numerous aunts and cousins. "There's not much
family likeness between you and these, Antoinette,"
pointing to a group of three plain girls with arms
stiffly twined about each other's persons, in a manner indicative of sisterly devotion, and one dear to
the heart of every conventional-minded photo-
grapher. "They may be very worthy, but they
don't appeal to me."

"My cousins Sidonie, Jeanne and Hélène from
Grenoble," Antoinette introduced them, "and

Grand'mère would tell you that the lack of resemblance between us is much to be regretted."

" But surely even grandmothers — even your grandmother, Antoinette—has eyes in her head?"

" I repeat that Grand'mère would beg you to remember that appearances are deceptive, and that embroidered cushion-covers are more maidenly than short hair, and would clinch the argument with the remark that Sidonie, at least, has found a husband!"

" However did she do that?" murmured Dennis, still intent upon the photograph.

" They had an awful time, doing it for her," Antoinette's eyes sparkled with mischief, " there was once a young man of blameless antecedents but of impecunious means, who was brought to the house, and proposed to her—or rather her ' dot '—and was refused by her father. The young man wreaked a horrible and subtle vengeance by going across the road and paying court to Sidonie's cousin, Adèle. Adèle is, if possible, even plainer than Sidonie—that's her photograph over there, between Raoul and Jacques, wearing English Eton suits, seven sizes too big for them."

" Thank you," said Dennis, gazing transfixed at the likeness of a fat young thing with a yearnful expression, leaning over a stucco balustrade with a tennis racket in her hand.

Antoinette continued : " Adèle accepted the young man : her dowry being slightly larger than Sidonie's, she could afford the luxury. But hereupon Sidonie's parents began to realise what they had missed, and to scheme to get the young man back again. This was easily effected by clapping a few thousand more francs on to Sidonie's dowry.

. . . They're the happiest couple in Grenoble now, I believe."

" There is, of course, also Adèle's point of view to be considered."

" Well, she has at least the consolation of having started a family-feud so bloodthirsty that it will not end as long as there is a single one of them left to carry it on. And think how difficult it will be for my uncle and aunt to get their two remaining daughters married, with Nemesis—or rather Adèle's parents—watching from the other side of the road !"

" Antoinette, I'm enjoying you most awfully. . . ." Enjoying, also, a feeling of security in her presence—in this absurd, hideous room with the family-photographs. He had escaped from the danger that threatened. He was safe—with Antoinette.

The door opened to admit old Madame de Courcy and her daughter-in-law. Grand'mère's pleasurable anticipation of interviewing her grand-daughter's suitor—it was doubtless in this capacity that young Blackwood was making his visit—was tempered by the thought that this suitor was not one of her own selection. She was therefore prepared to regard Dennis with a critical, not to say a disparaging eye. There was also the little matter of his income : Madame de Courcy had cross-questioned Antoinette very closely on the subject, without obtaining any results whatever. Apparently Dennis had been reticent concerning his financial position, a point greatly in his disfavour. A young man in a *good* financial position, had no need to be reticent about it. " *Il doit y avoir quelque chose de louche*," as she had suspiciously remarked to Anatole, who agreed with her.

It therefore behoved Grand'mère first of all, to put the young man at his ease, and then with her usual tact and discretion, to make him admit the exact figure of his income.

With this end in view, she commenced by assuring Dennis how much Antoinette had enjoyed herself at Eastwold, and how kind it was of his mother to have invited her. Dennis replied with becoming courtesy, that his mother had been delighted to have her. Which ended the first round. The next was more directly personal.

" I see, Monsieur, that you are not in uniform."

" No, Madame," Dennis replied superfluously.

Henriette was gazing out of the window, a look of profound abstraction in her cavernous dark eyes. Suddenly the sound of her voice vibrated through the room. " When I think of martyred Belgium, my heart bleeds. . . ." Her hand was clenched against her breast.

Dennis began to understand why Antoinette had said that genuine patriotism had been spoilt for her : small wonder, if she had to listen to much of this sort of thing ! He glanced at her, as she sat beside her grandmother on the hard sofa, hands sedately folded in her lap, eyelids lowered, the picture of the typical " jeune fille " decorously awaiting the advances of her suitor. She was adorable, he thought with a warm glow of affection . . . . and again something within him consciously registered that glow, and was satisfied. . . .

Madame de Courcy once more took up the thread of conversation. " My grand-daughters in Grenoble occupy themselves with cooking for the soldiers, and nursing them."

" Not specifying if the latter is necessitated by

the former," murmured Antoinette, who was on the
old lady's deafer side.

Madame de Courcy, catching the murmur but not
the drift of it, yet being convinced of its seditious-
ness, continued severely : " Antoinette does not
occupy herself with anything. . . ."   To which
Dennis, in the manner of the best French exercise,
responded : " Er—no, but my sister knits socks."

Henriette embarked upon a monologue directed
seemingly to the atmosphere in general. " Would
that I had a son to give to France. . . . Gladly
would I have sent him forth to do his duty, though
my maternal heart had been torn with anguish ! "

Madame de Courcy took the occasion to remind
her daughter-in-law that it was indeed regrettable
that she had no son ; and that she and Anatole had
always said so ; and that it must be entirely her—
Henriette's—fault, as all the other members of the
house of de Courcy had been blessed with male
offspring.

Antoinette hastily changed the subject by asking
Dennis what had become of Crispin.

" Crispin—no, he's not in the Army. He's
engaged upon a private and personal war against
the people who are trying to bar Wagner and Bach
from our concert programmes."

Madame de Courcy broke in again : " I hear you
are an artist, Monsieur, a sculptor, is it not ? "

" No, a musician," Antoinette corrected her, and
the old lady nodded her head.

" Ah, he visits the museums ? But that is indeed interesting."

" He is a musician, I tell you ! " shouted
Antoinette.

" *Comment* — he gives piano-lessons ? " cried

Grand'mère in great consternation. Dennis, very
gently, succeeded in making her understand that
he " wrote pieces for the piano " ; she looked relieved ; asked him if he were well paid ; and in a
loud aside demanded of Henriette if musical con-
ductors received pensions from the State in England. . . .

Henriette languidly shrugged her shoulders.
" Who thinks—who has the heart to think of music
now ? For me, if I were a man, there would be but
one music thrilling my soul : the roar of cannons—"
crescendo—" and the beat of drums. . . ." She
let the sound of her deep voice slowly die away on
the word.

Dennis was sorrier than ever for Antoinette.

When he took his leave, Madame de Courcy
pressed him to come again, and Antoinette gave
him a most decorous " Good-bye, Mr. Blackwood,"
with a blush and lowered lids, and then one second's
impish gleam from the grey eyes under their thick
black lashes.

Dennis walked away with a light heart. " It's
all right," he told himself, " quite all right. . . ."
He was struggling up out of the nightmare into
which he had been sinking, as a person sinks into a
dark, weed-clogged pool.   The weeds still clung
about him : there were several things from which he
must avert his mental gaze—or, better still, he must
pretend that they were not there. The picture of a
boy's lean body, lit by the glow of a forge, was one
of them. . . . But he could pretend quite easily,
and it would be all right, he repeated—if only Antoinette would give him a hand.

Antoinette felt stimulated by Dennis's visit. She

was liking him more than ever before. His whimsical sense of humour appealed to her, also his delight in the eccentricities of the de Courcy family, as recounted by herself. And there was still about him that air of mystery which offered food for the wildest speculations. Half idly, and yet not without a certain thrill, she began to wonder what sort of a lover he would make.

It was two nights later, and he had taken her to a theatre. They had laughed a great deal, and had had a very good evening, but now, as they drove in the taxi towards Cadogan Gardens, a silence fell upon them. Antoinette's heart throbbed with excitement that was mingled with a remote inexplicable dread ; but she did not know whether it was the dread of a repeated anticlimax, or dread of the climax for which she longed, and which she sensed near at hand. Yes, she decided, she *did* want it—but still the oppression remained.

Abruptly he ended the strain ; put his arms round her. " Antoinette, will you marry me ? It will be quite all right, dear . . . really it will."

And now that it had come, that for which she had waited, she was conscious only of a feeling of withdrawal, that amounted almost to recoil.

" Will you, Antoinette . . . ? "

She wished that after all, he had not come to the point so quickly ; wished he had prolonged the rather charming uncertainty of their intercourse ; wished that he were not already claiming a definite answer. . . . All this, while his arms were around her, his lips very gently straying over her cheeks, her eyelids. As one soothes a child, he murmured again : " You'll see, it will be all right."

Of what was he thus persistently reassuring her, she wondered with a touch of impatience ; and freed herself from his arms. " I'm not sure, Dennis . . . d'you know," with a little burst of hysterical laughter, " I've an awful longing to say that this is so sudden."

" But you must have always known that it was bound to come," he pleaded.

" Y-yes, but——" She could not put into words the feeling of flat disappointment that was upon her. He had kissed her—asked her to marry him : climax stirring enough ; and yet something in her that was not satisfied, protested : " This can't be all ! Is this really all. . . . ? "

" Well?" he smiled down at her, and she was irritated by his calm.   Surely a man who cared deeply for her must have behaved differently in the face of her vague answer ; must have sought by his passion to kindle a like passion in her.

" I don't love you," she said very low, knowing that she spoke the truth, and wondering what effect this statement would have upon him. He considered it in silence, as the cab drew up at the door. He helped her out and dismissed the driver. Antoinette, on the door-step, had one moment of fear lest Dennis should take his dismissal to be final. She had not meant to be quite so drastic as all that ; she liked him too much to want to hurt him.

. . . To her relief he was beside her on the door-step now, and in the darkness, his arms were round her again. " Dear child, believe me—it will be all right. . . ." Very lightly he kissed her lips, and as he ran down the steps : " I'll write to you to-night."

Antoinette, rather dazed, rather irritated, and

more disappointed than ever, let herself into the house. She reflected, quite irrelevantly, that Dennis had omitted to lay stress on the fact that he loved her. Now she came to think of it, he had not even mentioned it.

CHAPTER III

". . . I DIDN'T think it was possible to be quite so
happy as this. I want to thank you for it again
and again, but I simply can't find words. You've
made me so glad and triumphant. I know now that
nothing else matters, and that nothing can ever
come between us. Please say you know it too, because you do, deep down in your heart, don't you?
Oh, I can't say one fraction of what I want to, but
I can hardly wait till to-morrow, to have you in my
arms again . . . God bless you, my dear. . . ."

The sight of the scrawled phrases sent the blood
rushing to Antoinette's cheeks; and yet—she had
given him no reason to burst into these pæans of
joy. Was he so dense, then, that he did not perceive that there was no answering joy in her? Dense
and selfish he must be, with that peculiar masculine
denseness and selfishness that she had always
abhorred in the men who had hitherto flirted with
her—men who had taken for granted that her pleasure in receiving their attentions must equal their
pleasure in bestowing them. What right had
Dennis to take so much for granted? She had
credited him with more subtlety of insight than was
common to the average male. His caresses had
lacked the masculine brutality that had always
frightened her. Dennis had not frightened her : he
had merely bored her.

She read the letter through again, and again
thrilled at the sight of the words. Which of her
impressions of him was correct? How was it that

his letter could thrill her, when under his kisses
she had remained as cold as ice? Obviously, there
was still some mystery that awaited solution.

Perhaps it would be solved this morning! He
had rung her up, and asked her to meet him for a
good long talk . . . and at the sound of his voice,
tense and controlled, over the telephone, she was
aware of an intense desire to avoid hurting him,
and to find that everything was really " all right."

He took her to a little underground tea-shop in
the Strand much frequented by Barnaby and his
journalistic friends. It was empty at this hour of
the morning, and no sooner had Dennis given his
order for coffee, than he took Antoinette in his
arms, kissed her and kissed her. . . . And Antoinette let him kiss her and kissed him back, trying
to act the part, shamming the passion she was far
from feeling, and that she longed so genuinely to
call into existence by shamming if it could not be
otherwise, and wondered all the while that he did
not seem to notice the coldness beneath this sham
passion of hers, and that he could still murmur
brokenly between their kisses : " I'm so glad—so
very glad. . . ."

" Let's go and tell your people when we leave
here, shall we? " he cried, as he released her, " do
you think your grandmother will die of the shock?"

" Oh, she needn't know just yet. There's not
such a hurry, is there? " . . . Again that twinge
of alarm. She must know that she could still escape
in case of need. If her people were told at once,
and an engagement between herself and Dennis for-
mally announced, all possibility of escape would be
barred.

" But there's no need to keep it a secret," he pro-

tested, " I feel I can't keep it to myself a moment
longer. I want to tell everybody I meet—Crispin—
Barnaby—and to wire to them at home—Mother
will be ever so glad. I may just tell her, mayn't
I? "

" I'd much rather you didn't, Dennis. . . ."
More and more real her alarm, now. She must succeed in combating this desire of his to take people
into his confidence. For once his family knew, and
her family, and his friends, and her friends, she
would be bound hand and foot to carry out her
portion of an agreement into which she had not yet
entered. Not yet. . . . She was frightened of
being rushed into a decision; determined to play for
time.

" I'm not sure of myself, Dennis. I told you so
last night, and it's true. Won't you give me a
chance to be really sure? "

He avoided answering the direct question and
argued : " We could tell them all the same, couldn't
we? Whether we tell them now, or in six months,
doesn't make much difference."

" Yes, it does. It makes all the difference in the
world to me—it should make all the difference in
the world to you, if you care that I should really
care for you."

He said sadly, " But don't you, Antoinette? "

" Not yet. . . . Not as I want to be able to care
for the man I marry. Not as I have cared for—
other people." A fleeting recollection of some of
her feelings for Hester crossed her mind.

" Oh, don't talk like that," Dennis begged her.

" But I must ! " she cried impatiently, " not to
make you jealous, or anything as absurd as that,
but just to get things clear, to show you that I do

know the difference between the real thing, and what isn't the real thing."

"And this—isn't the real thing?" He spoke without looking at her.

"I've told you it isn't—yet."

"But it may be? You think it will be?"

For the sake of the eagerness in his voice and eyes, she smothered doubt, and replied, "Give me six months, and I'll tell you then."

As they climbed the little stairway that led from the tea-shop to the street-level, she had the ridiculous sensation of having been reprieved. . . .

He had to rest content with her decision. His belief that all was well was still unshaken; but it was a pity that she had chilled his first enthusiasm; a pity, also, that she had not let him tell his mother. Once his family knew, and her family, and his friends, and her friends, withdrawal would be made impossible. Not that he had the slightest desire to withdraw : this *was* the real thing, he assured himself over and over again, as he held her in his arms and kissed her.

All the same it would have been safer to make withdrawal absolutely out of the question. . . .

In order to avoid the curiosity which her family would have displayed, had it been known that she was seeing Dennis three or four times a week, Antoinette stated airily that he had returned to Eastwold; and accounted for her frequent outings, by manufacturing an entirely fictitious set of invitations from an entirely fictitious set of friends. Sometimes, to vary the monotony, she threw in some equally fictitious friends of Rosabel's, with the result that she was able, in comparative peace, to continue her experiment with Dennis.

It certainly was an experiment from Antoinette's point of view, but she wished with all her heart, that it was something more than that, or that it would become something more. . . . At present there was not much hope. He seemed incapable of arousing her, even though on their long drives home through the darkened streets she lay in his arms and returned his kisses, and tried so hard, for his sake as well as for her own, to catch fire. She resented the lack of mastery in him—mastery that should have demanded and compelled love, instead of gently pleading for it. Was it love, though, for which he pleaded? She was still aware that he did not reiterate that he loved her; did not use the words that love would have used, and that she longed to hear. . . . . But he wanted to marry her; he was taking for granted that at the end of six months she would marry him.

Of that queer glamorous mystery that had once enshrouded his personality, nothing remained. All the promise that he had held out in his letters from Devonshire was yet unfulfilled. When she tried to lead him to talk openly of himself, he fell silent, or changed the subject—and kissed her. It seemed to her that she knew even less about him now than at the beginning. And he knew nothing about her. She was convinced of that. He never made any attempt to fathom her moods and feelings; to discover what her thoughts had been in the past, or what were her ideas concerning the future. Nor would he discuss their relations to each other; always silenced her questionings with : " It must be all right—it was meant to be."

" I don't feel that it was," she argued uneasily.

" You will—in time."

" And . . . if I don't? "

" Oh, don't let's think of that."

" But why do you wilfully blind yourself like this? " she cried.

He said mournfully, " Because life is so full of cruelties, that the less one sees of them the better."

" It's cowardly, just to pretend that they aren't there ! "

He flushed and started at that; and she hoped it might lead to some further explanation.

" Much better to face them out."

He shook his head. " No . . ." and relapsed into silence.

Exasperated, she gave it up.

Often she wondered what his relations with other women had been, and tried to sound him on the subject.

He answered : " There's never been any other woman," and she knew by instinct that he did not say this merely to please her, or to assuage a non-existent jealousy, but that it was the truth . . . and she could not tell why it filled her with a new uneasiness. Yet she could not bear to sever their connection entirely. Sometimes, for days together, he did not see her; left her without news of his whereabouts. Then she began to believe that he would never return, and was conscious of a fear quite disproportionate to her real feelings for him. It was always with immense relief that she welcomed him back. There were so many little things for which she liked him. On rare occasions, she released him from his fictitious exile in Eastwold, and he was allowed to lunch in state at Cadogan Gardens. Antoinette enjoyed watching him as he made conversation with her grandmother, who

thought him a very backward young man, and strove
by an increased amiability to give him the courage
necessary to demand Antoinette's hand in marriage.
Grand'mère was not at all sure that she would accede
to such a demand, but then, from her own point of
view, it was almost as enjoyable to refuse as to
accept an offer of marriage for her grand-daughter.
Antoinette had explained the subtlety of Grand'-
mère's attitude to Dennis, who, sharing her delight
in it, solemnly acted up to it. It added, also, to the
pleasant feeling of truancy appertaining to all her
expeditions with him. Yes, in their lighter moods,
they harmonized well enough. It was only in moods
that were not light—

And yet she could never quite rid herself of the
hope that they must one day stumble upon the
thing which would dispel, as if by magic, the mental
fog that had descended between them. Some quite
little thing . . . something equivalent to a mere
click or switching-on of machinery that would be in
perfect working-order, if only one knew how to set
it in motion. The hope that one day it would be
set in motion, sprang up afresh whenever she was
not with him, but it died down inevitably at their
next meeting, died under his queer silences and
evasions, and under his kisses. . . .

Once, in one of his more clear-sighted moments,
he cried out to her : " Oh, why can't you care for
me more ? "

And all the longing of her soul was in her voice,
as she replied : " My dear—if only I could. . . ."

Dennis's music alone thrilled her, as could nothing else about him. In it, he seemed to give something of himself that he otherwise withheld ; and
yet she felt that it was not to her that it was being

given. He played her his old songs or bits of his opera, but nothing that had been dedicated to her or that had been composed because of her. Lacking the power to inspire him, she was completely shut out of his music.

Thus they drifted, for the six months and over the six months. He was no longer pressing her to make a decision, as he had done at first. She was guiltily aware that she ought to do so, that the situation was absurd, anomalous, and that she ought to end it—one way or another. But which way? She was no nearer to loving him than she had been six months ago; but she dreaded the idea of the blank there would be in her life, if she put him out of it altogether, as she surely must do, once she spoke the decisive word. So she did not speak it. . . .

More and more silences and evasions now; the fog between them thicker and thicker. . . . And always he kissed her; kissed her with a fervour that seemed to increase in the same proportion as their mental affinity seemed to diminish.

At the end of a hot August day, they drifted in their punt down one of the backwaters at Wargrave. Antoinette had done most of the punting; and now, deliciously tired, she lay back among the cushions, while he paddled down-stream. Through half-closed eyes she watched him, noted the contrast between his athletic build and sensitive features. He was gazing straight ahead, into the green-gold tunnel formed by the overhanging branches. What was he thinking of, she wondered. Was it some new musical inspiration that had come to him, and that was absorbing his entire thoughts? He was rather

a wonderful person altogether; good-looking, and a
genius. She was musician enough herself to recognise that he was a genius. It was absurd that she
should not love him. . . . Perhaps, unbeknown
even to herself, already she was beginning to love
him? Perhaps—with a sudden quickening of her
pulses—perhaps someone had spoken the magic pass-
word. . . . ?

He put down the paddle, tied up the boat, and
came and flung himself down on the cushions beside
her. He had chosen his moment well. For the first
time she was glad of the storm of kisses that he
showered upon her. No need to complain of his
gentleness now—not now, with his hands clenched
into the short warm tangle of her hair, his hard
kisses beating down upon her lips and upon her
throat. She lay passive under the storm, rejoicing
in this new fierceness and mastery that had come
to him—fierceness and mastery that in any other
man would have terrified her—and thought : " It's
going to be all right—it *is* all right now. . . ."

Suddenly, without a word, he pulled himself away
from her, untied the punt and paddled back to the
landing-stage. All the way to Paddington, their
compartment was crowded and conversation impossible; but Antoinette was satisfied with what the
day had already given her—knowledge that it would
be easy to make her decision now. Should she tell
him to-night, she debated as the taxi bore them
homewards, or should she leave it till to-morrow,
and let to-day be sufficient unto itself? She decided
on the latter course, convinced that it would harmo-
nize better with his mood. He was exceptionally
silent; and on her doorstep, he bade her good-bye
without kissing her again, without so much as

touching her. And she was well pleased with his behaviour that showed a fine appreciation of a mood for once shared.

Oh, but she was looking forward to seeing him to-morrow!

And to-morrow, at breakfast, there was a letter from him waiting beside her plate. Joyfully she swooped down upon it. After all, he had been quicker than herself to seize the moment. This would be one of his perfect letters, and at last she would be able to give in response to it, all that he might ask of her.

Grand'mère, who had of course recognised the handwriting, looked inquisitively over the tops of her spectacles.

" What has he to tell you, the young Blackwood? Would it not be time to ask him to lunch again? " And aside to Henriette : " *Cela lui donnerait peut-être l'entrain qui lui manque. . . .*"

. . . One of his perfect letters : Antoinette's heart fluttered wildly—and then stopped.

". . . I'm sorry, but we can't go on like this. I've known it for a long time, and I am to blame for not having acted on my knowledge sooner. You were right and I was wrong—it wasn't the ' real thing.' I should have broken with you completely when I first began to realise it, but for your sake I tried to go on pretending, long after I knew it was useless. So I'm afraid it must be good-bye."

" *Eh bien,*" persisted Grand'mère, " he has at last made you his declaration . . . ? "

But Antoinette sat staring at the letter, stunned and bewildered as from a blow between the eyes. This—after yesterday. . . . She was dazed with the sheer incredibility of the thing; too dazed, even, to be conscious of pain. That would come later.

" For your sake I tried to go on pretending——"

So yesterday, also, had been mere pretence on his part, yesterday, when for the first time she had been genuine in her response to his passion—his sham passion.   It was fantastic, this reversal of their original positions!

" So I'm afraid it must be good-bye."

The words, read and re-read till they seemed to become devoid of all meaning, swam before her eyes. If only he had indeed chosen to break sooner, he would have left a blank in her life; but no more. Why must he have waited until this moment, when it meant leaving far more than a blank?   One did not suffer when it was only a blank, but when it was more. . . .

" For your sake I tried to go on pretending, long after I knew it was useless."

That was the answer; and it stung.   Between the lines, she thought she read contempt of herself; contempt and dislike.

But was it entirely her fault that she had never possessed the key to any of his moods?   He had always shut himself away, hidden from her the workings of his mind, so no wonder that this revelation of an attitude that must have been crystallizing gradually during the past months came as such a shock.

She folded up the letter, and put it away with the one he had written the night he had asked her to marry him.

" I know now that nothing else matters, and that nothing can ever come between us. . . ."

As contrasts, she reflected, the two letters were quite effective.

CHAPTER IV

AT last, thank goodness, he had found sufficient energy to break away from this deadlock, to end this weary game of pretence! He had thought that with Antoinette he could escape definitely from his abnormality; escape from his loneliness; from the ever-present terror of himself; from the nightmare of his own music; and his thoughts of Alan. . . . From all these things he had sought refuge in Antoinette's arms; she would make him forget that they existed. And besides, Antoinette was of those who understood; he had not the slightest intention of deceiving her; some day they would talk everything out openly together.

But Antoinette had failed him; failed him in her moments of recoil, as she had failed him in her moments of insincere passion. He knew all along that her passion was insincere, and it frightened him. Was he, then, in truth so abnormal, so different from other men, that he was incapable of rousing real passion in a woman, real love? She did not love him; yet she would not let him go, even when he begged her to make her decision.

" We must go on, dear—or go back."

" I can't go on yet, and . . . and I don't want to go back. It'll leave such a big hole in my world if you're not there, Dennis." . . . Always appearing to give herself with one hand, and to withhold herself with the other.

He began more and more to doubt the possibility of her understanding, and to revise his previous judgment of her—judgment based upon some flimsy illusion created that night at Amberhurst. She was after all just an ordinary normal girl, who would turn from him in shuddering aversion, if she knew. . . . And she was rather immoral, he thought, in her simulation of passion that she did not feel; and endowed too, with the ordinary woman's vanity, that could not bear to lose an admirer, and must keep him dangling, even though he meant nothing to her.

But it became more and more difficult to break as time went on; he knew that there would have to be scenes and explanations. And he dreaded the idea of explanations now. . . . Of mental kinship between them, there was no longer any trace; neither of the warm tenderness which he had felt for her at first. He shut his inner self away from her, and, when they met, since they could not talk—he kissed her. It was evidently what she wanted, now that she had overcome her first distaste, and what he— well, not what he wanted, but what for the moment, could in some small measure content him.

He was rapidly sinking back into the nightmare out of which he had hoped to rise; nightmare of loneliness and strangeness and being different. . . . And the old hunting-mood had him again, when for hours together he paced the streets, courting danger and the thrill of danger from a flung glance or smile or whispered word . . . and with burning cheeks and beating heart, fleeing danger . . . and courting it again.

And all Antoinette's kisses could not content him now, even though she gave them so lavishly in response to the passion that was not for her, but only venting itself on her. That last day at War- grave—surely some instinct must have told her?

Was she so dense or so insatiable that she had really perceived nothing? She must have perceived nothing, or she could not for an instant have endured his kisses. More than time for them to break—so at last he had broken with her; and his letter would eliminate all possibility of a further compromise—of further drifting. He was not hurting her, at the most her vanity; and that did not matter. She would console herself easily enough; find some other man to fill his place.

And now he was free—for what, though? Free to take anybody, anything that could reach him through his charmed circle of isolation. For in this isolation of a soul terrified of itself, and doomed to eternal misunderstanding and misjudgment, lay the greatest temptation of all : the temptation to stretch out a hand to others like himself, and to own himself frankly to be one of them. It would be so much easier. . . . But his abhorrence of himself, and his honest desire to be as other men; above all, the æsthete in him insisted on a perpetual wearying struggle between his principles and instincts for the existence of which he was no more responsible than for the colour of his eyes. He had done his best to fight them down, only sometimes he was very tired, tired of having to keep this ceaseless watch over himself, tired of having to suppress and thwart desires that were natural to him, but would be classified as vicious and perverted by the world of ordinary people, lacking understanding of his peculiar temperament. Yet, even while he craved for understanding, he dreaded it : for this reason he had not been near Barnaby for weeks. He guessed that Barnaby's attitude would not be one of conventional intolerance, and therefore deliberately

avoided him.   Once he allowed himself the luxury
of confiding in someone, he could not tell what effect
this greater freedom might have upon him.   Fear,
mingled with some strain of asceticism, made him
deny himself that luxury, even as in his schooldays,
it had prevented him from accepting Eric Rubenstein's sympathy and friendship.

But London was too dangerous to him in his present condition.   He almost welcomed a letter from
his mother, asking him to come down to Eastwold.
Hugh Clavering was expected home on leave, and
his engagement to Doreen was to be made public.
Dennis went; but Hugh's leave was several times
postponed, so that he did not actually arrive till
after Christmas.

Dennis soon realised that the ladies of Eastwold
were experiencing considerable difficulty in the
matter of how to treat his mother.   Of course if
Mrs. Blackwood had only been *his* mother, one
could quite simply have cut her; but as she was also
Clive's mother and Hugh's future mother-in-law,
it complicated things.   Clive was in the trenches
and had been mentioned in dispatches. . . . But
there was Dennis who steadily refused even to attest
under the Derby scheme, and who thought that all
war was wrong (which was ridiculous, at least as
far as the British were concerned) and said so on
every possible occasion.

Some of the ladies argued that one should condole
with Mrs. Blackwood on the subject of Dennis,
rather than reproach her; some thought that his
disgraceful views more than outweighed Clive's
deeds of valour, so that they felt justified in cold-
shouldering Mrs. Blackwood.   But the majority
contented themselves when they met her, with en-

quiring enthusiastically after each individual member of her family, and leaving a frigid gap in the conversation to mark the place where Dennis would have been enquired after, had he been worthy of such enquiries. . . .

Lily Hallard, very military indeed in her V.A.D. uniform, openly confessed that she didn't like the prospect of having a shirker for a brother-in-law; and in her loud-voiced aggressive manner tried to convert Dennis to a proper frame of mind.

"How you can bear to sit at home, while other men—while your own brother is in the trenches!"

"They're doing what they think is right—or rather, they don't think at all."

"And you think it's right to let others go out and be killed for you?"

"Killed for me. . . . Good Lord, do you think I *want* them to go out into that infernal mess and muddle? I'd hold every one of them back with my own hands, if it were in my power!"

"You make me sick," said Lily. "That's not a man's way of talking. Look at Tom Sanderson—he's exchanged into an infantry regiment, because he says there's nothing doing in the cavalry, and he's so eager to get to the Front. That's the proper spirit."

"Not unless you can believe, with all your intellect and soul, that you're doing some good by taking part in that wholesale butchery."

"A fat lot most of our boys think of 'intellect and soul.' They just go and do their bit, and don't talk about it."

"If they did—if people talked and thought about it more, there might be some hope of ending the war altogether."

" We don't want the war ended that way ! "

" No, you want it to be ended by fighting, rather than by thinking. . . . To hear you, one would positively imagine that you enjoyed the idea of the war going on and on."

" It must go on till we win. Oh, if only I were a man ! I'd give anything to lead a fine cavalry charge. . . ."

Dennis did not doubt that she was quite competent to do so.

Altogether, he suffered no lack of attempts to convert him.

There was Griggs—Lance-corporal Griggs—who had not been out yet, but was dying to go, and expecting to do so next week, as he had been expecting every week since the outbreak of war.

" What—not yet in khaki, Dennis, old man ? What's all this about pacifism ? Come, come, come, that's nonsense—artistic temperament, that's all. You'll make as good a soldier as anyone, just the same. We're all in this—don't let anyone stand out. What I say is, rope 'em all in—rope 'em all in."

Dennis was reminded of the day at Amberhurst, when Griggs with just as much fervour, had sought to induce him to play the piano during the theatricals. " Rope 'em all in—everybody's got to do something. . . ."

No one must stand out. No one must be an exception. Not even if they had no leanings towards the particular form of entertainment advocated by Griggs.

Even Doreen, gentlest of sisters, did her best with Dennis.

" Don't you think you ought to go, Denny dear, now that everybody else has gone ? "

" Do you imagine, Doreen darling, that I should have waited till now—waited till everybody else had gone—if I had intended to go at all? "

A letter from Ottilie had come through *via* Switzerland, saying that " she herself with a hotly-beloved Bavarian officer on the West Front engaged had; " also that she hoped to see her dear friend Doreen again " as soon as the dreadful war over was."

Dennis went on : ' Surely you'd rather that your Hugh and Ottilie's soldier-man didn't have the chance of shooting each other to bits? "

" But the Army's so big, Denny : they're not likely to meet."

" In all probability they won't. But there are thousands of others in the same respective positions, facing each other in battle. Don't you wish they weren't? "

" Y-yes, of course I do, but . . . everybody's going, Denny."

And then the Ryan girls. . . . Millie cut him dead when she met him in the town, but Amy, not prompt enough to achieve the cut direct, had begun to smile before she realised what she was doing . . . tried to retrieve the smile, blushed, and finally stopped to say : " We all think it'th thuch a pity about you, Dennith. All really nithe men go and fight, don't they? " Then, having said so much, she could not resist the temptation to continue : " I'm keeping up a Correthpondeth with *three* Lonely Tholdierth—jutht ordinary Tommieth, of courthe, but being in khaki maketh all the difference, doethn't it? Ethpethially if you never thee them . . ." with which somewhat ambiguous statement, she vanished.

The only one who made no assaults upon Dennis's convictions, was young Hugh himself, very tanned and handsome, very much the hero of his native village, and the same unspoilt and charming boy he had always been.

"Doesn't want to kill the Huns? Well, neither do we—part of the time. Some of them are awful decent little chaps, quite pally with our men. Still, I suppose it's our job to do 'em in, if we can."

The biggest discussion took place at the Blackwoods' Sunday lunch party, the occasion on which the engagement was officially announced. Lily and her mother came, and Hugh and his parents, and Griggs, and the Ryans—poor Millie had to exchange a few civil words with Dennis after all, thus marring the effect of the previous cut.

The ladies had retired from the dinner-table; Hugh had vanished in Doreen's wake; and Griggs, as a non-smoker, had been accorded the freedom of the drawing-room. Dennis was alone with his father, Mr. Ryan and Dr. Clavering. Griggs, on his exit, gazing after Hugh and Doreen, provided the old gentlemen with the necessary cue.

"There they go—the gallant and the fair! Doesn't it make your heart envious to see them, Dennis? It's the uniform that does it, my lad, the uniform. . . ." He slapped his narrow chest, and went off, beaming.

"Yes, we believe you right enough," grumbled Mr. Blackwood, "if I were a young man, I'd be ashamed to be seen about in anything but khaki."

"They say conscription's coming in," Mr. Ryan wheezed hopefully.

"That'll be the end of all our slackers and shirkers, and a good job too. What'll you do then, my son?"

" Precisely what I'm doing now."

" What do you mean? "

" Refuse to fight."

" But you can't," cried Mr. Blackwood, " they'll put you in prison, or shoot you as a deserter."

" Let them."

" You mean to tell me," expostulated Mr. Ryan, " that you're afraid to go out to the Front and die like a gentleman, and yet you've no objection to staying at home and being shot like a dog? It's monstrous, sir, monstrous."

" My objection to going to the Front isn't entirely fear for my own skin, Mr. Ryan, though I know you're convinced that that is my sole reason for staying behind. I don't suppose I'm any more or less afraid of death than the average man of my age."

" Prove it," muttered his father, " prove it. . . ."

" I daresay I shall prove it, when conscription comes in. I would rather be shot, as Mr. Ryan says, ' like a dog,' than submit to a law that orders me to murder men with whom I've no personal quarrel. And if I did have a quarrel with a man, I shouldn't murder him."

" There would be some cases in which it would be your duty to do so : what would you do if a German attacked your mother? "

Dennis smiled as Mr. Ryan put the inevitable question. " I could defend my mother by incapacitating him for the moment, without resorting to the extreme measure of taking his life."

" Tommy-rot !" snorted Mr. Blackwood, " when a man's blood is up, he kills."

" Perhaps in the case of a personal quarrel. But you can't say it's his duty to kill when he has no quarrel at all "

" It's his duty to his country——" began Mr. Blackwood, and Mr. Ryan's breathless voice broke in : " His country's quarrel should be good enough for him."

" But it's not the quarrel of the whole of this country, any more than it's the quarrel of the whole of Germany. Why not try and restrict the quarrel to those who made it, without dragging in millions of innocent people on either side . . . . people, some of whom don't even know what the quarrel is about, and what they're fighting for ? German peasant boys taken straight from the plough—English lads raked out of remote sleepy villages : how much do you think they know ?"

" There can be no doubt that every Englishman knows what he's fighting for," declared Mr. Blackwood.

" Yes, he's told that he's fighting for honour and glory and freedom, and to defend his home and country from a dastardly enemy. And the German boy is told exactly the same. And they both believe it, bless them. When they're both out there, dying a foul death side by side, perhaps they may wonder if it was true, and if it was worth while, and why they let themselves be driven out to kill and kill and be killed by each other."

" Yes, yes, yes," said Mr. Ryan testily, " we all know that war is very dreadful——"

" Yet you won't even attempt to stop it !" cried Dennis. " You encourage it to go on. It's like a fire that instead of confining to the smallest area possible, you're fanning and fanning till it spreads from one end of the country to the other, and flinging on more material every day to feed it. Why

G

in heaven's name won't you try to stamp out the blaze?"

" Yes, it's all very well to talk like that," said Mr. Blackwood, " but there always have been wars, and there always will be. Nations that have had no wars have become degenerate, and gone to the wall."

" Oh, I can't stick all this humbug about war being necessary, and war being good for us! How can people talk such stuff, if they have the slightest conception of what war really implies?"

" Well, you won't alter human nature," answered Mr. Blackwood, " man is a fighting animal, and for my part I should be very sorry to see the fighting instinct knocked out of him."

" That's setting yourself deliberately against all idea of progress, Father : because certain evils have existed up to the present, is that a reason to declare categorically that they are bound to exist in the future? Why not root them out? What is there to be proud of in the instinct that leads one man to kill another? Why deny all possibility of conquering an instinct that can only make for misery?"

He looked from one to the other of the two red-faced elderly gentlemen; his father angrily fingering the stem of his wine-glass; Mr. Ryan glowering at him through the heavy wreaths of his cigar-smoke. Only the doctor, on the opposite side of the table, gave the impression of an impartial spectator.

" I've no patience with all this rot!" cried Mr. Blackwood, " if a man's got no fight in him, he's unnatural, that's what I say, unnatural."

" You'll allow a man to conquer nature with his ships and his railways—you'll allow him to widen

as much as possible the gulf that separates him
from the beast; but when it comes to rooting out
the war-instinct—*No!* He can't overcome that.
Why should he? It's always been there, always
will be. In fact, you're rather proud of it: it's part
of a gentleman's equipment. You want progress
and the conquest of natural difficulties in every possible direction, and yet you won't admit that a man
can conquer *himself*. You're shouted down as ' unnatural,' if you as much as speak of overcoming an
instinct that is nothing but a hindrance to civilisation and progress."

"Oh, you and your artist friends, I daresay you
talk a lot of twaddle, but you won't convince *me*."
Mr. Blackwood drained his glass of port, and rose
from the table. Mr. Ryan followed him.   Dr.
Clavering remained where he was.

Dennis smiled at him across the table. "Well,
Doctor, you've been very silent all through this."

"I was umpiring."

"They were two to one."

"Oh, you were quite capable of holding your
own. But you'll never convince them, Dennis, my
boy."

"And you, Doctor?"

"I don't say that you've convinced me, but I can
understand why, as an artist, you take that point
of view."

"Yes, but I don't want to have excuses made for
me on that ground," cried Dennis, " nor am I pretending for a moment that Clive and Hugh and
others like them, can go out and kill, because
they're more brutalised than I am. It's their belief
that I'm up against—their belief that they're doing
right."

" Dennis, Dennis, you're fighting a losing battle! It's too late for pacifism now. The war's started and the only thing for us to do is to make every effort in our power to end the unfortunate business; and that can only be done by fighting to a finish."

" And what then? Doctor, it's no use pretending that ' this is a war to end war.' I don't believe it. Do you believe that the British are fighting for disarmament, for democracy, for world-peace, any more than the Germans are? The governments of the big nations—not the mass-peoples, because they weren't asked—but the governments of all big nations organise warfare with the same ends in view —extension of power; consolidation of empire; commercial and political advantages. If we go on fighting till Germany has to cry ' Pax ' from exhaustion, it simply means that the balance of military power will be shifted, and that *we,* instead of the Germans, will be the war-lords of Europe. Do you call that a goal worth the sacrifice of one man's life-blood—let alone of millions?"

" But that's only a hypothesis, Dennis : you can't be certain what will happen after the war. We must end it first and then see. And surely, on the strength of a mere hypothesis, you wouldn't wish to see the Germans win?"

" Of course not. It'd be a tragedy for any one of the great powers to attain the complete military victory they're each striving for."

" But, my dear boy," the doctor protested with some heat, " now that we—now that all the nations —have sacrificed so much, we can't go back. Think of the utter futility of the whole thing ending in a draw!"

" I still maintain that that's better than fighting

till one side (whichever it is) is beaten to its knees, and the other in the position to dictate terms of bondage; and free to go on, through the years, preparing for wars more terrible even than this one."

" Well : and if it's a draw ?"

" If the so-called fruits of victory are withheld from them all alike, there's some chance that the people of each nation, seeing the true nature of the war-machine by which they've been driven, will clamour to have it broken up; will protest against the maintenance of great armies and navies for their mutual destruction. There'll be some chance of an era of real peace—not the sham peace of the lull before the storm, which will exist if the powers can be definitely divided into conquerors and conquered, with the conquered merely biding their time to reverse those titles, and the conquerors ever on the watch to see that they shan't do so. A lasting peace can never be achieved by war, because war only breeds war."

Dr. Clavering smiled. " You're a Utopian dreamer, Dennis, but I sincerely respect you, just as I respect my own boy, and all the other boys who do their bit in their particular way." He added after a moment : " And I doubt if you'll find your way easier than theirs. . . ."

.   .   .   .

Later that afternoon, Dennis wandered out for a walk in the hills surrounding Eastwold, thus cheating Mrs. Ryan of the opportunity to draw him into a renewed discussion on militarism versus pacifism.

The first breath of Spring lay upon the land; just a breath, and no more. The woods were not even faintly misted over with the green of budding foliage, but stood out as massed shadows of purple

and bronze against the pale sky. Except for the
deeper colouring of the woods, it was entirely a day
of half-tints; light fawn of the ploughed fields;
light green of the pastures where the cattle grazed;
tenderest blue of the sky. The hedges that separated the fields were lines of brown, curving rhyth-
mically about the undulations of the hills. Scattered farms nestled in the hollows, and from them
went up a medley of animal sounds; lowing of
cattle; barking of dogs; bleating of lambs; sounds
that were blended with the rapturous outpourings
of larks, and the drowsy distant peal of church bells,
rippling eight notes down the scale.

Dennis lay at full length on a ridge above a
chalk-pit, and looked out at the hazy blue view,
while the soft wind blew in his face, and flung up
the good strong scent of freshly-ploughed earth and
young grass. Railway-tracks gleamed in the sun;
chalk-white roads wound their crazy way up and
down the hilly country; and across fields to meet
them, just as the brooks and rivulets, born of the
winter's heavy rains, meandered along to join the
placid shining river that followed its leisurely course
to the sea.

And Dennis thought of all the roads and railways that had been made throughout Europe to
connect one country with another; of how these
same roads and railways had been torn up or
blocked and barred to form frontiers and sever the
connection between one country and another. And
he thought of the rivers that flowed through one
country and another; rivers, some of which ran red
now with the mingled blood of nations locked in
this death-grapple of hatred and lust and vengeance

—nations each and all inspired by the thought that they were fighting in self-defence for justice, for glory, for their honour, for their fatherland, for their God . . . . each and all fighting blindly against each other for the same abstract principles.

And the rivers flowed on, imperturbable; calm; oblivious of all artificial frontiers; oblivious if it was French or German or British or Austrian blood that reddened them.

If there remained enough sane people in this world gone hideously mad, could they not put an end to it all? Could they not open the eyes of those blindly fighting—of those in government who organised and were responsible for the fighting? Surely it must be the aim of every rational human being to stop the war : not to secure the victory of this nation or that, but to lay the foundations of a lasting peace for all humanity? But people holding such views were looked upon as cowards, shirkers, traitors. And if they stood rigidly by their views, allowing themselves to be deviated neither by scorn nor insults; allowing themselves to be persuaded into no weak compromise or half-measures, they would in all probability be shot or put in prison.

It must come to that for him too. For months, the Harmsworth press had been agitating for con-scription; the Bill would be passed that *ordered* every man to go out and shed the blood of his fellow-men. And then. . . .

If only sufficient people had the courage to fight against the war, then might the other countries of Europe lie as peacefully as this spread, misty land-scape at his feet. The roads and the railways might link them together again; the barriers of racial hatred and racial envy be swept away; art and civilisation arise once more in place of murder and barbarity.

Already, as was usual with him, thought was translating itself into sound, into music that was no longer morbid as a nightmare, but strong, triumphant, a pæan of peace—the peace of all nations. Into it would be blended the characteristics of each; the steadfastness of the English and the indomitable fire of the French; the depth and the innate good-heartedness of the German people; and the easy tears and laughter of the Austrians; the Italians' hot-blooded rhetorical love of their country, and the incurable melancholy of the Irish, the Russians and the Poles.

The voice of each he would transfuse into his music. He would make himself the medium through which their individuality, their thoughts, their dreams, their yearnings should be expressed. His brain teemed with the new bold harmonies into which they would be orchestrated. This symphony of his should be as international as art itself; as international as the heart of the man who, seeing beyond hedges and frontiers and class-distinctions, claims the whole world as his " country," and claims kinship with all people who walk upon the face of it.

He got up and wandered back into the straggling little town. A new recruiting-poster on one of the hoardings caught his eye: a pink-kneed Highlander with arm outflung against a highly-coloured patchwork of field and hedge, demanding : " Isn't this worth fighting for?"

Dennis smiled as he answered the question : " It's worth more than that; it's worth—*not* fighting for !"

CHAPTER V

HE was in London again now, and the Conscription Bill had been passed. All men must go, except those who were medically unfit, indispensable in their present occupations, or had religious or conscientious scruples against the taking of life. These could appeal for exemption, and their cases would be heard before tribunals set up for the purpose. It sounded rational enough and humane enough that no man should be forced to fight against his convictions; but already there were howls of protest and indignation at this clause in the Military Service Act. It was offering a loophole of escape to cowards and shirkers . . . . easy enough for a man who was afraid to fight, to fake up scruples that would keep him safely at home, while better men went out and shed their blood for him. . . . The Government was too soft-hearted altogether . . . . scruples, indeed . . . . pampering a lot of weaklings. . . . Thus the " Daily Mail " and others of its kind. When it came to it, Dennis wondered, would the tribunals do justice, and how?

He was walking up the Strand one Saturday afternoon to meet Barnaby at Miss Mowbray's tea-shop. The matinée crowd from the Vaudeville Theatre was just pouring out on to the pavement when he came face to face with Antoinette and Rosabel Fayne. For a second he and Antoinette stared at each other, both blushing furiously, each doubtful as to whether the other intended to stop or pass on.

Rosabel ended their indecision for them. " Oh,

Mr. Blackwood, what a surprise, meeting you . . . .
isn't it a surprise, Antoinette? Do come along to
tea with us, won't you? It's my tea-party—I mean
it's Antoinette's birthday, and we've been to the
theatre—only the pit, of course, but very dissipated
in war-time, isn't it? Shall we go to Fuller's?"

Dennis, very embarrassed, glanced at Antoinette,
but her eyes were obstinately downcast, and she
gave him no assistance whatever.

"Do come," Rosabel rattled on, "it'll make it
so jolly. This is my afternoon off, but I have to be
back at the hospital by six."

"Then I think you'd both better come and have
tea with me," said Dennis. "I was on my way to
meet a friend at Miss Mowbray's." He expected
that Antoinette would protest here, or make some
excuse not to follow his suggestion, but still she
said nothing, and in silence walked along beside the
talkative Rosabel.

It was nearly six months since he had last seen
her. In the interval, after his first bitter resentment had died down, he had scarcely thought of her,
and he assumed that she had thought equally little
of him. Everything had been over between them
when he had made his final cut, long before that,
really . . . . so it was quite ridiculous that he
should now feel so constrained in her presence.
Why had she given her tacit consent to this three-
cornered party? What was her attitude? One of
curiosity, no doubt, he reflected sardonically, curiosity as to what his own attitude might be. She
wanted a fresh sensation; Antoinette was like that.
. . . He decided that at all events he would not
gratify that desire.

They turned up a stone-flagged passage between

the back of a theatre and a row of small shops, entered a narrow doorway, and descended the steep stairs into the tea-room. It was neither square nor oblong, neither circular nor octagonal; but seemed to be made up of a variety of odd corners of different shapes. A big fire burnt in the grate, and six or seven little tables of dark stained wood were spread for tea.

Rosabel gave a cry of delight. " Oh, how lovely . . . . isn't it too Bohemian for words? Such a quaint shape . . . . and the dim light . . . . and that cosy little table in the alcove . . . . have you ever been here before, Antoinette?"

" Yes," said Antoinette, speaking for the first time, " I've been here once before." Once . . . . The day after he had asked her to marry him. Did he remember that, too, she wondered, as, much to Rosabel's glee, they ensconced themselves at the table in the alcove, where Barnaby was already seated. She had met the crippled journalist several times before, and talked to him rather hectically while Dennis vanished behind the curtain which divided the tea-room from Miss Mowbray's private sanctum and the kitchen. He was rather a long time chatting to Miss Mowbray and ordering the tea. . . . . So much the better. When he came back she would no longer be able to talk; the beating of her heart choked her when she could actually look at him and hear his voice.

This accidental meeting had been anticipated and mentally dramatised a thousand times over. One swift look between them, one touch : " It was all a mistake, Antoinette, I had to come back—It's all right now . . . . dear . . . ." Herein the imaginary meeting had invariably culminated; meeting longed for, almost prayed for during six weary months.

He returned to their table, and still without seeking Antoinette's eyes, and without speaking to her directly, embarked upon a desultory conversation with Barnaby. Through the small barred window near the ceiling, that was on a level with the street, Antoinette watched the legs and feet of the passers-by; legs and feet without bodies or heads, continually passing and passing. She remembered that thus, with an odd sort of fascination, she had watched them that first time, while Dennis had stumblingly tried to assure her that it was all right —that he was so glad. How much did he remember, she wondered again. And the footsteps of those strange bodiless legs on the pavement outside, echoed: how much—how much—how much?

" Oh, but you're not seeing this place at its best," Dennis was informing Rosabel in answer to her enthusiastic praise of the tea-shop, " it's empty to-day, but as a rule it's crammed full of actors, journalists, artists and rebels of all descriptions."

(Thus he had played up to Grand'mère, when he had lunched at Cadogan Gardens, giving his audience what it wanted!)

" Oh, how *exquisite,*" cried Rosabel, feeling that here indeed she was having her money's worth, or rather Dennis's; " I do so love rebels. Sometimes I think I'm one myself . . . . but it's rather naughty of you not to be in khaki, isn't it, Mr. Blackwood?"

" Oh, you mustn't try to air any military views here, Miss Fayne," Barnaby twinkled at her from under his shaggy brows, " this is entirely a haunt of pacifists."

" What a sweet idea," murmured Rosabel, who could always adapt her views to the needs of the moment; with equal flexibility she had transferred her one-time adoration for Marie Antoinette to the present Queen of the Belgians as being just as unfortunate and more up-to-date. " And how clever of you to have discovered this ' haunt,' as you call it, tucked away behind the theatre like this."

" I knew Kitty Mowbray before ever the tea-shop existed," Barnaby explained, " she was on the staff of the ' Daily Standard ' at the same time as I was; then the paper went bust, and she took up this instead. She does a roaring trade now."

Antoinette puffed nervously at her cigarette, and, through the haze of smoke, cast occasional surreptitious glances at Dennis. Often enough, during those six months, she had wondered if, when she saw him again, she would discover, as she had once discovered with Hester, that he meant nothing to her. He should by rights mean nothing to her. The love that he had awakened one day, and had not even come to claim the next, should indeed have been a short-lived emotion; short-lived as those few fleeting hours in the punt . . . . memory upon which, in view of his letter, she could only dwell with shame-flushed cheeks . . . . memory upon which, nevertheless, she dwelt again and again, striving to draw from it a little warmth with which to animate the dull, lifeless present. That love had not died during dreary days and nights of self-reproach, and longing for him to return, and conviction that he would not return, and more self-reproach . . . . days and nights of hope that to-morrow, at last, would bring the letter, the wire, the telephone-call that said that he was coming back to her.

It was not dead now, but very acutely and painfully alive, as she sat looking at him; tracing with
a half-fearful joy the familiar outline of his chin
and jaw; listening to the familiar tones of his voice.
She was grateful to the others for talking; she felt
incapable of taking part in the conversation herself.

Miss Mowbray entered with the tea.

" Has O'Farrell been here to-day, Kitty?"

The ex-newspaper-reporter, a sunny little woman
in a blue linen overall, shook her head in reply to
Barnaby's question. " He's broke again, poor dear.
He had his last lot of sausages and mashed on tick
last Friday, and I haven't seen him since."

" Well, if he turns up after I'm gone, tell him,
with my love, that he's a confounded idiot, and that
if he doesn't deliver that cartoon of his in time
we shall never be able to get it into this week's
' Dove.' "

" I'll tell him all right," smiled Miss Mowbray.

" ' The Dove ' is the name of the pacifist paper
Barnaby is editing," Dennis explained for Rosabel's benefit.

Rosabel clasped her hands ecstatically. " ' The
Dove '—Oh, what a *sweet* name!"

Barnaby grunted. " Yes, that's all that is sweet
about it. It's a very vehement peace-dove, I assure you. We expect our office to be raided everyday. O'Farrell's political cartoon will do the trick,
I should think, if he delivers it in time, instead of
indulging in riotous orgies of sausages and mashed.
It's Lord Derby and the Kaiser playing a game of
Oranges and Lemons while a stream of unfit re-
cruits passes under their outstretched arms to their
death."

Later on, a very bad-tempered Crispin joined the group, nodded curtly to the two girls, and sat down between Dennis and Barnaby. " F-fools!" he ejaculated, when at last he became articulate. " N-narrowminded idiots!"

" There, there, what's the matter now?" Miss Mowbray, who had come to take his order for tea, tried to soothe him.

Crispin spluttered : " A b-beauty. F-full-sized g-grand. P-perfect tone." Then, with a rush : " S-said they wouldn't have it in the house any more."

" Who wouldn't have what in the house any more?" queried Rosabel, quite bewildered, but very interested.

" My uncle and aunt. Their B-blüthner piano. Because it was a Hun m-make. So I said they n-needn't have me in their b-beastly house any more either. And n-no more they shan't!" concluded the irate musician. After a deep draught of Dennis's tea he found strength to add : " D-don't deserve to win the war—p-people like that."

Antoinette smiled at the vision of Crispin and the Blüthner grand homeless upon the pavement in Fitzjohn's Avenue; but she began to wish that the party would diminish in size, instead of increasing. The larger the party, the easier for Dennis to avoid meeting her eyes. Perhaps if she were alone with him—was it possible that he was really so impervious to memory as he seemed, absorbed in some political discussion with Barnaby, while Rosabel strove to assure Crispin that she, too, was a rebel? . . . . assurance pathetically incongruous with her peaked little face under the hideous flat felt hat that constituted part of her nurse's uniform. If only

the others would go—the thought choked her. If
they went, would he throw off this pose of indifference? Was it only a pose, though? What if it
were genuine? Or what if it hid—not agitation
caused by this sudden meeting, but actual dislike
of her presence? There had been dislike between
the lines of that last letter, perhaps something even
stronger than dislike. And while all his other
letters, his charming letters, seemed mere faded
ghosts, that one letter had never lost its power to
sting. Did he still hate her? She must know. She
could not possibly make matters worse than they
were already by knowing the truth.

Eventually the others began to disperse. Barnaby hobbled up the stairs on his crutches, and returned to his office in Fleet Street; Crispin took
his grievance into Miss Mowbray's sanctum; Rosabel, suddenly aware that it was long past six,
scuttled off in the direction of her hospital.

Dennis and Antoinette were left standing at the
foot of the stairs.

" I must go, too," she said, hoping that he would
give some sign at last, or make some attempt to
detain her.

" Is Grand'mère waiting for you with an inquisi-
tion as to how and where the afternoon has been
spent, and isn't there a lie ready to meet the situation?"

So he remembered that much! She gave him
one swift look to ascertain if he were about to
betray how much else he remembered. But his
smile was quite inscrutable. For very shame at
having been mistaken in her impression that he
was on the point of behaving as he had always done
in the imaginary version of this meeting, she

flushed scarlet as she answered : " I have almost forgotten how to lie to Grand'mère."

" A pity that a practice which you have really brought to a fine art should be allowed to rust," he commented cynically; and his cynicism hurt her, as had his previous indifference and apparent lack of memory, and one or two other things, absurd little things . . . . like seeing that he had a new slouch hat and brushed his hair straight back, instead of parting it at the side . . . . things that she would scarcely have noticed in the days when she did not care for him. She felt as if she had been mentally skinned; as if every nerve were exposed and quivering, and as if there were nothing about him that had not some mysterious power to hurt her.

She said in reply to his remark : " You see, there has been no need to keep in practice."

He raised his eyebrows in amused astonishment. " Do you mean to tell me that you have altogether ceased to cast a veil of fiction over your goings and comings?"

She was silent. She could not tell him that she had expended all her store of unveracity on the invention of excuses that had to be plausible enough to account for the cessation of letters, outings and telephone-calls, and that yet had to be calculated not to put him in a bad light, so that in case he ever came back—she had not wanted to make the severance seem too abrupt, so for a while she let it be assumed that they were still seeing each other occasionally, and the hardest lies of all were those she had to tell when she went out with quite irrelevant people, and allowed the family to take it for granted that she was with Dennis.

" *Eh bien, il etait aimable, le jeune Blackwood ?*"

And for pride's sake : " *Oui, Grand'mère, très aimable.*" Easy enough to fib about a good time that one had had ; difficult beyond belief to fib about a good time that one had not had. Antoinette had lost her taste for fibbing since then. Besides, as she had told him, there had been nothing and no one in her life to justify or necessitate it. And she was too much of an artist to waste a good lie, when the truth would do as well.

She repeated : " I must go now . . . ." and thought how grotesque it was that they should be standing side by side, laboriously making conversation, when a year ago in this same place, he had held her in his arms and kissed her. Why couldn't he kiss her now, while there was no one about? Once, he would have been quick enough to seize the opportunity. And now, not one of those unwanted kisses that she was not paying for with a separate stab of longing.

" I'll see you to your station," he said, since he could not very well do otherwise. " Charing Cross Metropolitan for Sloane Square, isn't it?"

" Yes." She smiled in memory of the innumerable times that he had seen her home by that route.

They walked down the Strand together. After a while, he broke the silence with, " Does your mother's heart still bleed for France? It was France, wasn't it, or was it Belgium?"

She laughed feverishly. " It doesn't matter. Her heart is always bleeding for something—symbolically. Actually, she's never been as happy in her life as now."

" How's that?"

" She recites patriotic poems—the ' *Carillon* '

and ' *Belgique meurtrie* ' at all the fashionable
charity performances."

Dennis laughed aloud. He could so well imagine
Henriette de Courcy with her deep voice and her
dramatic gestures and her symbolically bleeding
heart, reciting with much relish to an audience
composed chiefly of foreign ambassadors and English ladies of title.

" Mother tried ever so hard to make me take it
up, too," said Antoinette, " I suppose it would have
made quite an effective picture, mother and daughter, both with Parisian accents, both moaning for
their lost Belgium. But I really couldn't bear it."

" I should think not ;" for the first time she de-
tected a note of genuine interest in his tone. " And
have they tried to persuade you into other sorts of
war-work ?"

" Oh, yes . . . . translating French into English (because you know both languages so well,
dear), or cutting bread and butter in a canteen, or
emptying slops in a hospital. I've not done anything."

" From conviction ?"

" Oh, no, not from conviction," she said in a
listless way, " more from laziness."   She added
wistfully, " I wish I had convictions—any sort of
convictions. Just to have them." If one had convictions, one had at least something in one's life
that would stand rock-firm ; something by which to
steer ; one was not helplessly buffeted about upon
shoreless seas of emotion.

Dennis smiled. " You seem to consider convictions a luxury : they have to be paid for pretty
dearly, I can tell you, if one stands by them."

She had been so absorbed in the conflicting sensations of the moment that she had not realised what might be in store for Dennis if he stood by his convictions.

" What—what is going to happen to you?" she asked tentatively.

He shrugged his shoulders. " I wait till I'm called up; then I lodge my appeal; then I appear before the tribunal; and then—heaven only knows!"

" I see," she murmured, too shy, almost too afraid of him to say more, or to express the hope that he would get his exemption.

Silence fell upon them again. They were nearly at the station now. And there he would take his leave of her, with that new, half-cynical politeness; and he would not ask if he could see her again, and she would not see him again until chance flung them together once more, perhaps in another six months, perhaps in a year, perhaps never. And there would be one horrible moment when she would have to watch him disappearing into the crowd, knowing that in this vast town, and amongst these vast shoals of people, the odds were a million to one against their meeting again. With every second the hope diminished that he would still say something, do something that would spare her that one moment.

He took her ticket at the booking-office and presented it to her. "Well—good-bye."

She disregarded his extended hand, yielded to her fear and to her frantic desire not merely to be dependent upon blind chance for her next glimpse of him. " Please—Dennis . . . ."

Something of her desperate anguish pierced at last through his assumption that all she wanted of him was a fresh sensation. He looked at her white face and quivering mouth. "Why, Antoinette, what is it?"

She shook her head, not daring to speak, lest the tears that scorched her downcast eyelids should fall.

"What is it?" he repeated gently.

She tried to smile; made a great effort to gain self-control, but nevertheless it sounded lame and piteous as she stammered: "C-can't we—just be friends?"

He knew then that it was not friendship that she asked of him; saw also that he was face to face with some very real emotion. A certain amount of curiosity, blended with a slight softening of his attitude towards her, was responsible for his next sentence.

"We can't very well leave things like this, can we? There's a great deal to be talked about."

A sigh of relief escaped her. She was to be spared the moment she had so dreaded; spared at least for a while.   She had been reprieved, and memory mocked her with a vivid picture of the last time she had experienced that sensation: going up the stairs of the tea-shop, after Dennis had unwillingly acceded to her plea for six months' time in which to make her decision.

"Come for a stroll now—it's nearly your dinner-time, though, isn't it? Hadn't you better telephone to say you're not coming home?"

She laughed tremulously, and found her voice again. "Yes, if you can think of a suitable lie for me to tell them. They mustn't know I'm with you."

"Oh, you've met a friend of my mother's, who insists on your dining and going to the theatre with her. That's the usual sort of tale, isn't it?

And it'll cover all emergencies in case we're late."

Antoinette nodded and disappeared into the telephone-box, where she spent considerable time placating a resentful father at the other end. Anatole declared that she ought to come home to dinner on her birthday, as she had been out the whole afternoon.

" I had to say that your mother's friend was sailing for America to-morrow, and that this was my last chance of seeing her," Antoinette told Dennis when she rejoined him, " and when Father began to argue, I rang off. . . ." She did not know what was in store for her now, but at least she had enjoyed those few uneasy minutes of lying to the irate Anatole.

They left the station, and walked down towards the Embankment.

" Have I been a brute to you, Antoinette?"

" No—Oh, no . . ." fervently she denied his self-accusation. " It wasn't your fault, not any of it. It was all my fault. I made you hate me."

" Yes," he admitted, " I did hate you. But it wasn't entirely your fault either. There were so many other difficulties and complications that helped."

She said : " Yes, I know. . . ."

" Do you know—do you?" At the intense eagerness of his voice, some instinct warned her to banish all trace of interest or curiosity from her own. She replied in dead level tones : " Yes, of course I know . . ." and wondered what had prompted her to the lie.

" Are you sure?" he persisted, as if he very much wanted her to be sure.

And again she repeated : " Yes . . ." and

waited in breathless tension for what he would say next. She had no idea as to the nature of the difficulties and complications to which he alluded; had vainly sought an explanation of them during the last six months. But she knew now why she had lied: perhaps he would solve the mystery for her, if she pretended that already she had solved it for herself.

" That makes things very much easier," he said, " it was that which first drew me to you at Amberhurst—thinking you'd understand, that you must understand, because you had the same kink of abnormality as I had."

" Just the same," she murmured, still utterly ignorant of his meaning.

" You see I always knew I was hopelessly different from other men. Women never appealed to me. All the attraction I ever felt was for——" He stopped, still uncertain of her, but it was beginning to dawn on her at last, and she helped him out again.

" Yes—I know."

" Well: then you came along, and I spotted you at once. And seeing that the taint was in you too, I thought it must make you as lonely and miserable as it made me, and I imagined that the two of us could fight the loneliness better together."

He broke off to let some people pass between them; and she, confused and bewildered, but also strangely excited by this revelation, wondered if she could succeed in hiding from him the fact that she had never been aware of any particular taint in herself!

" It might have been all right if you'd said ' yes ' at once," he resumed, " only you hung back."

" I'm sorry, Dennis."

" Ah, don't say that. You were only being true to yourself; I see that now, but at the time, it made me furious. You wouldn't go on and you wouldn't go back. You just kept me dangling."

He set these accusations forth in a mournful, passionless way, as if merely stating his case, and with no desire to wound her. But she felt the wound nevertheless, and the pain of it gave her a queer thrill of elation. Better a thousand times that he should hurt her like this, than that there should be between them that dense impenetrable veil of silences and evasions. Even now, whenever for a moment she lost the sound of his voice amid the noise of wheels and the blaring of motor-horns, she feared that he would say nothing more, and that the veil would fall again before it had been properly lifted. And strung up to an almost unbearable pitch of excitement, she waited to catch his jerked-out sentences again.

" I always thought that one day I'd be able to tell you all about myself——"

" Oh, if you had, if only you had . . . . I tried so often to make you tell me, and you never would."

" Yes, that was where I made my mistake. I let my first impression of you, the correct one, become obscured. . . ." Subtle fascination in the knowledge that only by reason of his discovery of some taint or kink which they had in common, could he at last reveal all that the veil had hidden of dark turmoil, dark moods and impulses.

" We couldn't go on as we were. I felt dishonourable and loathed myself for not telling you, or breaking with you, but one seemed as difficult and impossible as the other."

" I wouldn't let you break," she said softly, " I remember. . . . And of course you couldn't tell me anything. And you must have hated me more and more for making you hate yourself."

" You understand well enough now," he cried, " I was a fool ever to doubt that you would."

On and on they walked, and the rumble of traffic and the hurrying footsteps made a strange accompaniment to words that were more strange yet. On and on, dodging other pedestrians, plunging across roads. But she was stimulated beyond all consciousness of fatigue.

" What was it," hesitatingly she spoke, choosing her words with care, so that he might not divine her ignorance, " what was it, that time at Amberhurst, that showed you ?"

" My child, the way you looked at that woman, was quite enough."

Hester. . . . So that was it !

" You were in love with her, weren't you ?"

" Yes. . . ."

" And there had been others, hadn't there ? Other women ?"

" Yes—Oh, yes." Rapidly she cast her mind over those school-girl passions of her early youth— Miss Prescot—Natasha—passing flickers of emotion aroused here and there by the beauty or attraction of women she had met in hotels abroad—finally Hester. . . . This, then, was the taint of which he spoke ; the taint that they shared, he and she. Only whereas he had always striven against these tendencies in himself, in herself she had never regarded them as abnormal. It had seemed disappointing, but not in the least unnatural, that all her passionate longings should have been awakened by women, instead of by members of the opposite sex.

"And you were thinking of them, weren't you, when you said you'd known what the real thing was like?"

"Yes. . . ." This, at all events, was the truth.

"You've never known it with a man, have you?"

"Never, Dennis. . . ." Never until now.

"I've known it, once, with one of my own sex . . . . that was a long time ago. It was terrible . . . . and rather wonderful, but it had to be beaten down, and beaten down again, and the scar has never quite healed."

She stole a glance at him, as he strode along at her side, a furrow between his deep-set eyes. A wave of burning tenderness and longing came over her. It was a shame that he should have to suffer so horribly from the consciousness of his abnormality, while her own had never caused her the slightest uneasiness. She understood now all the misery of his schooldays, everything that he had half-told her in his letters. He had put the key into her hands, hoping that she would be able to fit it into the lock . . . . only she had never been able to do so. She had not even tried—furiously she lashed herself with reproach—she had been far too indifferent to him, far too much absorbed in her love for Hester, that very love which proved her so closely akin to him. But he had always suffered, as a boy, as a man . . . . and she had gone scot-free. If only she could make up to him for all that he had been through, for the times that he had in vain asked her for understanding, for the times that she had thought of him without love, and kissed him without love. She had been blind and insensible before, because she did not love him; but now it seemed

that every pang he had suffered, every tortured desire that had been his, found its reflection and
counterpart in her.

" I've never known what it was to love a woman.
Not really. I didn't love you, Antoinette . . . .
you know that. And you didn't love me, either,
did you?"

" No . . . ." she added under her breath : "Not
until it was too late."

She saw him flush ; caught his murmured : " Oh,
my dear . . . ." but if he said more, it was lost
in the rumble of wheels. Heedless of the direction
in which they had been walking, they had almost
worked their way back to Trafalgar Square. Over-
head the searchlights were flashing rapier-blades,
continually crossed and re-crossed upon the background of thick dark blue. Whitehall was crowded.
She had a moment's panic, lest she should lose sight
of Dennis. In this bewildering sea of faces and
figures that pressed in upon her from all sides, she
would never be able to find him again. They would
go different ways, each hunting for the other . . . .
but they would never find each other again in the
sickly half-light of the darkened streets. There
were so many different ways that they might go.

The next minute she was reassured by the pressure of his arm against hers. " Shall we go into
Lyons' for a meal? I saw you didn't eat anything
at tea."

Nor could she eat anything now. She was too
tired and excited ; but she was touched by his concern for her, and followed him through the swing-
doors into the crowded and garishly-lighted Corner
House. The strains of a rag-time band fell upon
their ears ; the sound of mingled voices and laughter, rattle of crockery, footsteps of waiters. . . .

"Not quite the right *mise-en-scène* for a psychological dissertation," Dennis smiled as they seated themselves at a small corner table.

"Oh, it's good enough as a contrast," she laughed, and reflected that she was indeed having an uncommon birthday-party . . . . uncommon birthday-presents, too. Meeting him had been the first; that moment at the station when she had had her reprieve, had been the second; the way he had suddenly taken her arm in the crowd, was another. Were there more to come, she wondered? She dared not hope for more, but accepted with gratitude each as it came.

"It's a case of 'like to like' with us." He had given his order for dinner and they faced each other across the narrow table. "And because there's a certain amount of the masculine element in you, and of the feminine element in me, we both have to suffer in the same way."

She felt suddenly compelled to honesty. "I haven't suffered—because I didn't quite realise . . . . about myself."

"And I've made you realise . . . . ? Oh, I'm sorry."

"Don't be sorry," she implored, "I should have had to know sooner or later." And she was glad that it was he who had made her realise . . . . glad . . . .

"Yes," he assented, "of course you would. Not much peace of oblivion for people like us. Not much happiness either, so far as I can see. Not when one always has to fight and watch and take care, and pay the penalty for having instincts that aren't like other people's."

Yet she had been happy, blissfully happy during

her brief passion for Hester. She had not fought nor watched nor taken care, for she had never realised the need of doing either. She felt as if she had not been justified in being happy, as if it were unfair to him that she should have escaped paying the penalty. But in future she would not escape. Suffering must inevitably accompany realisation. Again she was glad : for by suffering shared, she would earn the right to stand by him in his loneliness.

Clatter of plates ; the continual coming and going of people between the tables ; the rattle of money on the cashier's desk ; the cloying sweetness of " Until," played by the band. And Dennis's low voice reaching her across all the other conflicting sounds.

" We're disinherited from the legitimate ways of happiness, you and I. We're Ishmaelites, outcast for ever from the world of normal men and women. Yet it isn't our fault that we were born with unusual natures any more than it's a cripple's fault that he's born with a deformed body. But they turn from us as if we were lepers. What do they know of the continual struggle to be decent, and to keep decent, with something always tugging you the other way? They don't know the ghastliness of having to pretend to be as normal as they, and all the while to be stifling and suppressing the most vital side of yourself—the love-side. And they don't know what it's like to go in perpetual fear of discovery, and fear of your own condemnation as well as theirs. . . . I'm twenty-six, Antoinette, and I've known, or almost known ever since I was fifteen ; and in all those eleven years I've never told a soul."

" I'm glad you're telling me now. . . ."

" My dear, whom should I tell, if not you?"

Swiftly she raised her eyes to his and dropped them again. " Thank you, Dennis. . . ."

. . . . They stood outside the swing-doors and shivered in the night air. The music and light and voices were cut off behind them, and they were caught up in the dark swirl of traffic again. He piloted her across the road and into a taxi; gave the address to the driver; slammed the door.

And then his arms were round her, his lips clinging to hers . . . . and the shock of joy was so poignant, that she averted her face and buried it against his coat-sleeve, so that he might not find her lips again, nor kiss them again just yet—not just yet. . . . Let her hold this moment fast, hold it and hold it against memory of all the days and nights of fruitless yearning, against the dread of days and nights that might perhaps still be to come.

She stirred a little in his arms, and he kissed her again.

" Dennis—I love you . . . ."

Strange for him also, to hear this from a woman. " My dear . . . ."

Her arm stole round his neck, drew his cheek down beside hers. And she remembered how with just these gestures she had formerly counterfeited passion.

" I love you, Dennis . . . ." Words breathed scarcely above a whisper; words that she had not spoken to him before; words that she derived a queer sort of delight from repeating now, as if only by admitting and re-admitting her love for him could she atone for her past insincerity.

After a while she said : " Will you tell me what it means, Dennis, that I can care for you like this?" She really meant : " Doesn't it prove me perfectly normal after all?"

And he understood and answered the unspoken part of her question. " It's only another proof of your abnormality, my poor child. No normal woman could care for me, I'm sure. You only do, because you are what you are, and I am what I am. It's ' like to like,' as I said."

" Then I'm glad I'm like that." Glad of anything that enabled her to love him so well.

" You mustn't be glad; it's a curse, a terrible curse. You'll know some day !"

Yes, some day she might know, but what matter now, while he held her close, and between his warnings kissed her, and kissed her again, so that her face and throat and hands alike burned with the touch of his lips. . . . Exhausted, finally, she leant back against his shoulder.

" Tired, dear?"

She nodded; too tired even for speech now; dead tired with tramping up and down the streets while they talked; and with the nervous tension and excitement; dead tired, but happy, she told herself triumphantly, even if she were never to be happy again.

He almost lifted her out of the cab. " You've had a strenuous day—your birthday, too, isn't it? Many happy returns. . . . Did your grandmother give you a needle-case or a pair of embroidery-scissors? Good-night, my dear. . . ."

.   .   .   .   .

She asked no questions of the future; scarcely allowed herself to wonder into what strange chan-

nels they were about to drift. Not for a moment
did she delude herself into belief that she could save
him from the shadowy danger which had always
threatened him, nor into belief that he loved her,
or could ever love her. But at least all was clear
between them; it was to her that he had first spoken
after his years of self-imposed silence; he no longer
hated her. . . . . Therefore she was happy, even
though she knew that her hold on happiness was as
precarious as that of a person clinging to a very
small raft in a very stormy sea.

" It's wrong of me to do this, and wrong of you
to let me," he declared at their next meeting, when
without an instant's hesitation, they found their
way into each other's arms.

She laughed up at him. " Why is it wrong? I
know, and you know, and we each know that the
other knows, so nobody is deceiving anybody."

" You're an immoral woman," he teased her.

" I don't care if I am !"

" Yes, but what's going to become of us, Antoinette?"

With fast-beating heart, she yet managed to say
lightly : " I'm sure I don't know, dear."

As it was she who had been responsible for
bringing about yesterday's situation, she must not
let him imagine for an instant that she thought she
had any claim upon him, or that she expected him
to marry her. *Marry* her—she had forgotten : marriage was not for such as she, Antoinette reminded
herself severely. . . . Only it was a pity that she
could not take the same serious view of her "taint"
as he did of his. It seemed so absolutely normal
and right that she should love him. But she must

remember that she was an outcast and an Ishmaelite, and it was all great fun, as long as they could be outcasts and Ishmaelites together! She seemed to have recaptured some of the exuberant joyousness and vitality of the Amberhurst days.

" And I'm sure I don't know either," he replied, " there's all this military business hanging over me, too; it's impossible to decide anything yet."

" Quite impossible," she agreed; and finally, to put him at his ease and free him from all sense of responsibility towards her : " So don't let's bother."

" Idiot-child," he laughed and kissed her.

She had to cloak her outings with him now under a most elaborate set of falsehoods. Already Dennis was in the family's bad books for having taken no decisive steps towards proposing for her hand in marriage; and since that explanation the other night, it was more necessary than ever that he should be kept a " guilty secret " from the family. She revelled in having this secret to keep. It heightened her enjoyment of the good hours with him, as contrasted with the dull ones spent with her family. If, as he had said, people like themselves were " disinherited from the legitimate ways of happiness," then it behoved her to snatch what happiness she could, when and where she could.

They had had dinner at Lyons' one night and were walking up Shaftesbury Avenue towards the Coliseum. She always loved these evening expeditions; loved the mingled excitement and security that she felt in knowing that he was beside her in the shifting crowds.

They had to halt on the kerb at Charing Cross Road, while the stream of traffic flowed past them; and suddenly, from the crowd on the opposite side

H

of the street, a figure detached itself for Antoinette;
a man, stalking hurriedly in the direction of Trafalgar Square. Something in the walk, graceful
and yet athletic, attracted her notice. She turned
to Dennis, and saw that his eyes were riveted to the
same figure, now rapidly vanishing from sight.

" Is that someone you know?" she asked.

He started, like a person awakened from heavy
slumbers. " Someone I—thought I knew. . . ."

He said nothing more, but all that evening remained abstracted and curiously restless.

CHAPTER VI

SOME days later, Dennis and Antoinette, on their way to Miss Mowbray's, fetched Barnaby from his office.

"We've got a new acquisition at the tea-shop," he said, "a man called Rutherford. He's an absolute firebrand."

"Pacifist?" queried Dennis.

"Of course. The most passionate pacifist I've ever encountered. Your most eloquent tirades, and mine, and even O'Farrell's pale to insignificance beside his. He's a friend of O'Farrell's—came down the other day with him and the Taylor woman."

Dennis laughed. "How is the O'Farrell *ménage* progressing?"

"Don't ask me," returned Barnaby, "it's Benny Joseph's affair just now. He's been acting as go-between for the two parties. I believe the spirit of melodrama which they exhale appeals to him as an actor."

"I hope they'll be there to-day," said Antoinette. She was enjoying more and more these afternoons at Miss Mowbray's, and the haphazard meetings with people different enough from her family's set of acquaintances. "I love melodrama."

Barnaby smiled at her eagerness. "They can supply you with plenty of it. She's a mad Irish-woman, married to an intensely worthy British husband. They live with his people in Chelsea, and they've let the studio that's attached to their house, to Conn O'Farrell, who is also Irish, also

mad, and a bit of a genius into the bargain. . . .
Well, you can do the rest in your head, can't
you?"

"Some of it, perhaps," laughed Antoinette,
"but not all."

"No, you're right, there is rather a lot. This
Rutherford man has been lecturing Conn on the
folly of wasting his time with a woman, when he
ought to be devoting himself entirely to the Cause
—and then the woman goes and weeps on Benny
Joseph's shoulder, and says she's going to commit
suicide because Conn doesn't love her any more—
and then Conn comes and weeps on Benny's other
shoulder, and says he's going to commit suicide
because *she* doesn't love him any more. And so
on *ad infinitum*. If Benny has succeeded in
snatching them both back simultaneously from the
brink of suicide, I expect they'll be there to-day."

They were. When Dennis, Barnaby and
Antoinette descended into the tea-shop they found
Conn O'Farrell and Mrs. Taylor seated at a table
with Benny Joseph and Everard Walters, a very
handsome, dark-eyed young man who was acting
at the theatre next door.

Dennis introduced Antoinette all round, adding:
"You'd better sit down and talk to Benny, child.
He's got a perfectly respectable family in Hamp-
stead, even if he *is* on the stage."

"I don't see why a family in Hampstead should
render me entirely innocuous," protested the young
Jew.

"Oh, but it does, Benny. You know that your
wild Bohemian ways are only skin-deep, and that
one day you'll settle down with some nice little girl

of your own people, and forget that you ever knew the smell of grease-paint."

Benny looked hurt, and Antoinette said : " Never mind; I'll talk to you, even if you are respectable."

" That's nice of you!" Benny turned to Dennis : "Is the lady a sympathiser?"

Dennis laughed. " She hasn't got any convictions, or if she has, they're entirely plastic, aren't they, Antoinette? But we'll make a real convert of her before we've done. Here's the one before last!" He broke off to greet the lank-haired undersized youth who had entered shortly after them, " you're a first-rate advertisement for the Cause, Oswald."

Oswald Forsyth turned a pair of mournful grey eyes up to the ceiling, and struck an attitude. "Plucked from the very doors of the recruiting-office," he declaimed, " and made to see the light of the true faith by Barnaby's persuasive eloquence. Now on the staff of ' The Dove,' and one of the most inspired pacifist poets of the age, eh, Barnaby?"

" Not so bad," grunted Barnaby, and disposed his crutches under the table, " not so bad, considering you've only just left your slate and copy-books behind you. Have you had tea yet, O'Farrell, or shall I order it?"

" You may order it," laughed the Irishman, " but it's divil a chance that you'll get it. I did order a pot of China tea and some cakes, but Miss Mowbray has forgotten us the day, and Pegeen here starving for sight of a penny bun. It's Roy Radford and his performing Flappers that have consumed all the food, and there's himself in the midst of them, devouring the last muffin in the establishment!"

The plump little theatrical producer, who had overheard this from his table in the far corner, looked up and beamed; and the half dozen long-haired, long-legged and very pretty flappers who were with him, protested hotly against Conn's accusation of greed.

"You story!" . . . "When Flossie hasn't even had her third cup of tea yet!" . . . . "And I've only had four cakes—teeny ones." . . . "You're a mean cat, Mr. O'Farrell!"

Miss Mowbray bustled in with a heavily-laden tray. "Sorry to keep you waiting, Mr. O'Farrell. Here's your Welsh Rarebit."

"That's m-my Welsh Rarebit," declared Crispin Burgess, sitting in lonely grandeur at a table all by himself, "I ordered it y-yesterday."

"I don't care if you ordered it last year," returned Conn, "I'll keep it in pawn till our tea and cakes appear."

"It'll be s-stone-cold by then."

"It will not," said Pegeen, "for I will eat it this very minute. I like Welsh Rarebit. Mr. Burgess can have our cakes, if they come this side of Christmas."

Crispin spluttered: "I hate c-cakes," and came over to dispute his claim upon the Welsh Rarebit, which Pegeen was already in the act of demolish-ing, the while she twinkled mischievously across at the six flappers, who one and all smiled back at her. There was something about her that irresistibly drew smiles, Antoinette thought; not beauty, for there was little enough of that in the wide generous mouth, the tilted nose, and the untidy tangle of black hair, but something more subtle than beauty; fascination, perhaps.

"Dear me, have I made a muddle again?" enquired Miss Mowbray sunnily, returning with relays of cake and jam for Roy Radford's voracious troupe, "doesn't Mr. Burgess look cross? Was it baked beans and tomatoes you ordered? I do hope not, because I gave them to Mr. Walters, and he's eaten them up long ago."

"I took what the gods gave me—in lieu of the fruit-salad and wafers I had ordered—and was content," said the actor in his beautiful purring voice.

"There now, isn't that too tiresome of me? But I do wonder whom those baked beans can have belonged to . . . ." Miss Mowbray, balancing a trayful of crockery, relapsed into a profound reverie, from which she presently emerged to say: "There's Vera Mansfield, I must go and talk to her. She was married two days ago, just before Mr. Mansfield was arrested. Wasn't it splendid of her?"

Antoinette looked up with eager interest; caught an impression of a plain little woman with earnest eyes; and she was thrilled and rather awe-struck at the idea that this woman had " stood by " the conscientious objector, up to the very gates of prison.

Evidently it appealed in just the same way to young Oswald. " Splendid "—with shining eyes he echoed Miss Mowbray, " it's great, it's—it's almost unbelievable, people going through with it like that to the last."

Antoinette smiled. " Well, you're going through with it too, aren't you?"

"Me? Oh, rather! None of your half-and-half for this child . . . ." He added with a slightly wistful expression : " But it is splendid, isn't it ?"

Mrs. Mansfield spent a few minutes in conversation with Miss Mowbray, and went out again; and as she did so, a short young man wearing a yellow felt hat and a green muffler, pelted down the stairs, fell over Barnaby's crutches, and announced in a breathless, husky voice : *"Everard—Benny— I've got it, actually got it !"*

" Got what ?" Everard enquired languidly.

" My exemption, you ass, three months' exemption."

" And on whatever grounds did you appeal ?" demanded Barnaby, " you haven't any convictions that I'm aware of."

" Sole-support-of-widowed-mother," said Harry Hope glibly, " but if someone doesn't give me a part in something soon, my widowed mother will be the sole support of *me !*"

" A pity they've only allowed her three months of existence," mused Everard.

Harry looked perturbed. He was fond of his mother.

" I expect he can appeal again," said Benny.

" I can—they said I could—but that won't prolong the old lady's life."

" It is you who will have to seek to prolong it with every care and attention in your power."

Harry burst into peals of raucous laughter, and Everard winced. " For heavens' sake, curb that high-explosive laugh. It shatters the nerves, Harry, it grates . . . ."

The flappers looked over at him and giggled, and wearily Everard shrugged his shoulders. During

his career on the stage, he had specialised in playing
the parts of cardinals; majestic cardinals; wily
cardinals; jovial cardinals; suave cardinals. And
although at present, work being scarce, he was
playing a German spy in the farce next door, and
masking his beautiful diction with a guttural
Teutonic accent, the peculiar pussy-cat manner that
had made him invaluable as the cardinal in " Pippa
Passes," still clung to him in everyday life.

Pegeen, in the intervals of consuming Crispin's
Welsh Rarebit, was taking Antoinette into her confidence. " Is it a friend of Dennis Blackwood's
you are, my dear? Then you must come and
see Conn and me in the studio one day. We'll
have a party, we will that. I am so happy this
day, that I could kiss everybody. I could kiss
Benny Joseph this very minute, for glory be to
God, we owe it all to him !"

" Oh, I don't wish to compete with the deity,
Mrs. Taylor," murmured Benny.

" ' Mrs. Taylor,' indeed; My name's Pegeen.
I would just as soon you called me ' Margaret,' as
my parents-in-law do, and my husband, God rest
his soul——"

" D-didn't know he was d-dead," pronounced
Crispin.

" He's not, dearie, he's not . . . . but he may
be by to-night, for all we know. 'Tis a dangerous
job, it is, walking up and down the King's Road,
Chelsea, and flashing a wee bull's-eye lantern up
at all the houses and into all the gardens."

" And not knowing that all the while we're in
the studio together, Pegeen and I," Conn put in,
" talking of this and of that, and of the great day
that's coming for Ireland; and I doing a bit of a

drawing of her, perhaps, and she getting a bit of supper for the two of us."

The two "Irish lunatics," as Barnaby called them, gazed at each other in undisguised adoration; then Pegeen resumed : "He is a stick, is William, my husband. A real English stick. I said to him one night when the moon was full, ' William,' I said, ' will we be taking a Thermos flask and a packet of sandwiches up on to Hampstead Heath for a picnic ?' And he looked at me, my dear . . . . he just looked, and said, ' Margaret, are you mad ?' "

Antoinette, convulsed with laughter, could not resist the temptation to ask : " Whatever made you marry him ?"

" I thought I might be able to do him good," Pegeen replied simply, " but that man is past doing good to."

" He is that . . . ." O'Farrell concurred.

" But now we know what true happiness is, thanks to that ungrateful Jew-boy, who won't even let me kiss him !"

Dennis and Antoinette exchanged a look of amusement and again, as previously in the crowd, she felt conscious of a delicious feeling of security. It was good to be with him, and to be enjoying these people with him. Outside, the strange bodiless legs passed and passed; the cries of the newspaper boys echoed down the stone passage; and inside, the atmosphere became smokier and smokier, and bits of *risqué* stories became mingled with political arguments, theatrical jargon with the orders for meals; and the mournful lilt of the Irish voices was a queer contrast to the high-pitched shrieks and giggles of the flappers. And it was all

very delightful and unconventional and unlike
Cadogan Gardens. And Dennis was being nice to
her. And she was very happy.

The door to the street banged, and quick footsteps came down the stairs. A voice, youthful and
eager, was heard asking: "Is Mr. Barnaby in
there?"

Dennis started. Was it hallucination again that
made him believe it was Alan's voice, the same
hallucination that only a few days ago had made
him believe that it was Alan's figure he had seen
in the crowd? He had suffered from so much of
this kind of hallucination at one time . . . .

"Yes, we're all here, Rutherford, come in,"
cried Barnaby. Antoinette glanced at Dennis's
face. And had no need to be told that already her
precarious hold on happiness was threatened.

"This is the man I was telling you about,
Dennis, I wanted you to meet——"

Alan cut him short. "We met ages ago. I've
still got one of his handkerchiefs in my possession.
Do you remember tying up my gory wound for me,
Dennis?"

"I remember," said Dennis, and Alan grinned
at Conn and Pegeen, flung off his hat, and seated
himself between Everard and Barnaby.

"What about your tribunal?" asked the journalist.

"The local tribunal has already passed me for
Combatant Service," replied Alan, "but I'm
appealing again at the House of Commons next
week. And then—good-bye to freedom for me, I
suppose! But I'll tell 'em a few home-truths
before I'm locked up. Beefy, sanctimonious old
men, sitting there to tell me it's my duty to go out

and take my share in murdering peasant-boys and students and labourers . . . And the same sort of old men on their side, egging *them* on to fight us, with just the same platitudes about duty and honour and self-defence, saying that we declared war first, just as we say they sprung the war on us! And the capitalists of all countries coining money out of bloodshed . . . . Do they want the war to stop, those government contractors, making their millions by supplying munitions or boots or food for the armies?"

Dennis watched him through narrowed eyes. He had not altered much. He was eighteen months older, that was all. But there was the same quick impatience in phrase and gesture, the same vivid look.

He went on: "The only way to stop the war—not only this war, but all future wars, is by opposing conscription. You're all for the good cause here, I suppose?"

Barnaby answered for the company in general: "Yes, they're all appealing on different grounds. Everard, I forget what yours are?"

"I've not had the honour of being called up yet," the actor replied evasively.

"And yours, Crispin?"

By a series of grunts, Crispin made it know that he did not intend to fight against the nation that had produced Beethoven and Bach.

"I'd like to appeal on every ground there is!" Oswald cried excitably, "one can't do enough to keep the horror from going on."

"I'm appealing on racial and personal grounds," declared Benny, "I won't be made to fight the Jews

of other countries, even to avenge Brave Little
Belgium, or prove myself a true patriot!"

Oswald began :

　　" ' Breathes there a man with soul so dead
　　　Who never to himself has said——' "

" I've said ' This is my own, my native land ' at
least half a dozen times in half a dozen different
lands," Benny interrupted, "I have relatives
scattered about in allied, enemy and neutral
countries alike.　And how can a man fight for any
particular country, when he's got an aunt in every
port ?"

" And England talks of defending the honour of
small nations," murmured Conn, "has she forgotten Ireland at her very door, Ireland that she's
oppressed and ground under her heel these many
years?　Let her recognise Ireland as an equal and
raise her up from the thraldom of a vassal before
she's takes Belgium's name in vain to hide her
desire for gain."

" Well, at least you're free from the necessity
of appealing," said Barnaby, "they'll never dare
introduce conscription into Ireland.　It'll mean
revolution if they do."

" And may I be the first to fly the *Sinn Féin*
flag in the streets of Dublin that day!"

" What about you, Dennis?" said Alan.

" Humanitarian grounds."

" Good!"　For a second their eyes met, and then
parted again.　There was chaos in Dennis's mind.
Alan's personality had lost none of its potent spell
. . . . and there was Antoinette beside him . . . .
and he longing and longing to have the boy all to
himself . . . . And he knew that all his energies
must go to the concealment of that desire.　He

leant back in his chair and listened to Alan's voice
—and was aware that Antoinette's gaze rested
always on himself.

"Conscription has got to be fought," Alan repeated, "without conscription, Germany could
never have gone to war. And the people have got
to be made to see reason, those who say that we
must go on with the war ' for the sake of the men
who have fallen.' What sense is there in that?
Because we have wasted a million good lives already,
why should we throw another million on to the
same refuse-heap? ' To make their sacrifice worth
while !' As if anything could make their sacrifice
in such an iniquitous cause worth while ! ' They
died gladly for their country '—it's all cant, cruel
sickening cant to make the people at home see the
war through rose-coloured spectacles. If they saw
it without the spectacles, they wouldn't be so willing to go on paying for the continuation of it.
' We must fight until the whole of Germany is
crushed '—is the whole of Germany to blame for
this war, any more than the whole of England?
Blame it on the German High Command, if you
like, and on the Prussian Junkers and their kind,
but not on the people—people as straight and decent
as ours, only maddened by this artificially worked-
up hatred, this dizzy vision of world-power and
world-empire. But in Germany, just as in every
other country, there are people who don't let themselves be dazzled by that vision, and who are ready
to work for the overthrow of governments that can
organise wholesale butchery as a means by which
to extend dominion."

"The pity of it is, that we're so few," said
Benny, " such a small and unpopular minority."

Alan returned impatiently : " We're not out for laurels."

" No, it's more likely to be the broad arrow," said Oswald.

" Let it be the broad arrow, then ! It'll be the badge of freedom of the future, badge of honour for those who have struggled against the tide of public opinion.   The militarists' hatred of us is much more bloodthirsty than their hatred of the Germans; we are the cowards and the traitors who are deliberately delaying victory.   ' If we don't give Germany a knock-out blow now, the war will start all over again for the next generation—you hear the ignorant and the thoughtless reiterating that catch-phrase like a lot of parrots.   The war all over again—that's exactly what they will have if they do win their complete military victory. When the ' knock-out blow ' has been dealt, they'll have to go on keeping big armies and building big ships, to consolidate their position as top-dog. And as long as we have big armies and navies, we shall always have wars.   The pretty toys have to be used—they can't be kept for show . . . People call us ' Pro-Germans '—it's laughable.   If I'd been in Germany or anywhere else, I'd have fought just as hard against being turned into a cog in the infernal machinery of war.   It's the whole system of militarism I'm up against, not the individual wrongs of one country or another.   No civilised industrial population of any country wants war. Miners in Cornwall and Lancashire or Galicia and Siberia; poor devils sweating in our factories and in *their* factories; railwaymen, schoolmasters, farmers—what do they want with war?   Nothing . . . . until the idea is drilled into them by those

in power. The people who want war and believe
that war is good, should be allowed to make a
private picnic of it. The government officials and
cabinet ministers and war profiteers on both sides;
the people who say they'd rather lose all their sons,
than that they shouldn't go out and fight——"

"The khaki-clad females who say they wish they
were men, so that they could kill a few Huns themselves," Dennis put in.

"Yes, if only that small handful who started
the war, and are continuing it, could finish it up
amongst themselves, without implicating the
masses!"

"Without the masses, there would be no war,"
said Barnaby.

"Exactly!" cried Alan, "without the masses,
there *could* be no war, and that is the solution of it
all, and the end and the aim of socialism—to free
the masses from the tyranny of governments that
can drive them like cattle to be slaughtered in this
crazy campaign of greed and hatred. Look at the
wonderfully organised man-power of all the nations,
with all the woman-power behind it; look at the
scientific miracles and the ceaseless labour and
energy that go to the production of big guns, submarines, aeroplanes, poison-gas; think of all this
employed in the cause of destruction . . . . And
think of the heroism and self-sacrifice of those who
really 'die gladly' for a mistaken ideal; and the
tremendous flame of patriotism that's burning in
the hearts of all the peoples alike: if all these
tangible and intangible splendours could have been
used in the furtherance, instead of in the destruction of civilisation!

"And you're expected to take your share in the

destruction, without asking if it's right or wrong. All honour to the men who, when war broke out, almost as a matter of course left their homes and their loves and their careers, because they thought it was the only decent thing to do . . . . And all blame to the old men at home, and to the narrow-minded women and unimaginative girls who made it appear the only decent thing! We're convinced that it isn't, and *we must stand firm*, cost what it may! We're few : that doesn't matter. We shall be pilloried : that doesn't matter. All that matters is that we shall have striven against what our brains and our hearts recognised as evil—Oh, not only evil, but stupid and petty and beastly—and that we shall have done our bit towards bringing nearer the day when militarism will be supplanted by industry, and we may hope to have an international system of legislation that'll knock out the possibility of disputes having to be settled by the barbarous and unintelligent means of bloodshed."

"Unintelligent, good Lord, yes !" cried Barnaby, "the whole thing is unintelligent, even from the militarist point of view. There are thousands of men being forced to fight, who are physically and mentally unfit to be of the least use in battle, but whose brains might have given us scientific inventions that would have benefited humanity, works of art, books, music . . . . No, they won't let them stop at home and do what they *can* do, but must send them out to do incompetently things against which their whole nature rises in revolt. From the general utility standpoint : in which capacity is the artist of more value to the nation ? As a creator of a work that may live, or as a mass of shattered nerves, totally incapable either of fulfilling the requirements of the army or of carrying out his own ideas?"

" Oh, how much does the general public care about art or the artist these days?" exclaimed Dennis.

" They may not care now," rejoined Barnaby, " but it's the sacred duty of everyone who's got the gift of creation to try and keep it intact. When the war is over we shall be grateful to those who through the long night of destruction have kept alight the torch of art and intellect. That's rendering a greater service to mankind than putting your life at the disposal of the war-machine."

" And the sight of all those war-shrines makes me sick!" cried Alan. " ' *Greater love hath no man*——' How dare they profane the words? It's not that a man is merely ' laying down his life for his friends,' but trying to do some other man in at the same time. How does that fit in with ' *Thou shalt not kill?* ' "

An unobtrusive-looking spectacled man, who all this while had sat silent at the corner table which Crispin had vacated, looked over at the group. " It does not fit in, and it never will, but the Church has become untrue to herself, as those who serve her have become untrue, perverting her words until they seem to serve the ends of the State."

Alan asked eagerly : " Are you appealing on religious grounds, then?"

The man replied, " Yes. And I daresay I'll get partial exemption. Non-Combatant Service. The despicable compromise that some men can make with their conscience. ' *Thou shalt not kill* '—they think they're obeying the letter of the law if they don't bear arms and go to the fighting-line ; but they're scarcely obeying the spirit when they accept work in munition-factories, or otherwise help to release men to be killed in their place."

" Yes, I'm up against people of that sort, as much as I'm up against rabid militarists," said Alan ; " they are the cowards and shirkers who deserve all the onus heaped upon the community of pacifists and socialists as a whole. Men whose conscience won't let them kill, but who haven't the courage to back their opinions—I've no use for them. Passive pacifism won't do any good. What we want is active pacifism, fearless and unashamed, ready to join hands with the workers of all other countries ; to stand firm against their immoral, gain-seeking governments ; and ready to suffer the utmost penalty of their idiotic and benighted law."

Crispin rose from his chair. " You b-bloody pacifists make as much noise as b-bloody militarists. One c-can't hearoneselfthink. . . ." And on this cryptic utterance he made his exit.

The cloud of smoke became denser and more dense. Roy Radford and the flappers had long since departed, and the remaining company, having abandoned their separate tables, formed one collective straggling group. Through the smoke, Antoinette watched them ; O'Farrell's fine sensitive features and visionary eyes shadowed by a thatch of wild auburn hair ; Barnaby's rough-hewn head and hunched shoulders ; Everard's sleek good looks ; Harry Hope's chubbiness ; Benny Joseph's dark eyes and Semitic profile ; the nondescript appearance of the religious " objector " who had joined in the conversation ; Oswald's thin pale face and jerkiness of movement ; Pegeen's tilted nose, and the cigarette stuck impertinently in one corner of her mouth. . . . Picturesque enough, the whole group, only now Antoinette dared not glance at that slim boy with his dark flaming eyes, nor at Dennis . . . . not since she had seen that look on his face when Alan had entered.

Barnaby was saying: "From every possible point of view, whether from religion, art, socialism or humanity, war is a disgrace to any civilised nation. Personally, I'm out of the running, altogether, but I envy you fit men for having the chance to do your bit in the cause of peace."

Antoinette got up to go, wondering if Dennis would accompany her as usual. He followed her up the stairs, but it was evidently his intention to return to the others when he had said good-bye to her.

At the top of the stairs she faced him.

"Is that—is that the boy we saw the other night?"

"Yes."

"It's the one you told me about?"

"Yes . . . ."

"You're still in love with him. . . .?"

And again: "Yes . . . ."

With one hand she was clutching the wooden balustrade. He saw her knuckles whiten under the strain, as she said in a dead, unemotional voice:

"D-do you want me to back out altogether?"

"My dear, it's for you to say."

He could not bring himself to make a quick, clean end to the situation then and there. He was too dazed and bewildered to think. He only knew that he could not speak the word that would hurt her so much, not now, although her head was defiantly raised, her eyes downcast, as if she were determined that nothing should be visible to him of the pain he might choose to inflict.

" It's for you to say."

She relaxed the tenseness of her attitude, and seemed suddenly to go limp. " Oh, I don't know what to say. . . ." The situation had come upon them both as a shock. Neither of them felt capable of coping with it at the moment, and in the door-way. . . .

" Meet me down here one day, and we'll talk it all out," he whispered hurriedly.

She nodded and turned away.

CHAPTER VII

" I HAD quite made up my mind that you were dead," said Dennis when, later on, he and Alan walked back to his rooms in Tavistock Square.

Alan laughed. " Did you think I'd been storming trenches single-handed, and that my V.C. had been sent home to my weeping mother?"

" Something of the sort. I knew well enough that you'd expose yourself to every possible risk—as you are doing, only on the right side, thank heaven, instead of the wrong."

" I'm running no greater risks than you are : perhaps imprisonment, perhaps death. I should think the latter quite probable if they attempt to force us to do war-work in prison—dirty trick, that, but they are quite capable of it."

Dennis said nothing. For himself, he had long ago contemplated these possibilities. It was different to contemplate them for Alan. He wished somehow that Alan need not incur such risks, and yet was proud of him for incurring them . . . . and realised that on the other side, the militarist side, they felt precisely the same : those who sent their lovers and sons to the fighting-line and dreaded their going, yet would not hold them back. . . .

" It's all a bloody shame," he said aloud, " such a bloody shame. . . ."

" Yes, and when you think of all the labour and ingenuity that are being spent in the invention of more and yet more diabolical means of destruction. . . . . I've watched big guns being made, and shells in munition-factories."

" And how did you contrive to get into a muni-tion-factory?"

" The name of my never-sufficiently-to-be-re-spected father was disguise enough for my revolu-tionary tendencies when I was up North," said Alan, " but when I was going about the country, trying to get at the people's outlook in various branches of industry, I had to assume alternately the disguise of a sanitary inspector, a newspaper-reporter or a workman. I've been temporary rail-way-porter and ship-builder's apprentice, and fol-lowed all manner of trades since I saw you last."

" And hasn't your father cast you off for ever yet? Mine would like to, but he can't quite do it because of mother. She, poor dear, is the victim of the complicated Eastwold table of weights and measures, namely : Do one son and one son-in-law in the trenches outweigh one conscientious objector, or do two in the trenches equal one in quod?"

" My father's done more than cast me off," said Alan, " he's tried to get me run in before now— beery old buffer, making pots of money out of the war ; sitting at home and joining in the hue-and-cry : ' We want more men—more ships—more mu-nitions. . . .' They're tearing up the young man-hood fast enough to make soldiers, and tearing up the forests to get wood to line the trenches and dug-outs. There was a pine-forest I passed through in Devon—or rather the remains of a pine-forest . . . a wilderness of prostrate tree-trunks, with sticky pale-red stumps, lying crippled and bruised, with their branches crushed under them. And the sight and the smell of the resin oozing from where the boughs had been sawn off was a thing that hurt you —a damnable thing !"—his voice suddenly tightened—" it was like seeing the forest bleed to death before your very eyes. And all the time men were at work hacking, hacking and sawing . . . . you couldn't get away from the rasping of those saws and the dull blows of the choppers. While I watched they were stabbing at the trunk of a great giant of a tree, and I saw its crown waver and rock and sway, and heard a sort of groaning crash as it fell to the ground among the litter of mutilated boughs and bleeding roots. . . . And all around were neat piles of stacked-up logs and sawn planks, ready to be despatched to France. The glory of that forest once—and now——"

" I know," replied Dennis, " they're felling the old beech-trees around my home, too—trees that have taken centuries and centuries to grow; and when I've cried out at the pity of it—' *Every tree that can be of service to the country must come down!*' It's terrible and wonderful, this ruthless, relentless concentration of will and effort. The men going out, and the women taking over their jobs— even inanimate nature pressed into service to ' help to win the war !' "

Alan nodded. " Yes, and with all that force pushing against us, we've got to use the same concentration of will and effort to win peace."

They had reached Tavistock Square. Dennis opened the door with his latch-key and went up to his room. Alan followed him. And thus he had once followed Alan, by the light of a guttering candle, up a rickety wooden staircase at Crannack. And thus, in imagination, he had often felt himself being followed by Alan. As they were about to enter the room, Dennis wheeled sharply round. Alan smiled back at him with half-impudent confidence. " Well ?"

" All right, I only wanted to see if you were really there—you've had such a way of dogging my heels, just like that, and then vanishing when I turned to look at you."

Alan said : " You were a coward to run away that time at Crannack, Dennis."

" You know why I had to run away—why I had to make myself run away. It wasn't easy, Alan."

" It's no use running away. Because you'll never *get* away. We're made like that ; why not look things straight in the face ?"

" Antoinette said something of that kind a long while ago, without having the vaguest idea what she was talking about."

" Antoinette ?"

" The girl who was with me at the tea-shop to-day. The girl with whom I sought safety from you."

" And did you find it ?"

" Do you need to ask ?"

Alan sat down on the floor, and with hands clasped round his knees, gazed into the fire.

" Then what do you want with the girl now ?"

Dennis shrugged his shoulders.

" She's mad on you," Alan persisted, " I could see that. But you don't want her, Dennis—we don't want her. . . . . Cut her out altogether !"

Dennis answered sadly : " She is out altogether, poor Antoinette, to all intents and purposes."

Alan turned his head with a slow smile. " Good . . . ." he murmured.

" Damn you, don't talk and look like that !" Dennis blazed out in sudden rage, " you might be a woman, intolerant of all favourites but yourself !"

" I am intolerant of other favourites. And

they're no good to you, no earthly good . . . . are
they?"

" No . . . ." said Dennis dully.

" You admit it! Then why continue to strive
after what can't really satisfy you?"

" Because I mustn't take what would really satisfy me."

" Then at least accept the fact that you are as
you are, and don't try to pervert yourself into something you never will be. We're both right over the
border-line of the normal—I more than you, because
no woman could ever attract me in the least—and
we've got to have the courage to face out that knowledge and, above all, to be true to ourselves. You
want to make our love an abstraction. Believe me,
you'll only succeed in making it unnatural."

" Unnatural, good Lord! Isn't it that already?"

" You've been brooding too much in secret,
Dennis, you've grown morbid. Why will you per-
sist in regarding it as something vicious and degenerate? For people made as we are it's natural and
it's beautiful to love as we love, and it's perversion
in the true sense to try and force ourselves to love
differently."

" I know . . . . I know all that, yet I can't accept it as justification . . . . even though love like
this is little short of crucifixion, as long as some
remote principle nails us to the cross and forbids
expression."

" Then in God's name, Dennis, why deny yourself and torture yourself like this?"

Dennis flung out his hands in a gesture of help-
lessness.

Alan looked at him. . . .

Then, very softly, he spoke. " All right, Dennis,

it shall be as you say. Hang on to your foolish
Quixotic principles, if you must . . . . if you must
. . . . but you'll never get away like that—never,
no, never in this life. . . ."

.   .   .   .

So now the shadowy danger, that she had perhaps not taken so very seriously, just because it
was shadowy, had materialised in the shape of that
boy. Dennis had warned her, and she had said :
" Yes, I know. . . ." With her brain she had
accepted his warning, with her brain understood
what it implied. But she had not felt anything.
Even now the poison had not begun properly to
work. . . . It was still difficult to overcome the
initial sense of absurdity, of having to be jealous
of a—man. Certainly, if Dennis had chosen to
make love to her at Amberhurst, she would have
given him every right to be jealous of—Hester.
Crazy world . . . . and all these years she had
lived with her eyes shut, never perceiving how crazy
it was ! She could not hazard any conjecture as to
the future. All her previous experience was powerless to assist imagination. She was on entirely new
ground now, ignorant of the significance of such
landmarks as she might encounter ; instinct her sole
guide, and one whom her reason and her sense of
humour were still half-inclined to mistrust.

At least she was glad that no decisive action was
called for on her part. On the spur of the moment
she had offered to back out, and he had not accepted her offer. She could remain passive now,
and await developments.

Mrs. Taylor rang her up while she was awaiting
them, and invited her to tea at the studio. Antoinette went, and found the Taylors' house a low,

rambling building in a tree-shaded street in Chelsea.
The studio was connected with the house by a glass
corridor, but it had another entrance that led
through a walled passage into the street. A third
door opened into a tangled garden, overgrown with
weeds.

Pegeen met Antoinette at the side entrance, and
impressed her to keep silence during the brief tran-
sit from the street to the studio. She explained in
her inimitable fashion that since the studio had
been let to Conn O'Farrell, her husband and
parents-in-law did not think it suitable for her to
frequent it.

"But glory be to God, I have a latchkey of my
own, so I say I'm taking a walk, and just pop out
of the front door and into here by this side-entrance,
when no one's about. It's like watch-dogs they are
over me, my dear. . . . William's at the office all
day and Special-Constabling most nights, but he's
always telling his mother and his father to look
after his ' little floweret '—that's me, dearie—while
he's gone."

"So they do their duty by you!" laughed Antoinette.

"They do that, in the true Christian-martyr
spirit; for it is a very, very bitter thing for Mother
Taylor to have a wild Irish scaramouch like me for
a daughter-in-law. Her Willie should have married
one of the Vicar's daughters from next door; they
play croquet all the afternoon. . . . It is really a
vicarage next door, my dear, and that's the truth
of it!"

Antoinette was taking in every detail of her environment. A square of blue was visible through
the big skylight; an oak chest, left untidily open,

disclosed a collection of gorgeous-coloured fabrics; garments of all hues and all periods; a very old carved table was littered with paints, cigarette-ends, lip-salve, pencil-stumps and chocolates; the originals of Conn's political cartoons were upon the walls, and formed a queer contrast to the more imaginative examples of his art—the illustrations to old Irish fairy-tales and the designs for scenic decorations. And then Pegeen, with a childish and charming absence of false shame, exhibited Conn's drawings of herself in all manner of poses. . . .

" But aren't you afraid that someone will see them and find out?" said Antoinette.

" Oh, there's never a soul in here but Conn and me and our friends. The servants from the house aren't allowed in. I do all his dusting for him, bless the lad! We want no strangers here, and for another reason that I'll be telling you now. . . ." Pegeen cast a glance over her shoulder, lowered her voice to a mysterious whisper, and kicking aside one of the rugs on the polished floor, disclosed a sliding panel. " Look!"

Antoinette looked, and as the panel slid back beheld a cavity some six feet deep. " A trap-door, Pegeen, a real trap-door?"

" Hush, my dear . . . . there are papers in there that could get the whole lot of us put in prison this very minute—" (Surely this was all a child's game of " conspirators?")—" we must get them safely over to Ireland and into the hands of our leaders before the month is out. We're going together, Conn and I, when the time comes."

. . . . This was more lurid even than anything Antoinette had anticipated from Barnaby's descriptions. Pegeen replaced the rug, offered her the cigarettes, and curled herself up in one of the deep armchairs. " To-night there'll be company in the house—they have a bishop to dinner, my dear, all in gaiters, and I talking to him as if butter wouldn't melt in my mouth. . . . And Conn will stand in the glass passage, just this side of the curtain, and strain his ears for a sound of my voice among the other voices . . . . and after dinner maybe I'll slip away and steal down the passage for one minute and feel his arms round me in the dark—then back again to old Gaiters, and the talk of how they'd like to have the parish church restored, and how well this bloody England is doing in the war."

" How marvellous, Pegeen, that's better than anything I've ever accomplished!" Antoinette told her of her own campaign of lies invented to elude Grand'mère's vigilance. " It's so neat, pretending to your parents-in-law that you are miles away, when you're really in here, separated from them only by a curtain."

" Yes, it was a happy thought, that curtain. I advised my mother-in-law to have it put there when we let the studio to Conn, because I said, 'tis for the look of the thing, and with artists you never know. . . . And she said I was after showing a bit of proper feeling at last!"

" Where did you meet Conn?" queried Antoinette, and was rewarded with the entire history of Pegeen's life.

" I was left an orphan at the age of six, my dear, and I had two aunts in Ireland and one in England. And they played battledore and shuttlecock with me right enough, for not one of them was pleased to have me in the house with her own brats. You see," Pegeen added with delightful simplicity,

" they were never quite sure if my mother had been married to my father, so they thought it best not to give me the benefit of the doubt. . . ." Followed the account of her marriage to Mr. Taylor, and the freakish impulse that had led her into it.

" It made me laugh so the way he said : ' Margaret, I don't understand you,' every time I opened my mouth . . . . and when he asked me to marry him I said ' Yes ' just to annoy my aunts, who said they never would have believed it of me."

Antoinette suggested that in the course of Pegeen's married life she might have heard that remark of Mr. Taylor's once too often.

" Yes, indeed, my dear. And the night I met Conn, I felt I'd be suffocated dead by the morning if something didn't happen ! So I wandered out for a walk by myself, and there in the middle of Trafalgar Square there was a recruiting-meeting, and a man with a big banner telling all those poor fools of Englishmen to go and fight for their country. . . . I made a face at him—I did that ! And Conn —he was in the crowd, too, with his friend Rutherford—he saw me make that face, and came and spoke to me. And, dearie, when I heard that boy's voice, I could have put my arms round his neck and wept. . . ."

" When Irish meets Irish," murmured Antoinette, " it must have been rather wonderful."

Pegeen's greenish eyes shone. " It was that . . ."

Later on Conn came in, having just returned from Rutherford's tribunal at the House of Commons. " They've not heard his case yet, but I thought I'd have time to slip down here for a cup of tea, and back again." He drew Pegeen towards him and kissed her lips. " I've brought you these primroses, the first I've seen this spring—let's have that great green bowl, and I'll be arranging them while you get the food."

Pegeen disappeared into the pantry adjoining the studio, and called to Antoinette to come and watch her fry the eggs. Conn was left dreamily putting the primroses one by one into the jade bowl.

" Wouldn't you rather I went ?" Antoinette suggested to Pegeen, " I'm sure you want to have him all to yourself."

Pegeen laughed. " What a child for talking nonsense ! We like to have you here. It's a poor sort of hospitality that wishes one friend to go, when another arrives."

But all the same when Conn joined them in the pantry, and kissed Pegeen's neck as she bent over the gas-ring, Antoinette felt that she was an intruder—a feeling which, to do them justice, neither Conn nor Pegeen seemed to share. They had a composite meal of eggs and tea and cakes, all among the cigarette-ends and the lip-salve, with the massed bowl of primroses as table-decoration in the centre. Then Conn declared that he must go. " I don't want to miss Rutherford's speech ; it'll be worth the hearing."

Pegeen made a grimace. " I hate that person."

Conn said warmly : " You've no need to say that now, Pegeen, love. . . ."

Antoinette asked, " Is anyone else at the tribunal, Mr. O'Farrell ?"

" Barnaby's there and Dennis Blackwood. Will I give him your love, Miss de Courcy ?"

" Oh, never mind about it . . . ." she laughed ; but the thought of Dennis as a spectator at Alan's tribunal made her heart give a sudden painful jump.

" Good-bye, Pegeen; it's William's night on duty, isn't it? Will I leave the side-door open . . . ?"

Pegeen shook her ruffled head. " It's the footsteps I'm thinking of, Conn, the two lots of footsteps all down the gravel-path. You've no idea how they show up !"

" Then I'll have to carry you "—Conn's eyes rested fondly on her—" that'll only make one lot."

" There's another way, too," Pegeen broke into her impish laughter, " the house on the left of this stands empty. If I can get into that garden from the street and over the wall into ours——"

Conn laughed. " Then William will spot you with his lantern, burgling your own house ! Well, I don't care how you find your way in, as long as you do—after the bishop's left . . . ."

The door banged behind him. Antoinette reflected that here indeed were combined melodrama and romance and farce of the most highly-coloured variety. Oh, certainly romance for those two mad, delightful people who loved each other ; romance in the need for secrecy, and their peculiar methods of ensuring it ; melodrama in the existence of the trap-door concealing the papers ; farce in the idea of the respectable household adjoining this anything but respectable studio, the vicarage next door, the stolid Special Constable patrolling the streets.

" And to think I might never have known this happiness !" said Pegeen, " that objectionable person Rutherford was for ever advising my Conn not to take the studio. He said I was a harpy and that I didn't really love him. So Conn believed him, and would not come near me, and I thought I would kill myself. . . . I told that to Benny Joseph, that

I

nice Jew-boy when he came to tea here. And I cried into his handkerchief. And he made it all right, speaking to Conn and saying I was not a harpy, and did really love him truly. Now, I'm asking you, do I look like a harpy?"

"You're a darling," laughed Antoinette, and Pegeen gave her a warm broad smile. "I liked you the first time I set eyes on you. I don't know why Dennis Blackwood didn't bring you here before; he and Mr. Barnaby often come to see Conn. . . . I like Dennis," she mused, "he's a dear fine fellow, he is that, and he plays the piano like an angel. Aren't you of the same opinion, my dear?"

Antoinette said softly : "I am. . . ."

"It's glad I am to hear that! It means that there's a great day of happiness coming for you just as it's come for me."

"I'm afraid not, Pegeen."

"But why, my dear?" Pegeen came and sat on the arm of Antoinette's chair. "Why not?"

"It—it's difficult to say. . . ." Incredibly difficult.

Pegeen put her arms round her with a gesture impulsive and almost maternal. "Oh, my dear, won't you tell me what it is?" She seemed to have lost for the moment her elfin devilry, and to have become softer, less of an imp, more of a woman. "I've had to go through sorrow too, to know happiness. . . . Tell me, dear : is it another woman that's come between you?"

"No, Pegeen, it's not another woman. . . ." She was beginning to feel frightened. Dennis was at the tribunal, every nerve drawn tense with the hope that Alan would get his exemption. Quickly she chased from her mind the half-hope that he would

not get it. That . . . . was ungenerous. . . . Was
it, though, in the face of such a dangerous enemy?
How dangerous, exactly, was Alan? Could he be
fought on equal terms, or was his advantage over
her so great that the conflict was already decided in
his favour? If only she knew. . . . But how, and
by what standards was she to measure the power
of this strange enemy? She was oppressed by fear
of the unknown; longed to be able to confide in
Pegeen.

" It's not another woman, it's——"

But that was the sort of thing one could not say.
Not to anyone. Not ever.

" Then it'll all come right in the end, you'll see "
—Pegeen was still gently stroking her hair—" he's
a silly fellow and perhaps doesn't know his own
mind yet, but one day you'll be as happy as
Conn and me, and that's what I'm wishing you with
all my heart."

Antoinette raised her head, and with an effort
smiled. " Yes, I expect it'll all come right. . . ."
She would not spoil the picture of herself and
Dennis pairing off as a secondary couple to Pegeen
and Conn. But it had been hard not to tell Pegeen.
Pegeen's warm-hearted sympathy would have
soothed, if not comforted her. It would have been
such a relief to tell someone. But—*one could not
tell that sort of thing*. However much one longed
to. However frightened one was. However lonely.

CHAPTER VIII

BY what standards was she to measure Alan's power . . . .? Instinct answered : by the power that Hester had once had over herself. There would have been little enough hope for Dennis pitted against Hester, or any of those other women; little enough, if it had come to it, against—Pegeen. Antoinette was fully alive to Pegeen's attraction, and realised that she might have had one of her swift burning passions for her, had she not been so entirely absorbed in Dennis, the greater love blotting out all possibility of a lesser. But if she had not cared for Dennis so much, he would have stood a poor chance against Pegeen; and according to that analogy, Antoinette stood a poor chance against Alan. She had not heard from Dennis; neither did she know the result of Alan's appeal. Inaction was becoming intolerable. If matters were decided one way or another, at least she would be rid of the uncertainty, and could try and adapt herself to the altered conditions. He had told her to meet him at Miss Mowbray's to discuss the position . . . . and it would be better, once she knew. This she told herself repeatedly, and it gave her a sort of spurious courage as she walked up the passage between the theatre and the tea-shop, and with fast beating heart descended the stairs.

Her hope that she would find Dennis alone was immediately dashed. The usual group was complete, save for Conn and Pegeen, and to-day it included Mrs. Mansfield and Ernest Strickland, the religious objector. Antoinette slipped into the vacant place that Dennis had made for her between himself and Everard. She gave an exclamation of surprise on seeing that the latter was in khaki. " Why—what's happened?"

" He's ratted!" cried Alan, " that's what's happened. Couldn't stand out, and took the easy way. The play has come off next door, and I suppose he fancies himself in the new part—' A better and a worthier part, laddie, than the one you used to play ' —can't you hear 'em?"

Everard stroked the cuffs of his ill-fitting private's uniform. " This is all so stupid . . . ." he remarked to the ceiling, leaving it doubtful as to whether he meant the war in general or Alan's gibes in particular.

" I can't say the costume suits you," Benny taunted him, "you were fastidious enough about the fit of your stage-clothes, and look at you now!"

Everard, with magnificent dignity, feigned complete ignorance of his too short sleeves and coat that had a baggy look about the waist-line; and turning to Antoinette, wondered aloud in his beautiful mellow voice, what effect war would have upon his psycholology.

" Speaking of costumes," said Alan, " I hear there are dozens of C.O.s at the various camps arrayed only in blankets. When they're handed over to the military and commanded to put on uniform they refuse to do so. Then their own clothes are taken away from them. . . . *Then* they tear up the nice khaki that the good kind Government gives them and wrap themselves in the blankets off their beds."

" As we're in England, I suppose the authorities won't remove the blankets?" murmured Benny.

" Oh, hardly. . . . But one really ought to
practise beforehand how to wear one's blanket in
the most artistic and effective manner. You'll look
hideous in yours, Benny, you're the wrong shape.
By next week I shall no doubt be quite an authority
on the latest fashions in bedclothes."

" So you are passed for General Service?" said
Strickland.

" Yes. I knew I hadn't any chance of getting off
entirely, and I wasn't playing for Non-com. . . .
They actually asked me what I'd do if I saw my
mother attacked by a German soldier. . . . I told
'em I was tired of that old chestnut and that I'd
go to the defence of the soldier !"

There was a burst of laughter, but to Antoinette
it sounded rather strained and hectic. She saw that
Alan's eyes were feverishly bright, his cheeks
flushed ; and that Dennis's gaze rested upon him
with an anxiety barely concealed by the laughter.

" Two policemen called at my rooms yesterday
when I was out, waited three hours for me, and then
got fed-up and said they'd call again to-morrow and
wait till I *did* appear, if they didn't cop me during
the day."

" You can't dodge them for long, though," said
Barnaby.

" I don't intend to—'tisn't dignified. But just
for a while it is a most stimulating experience to be
Wanted by the Police, and one which may never
repeat itself in the future course of my blameless
career."

" Child . . . ." murmured Dennis under his
breath, but Antoinette caught the murmur, and the
rueful tenderness of it.

" At any moment I may feel a heavy hand upon

my shoulder—handcuffs on my wrists! I thought
I was being shadowed by a plain-clothes detective
this afternoon. I gave him a couple of hours'
healthy exercise, dodging him up and down the
Strand, and finally shook him off when I reached
sanctuary here. . . . Oh, I'd rather run with the
hare than hunt with the hounds, any day. There's
something so smug and self-righteous about the
hounds, and the hare has all the sport!"

"The hounds win in the end . . . ." said
Dennis, and Everard quoted softly :

" *A la fin de l'envoi, je touche.* . . ."

Alan threw his head back and laughed. "Well,
never mind for the moment. Let's have cakes in
vast quantities, and regardless of expense, please,
Miss Mowbray, since this may be my last meal in
freedom.

Miss Mowbray begged him not to talk like that,
and expressed her willingness to hide him from the
police among the jam-jars in her store-cupboard.

"Oh, this place of yours is bound to be raided
sooner or later as it is, Kitty," said Barnaby,
"some outsider will stray in and, overhearing our
conversation, will warn the authorities that it's a
hornet's nest of nihilists, anarchists, socialists, and
other dangerous and seditious elements!"

"I expect you're right, Neil," Miss Mowbray
returned placidly, "but even if the worst comes to
the worst, I shall be glad that all you boys have
had some place where you could be together and air
your views in peace."

"And we can never be grateful enough to you
for supporting the cause of freedom as you've done
by letting us congregate here!" cried Alan warmly.
"When this country is proclaimed a democratic re-

public, we'll erect a statue to you on what was once the site of Buckingham Palace.''

Harry Hope plunged into the group, bursting with the news that he had got a part at last. '' Round town, too, and no commission to pay !''

Benny Joseph offered him heartfelt congratulations. '' You lucky beggar, being able to take work. I daren't settle anything till my beastly appeal is over. . . . When do you open?''

Even Everard was roused to a languid display of professional interest, and sighed : '' It is a beautiful thing to have a widowed mother to support. Her life should be very sacred to you.''

'' It is, Oh, it is,'' Harry assured him with husky eagerness. '' I'm thankful to say the old lady's keeping wonderfully well.'' He joined a small group of actors seated at the table in the alcove, and proceeded to answer more questions concerning his new part.

Barnaby asked Mrs. Mansfield if she had news of her husband, and she replied that he had contrived to communicate with her. '' It's too terrible, the way they're treated ; worse than ordinary criminals. He was kept in irons for twelve hours ; he drew a design of them—cruel-looking instruments that cut into the flesh.''

'' Oh, yes, we're a civilised and cultured race, we English,'' cried Alan, '' it's only the Huns who are barbarians. . . .''

Antoinette saw Dennis flush. Easy enough to guess that he was dreading that barbarous things might also befall Alan. Already he seemed to be quivering to the least shade of pain that Alan might have to undergo. But was it nothing to him, she wondered in a sudden surge of revolt, was it nothing

to him that she should be thus compelled to watch
him suffering for Alan and because of Alan? To
watch him alternately brooding over the boy with
absorbed gaze, and then averting his eyes, as if the
sight of him there, laughing and vivid, were too
poignant to be borne?

" They have to go to chapel every Sunday," Mrs.
Mansfield pursued; " that's the only time when the
prisoners who are in solitary confinement catch
sight of each other. Maurice says there's a perfectly hateful man who preaches to them—it's a
degradation to call it preaching! He was actually
brute enough to say to those poor wretches : ' God
has turned His face away from a lot like you.' . . ."

" It's difficult to believe that a man of God could
so profane the word of God to those dependent upon
him for spiritual consolation," said Strickland,
" but he's not the only one of his kind. So many
of the clergy, who call themselves followers of the
Prince of Peace, deny Him, by abuse of their power
—by preaching war from the pulpit and joining
hands with the misleaders of the people to exhort
them to take part in bloodshed and strife"

" Yes, it beats me how devout Christians can believe in war," said Benny, " don't they see it's the
negation of all that their Christ ever taught ?"

" They don't see now. It's they who have turned
their faces away from God. Christ wasn't thinking
of the Germans when He told us to turn the other
cheek. . . . That's a very favourite line of argument, I believe ; it tends to make the Bible seem
old-fashioned and out of date ; a good excuse for
going behind its teachings. If people had lived up
a little more closely to these antiquated teachings,
the world wouldn't be plunged in darkness and
misery now."

"Well, look what they do to those who strive against the darkness and misery," said Barnaby. "How long has your husband got, Mrs. Mansfield?"

"Six months penal servitude. But still I'm glad he didn't give in and take Non-Com. It's an unworthy compromise, and the men in the N.C.C. are being treated in the most despicable way."

"Yes, some of them, unarmed men, have actually been sent out to France," said Alan. "I've little sympathy with the Non-Coms., but it's a dirty trick all the same. It's an easy way, of course, for the authorities to get rid of them altogether: simpler to shoot them for disobeying military orders out there than it is here. . . . Downright murder! Oh, it's better by far to stick out your time in quod than to compromise, Mrs. Mansfield. It's accepting no favours from a rotten, sneaking government that can't keep its word."

"Six months is a long time, and it may be longer . . . ." said Dennis. And Antoinette knew that he was thinking neither of Mansfield nor of himself. It would be a long time—for Alan. A long time for her, if Dennis. . . . And if the war went on and on. . . . Suddenly she hated the whole group, working upon each other's nerves, exhorting each other to stand out at all costs. What did she care for pacifism if Dennis had to go to prison for it? She cared frankly only for her man, and it seemed appalling to her that he should thus subordinate his life to his convictions.

. . . . And Dennis had no eyes and no thoughts for her now. It was not difficult to see wherein Alan's attraction lay: he *was* attractive, no doubt of it, with his feverish dark eyes and sensitive well-cut mouth. He gave her the impression of a very high-spirited race-horse. She could quite well imagine how he would appeal to Dennis .... this terrible boy against whom she was utterly powerless, for he seemed to possess all the fascination of her own sex as well as of his.

" There's a good time ahead the day the C.O.s come out of prison!" cried Alan, " we'll have a word to say then, in the name of freedom and democracy, and we'll have earned the right to say it. We'll eat and drink to the day! Let's toss down one Welsh Rarebit after the other, in the true spirit of devil-may-care recklessness. . . ."
How much of this burlesque was genuine, Antoinette wondered, and how much a disguise to hide real terror? With a shudder she realised that most of those who sat here, laughing, smoking, arguing, blaspheming, would sooner or later be in prison. Small wonder if terror lurked beneath these spasmodic bursts of laughter. If Alan were afraid—small blame to him. And if Dennis were afraid for Alan—small blame to him. And if she were afraid for Dennis. . . .

She was studying Alan carefully; and came to the conclusion that no terror would ever be great enough to deflect him from his purpose. Alan would never " rat." . . . Perhaps his present attitude betokened an inability to resist obeying the highly theatrical demands of the situation. She could appreciate and understand that . . . funny to have discovered something in common with Alan. Very funny. . . . She must hang on tight to her sense of humour, and not allow herself to wonder if the world contained anything else for her to hang on to!

The men were deep in political conversation now; none of the sense of it penetrated her mind. She only knew that Alan, in his explosive, jerky sentences, was doing most of the talk, with occasional interruptions from Benny Joseph and Barnaby; that Strickland sat silent and thoughtful; and that Dennis's troubled eyes rested ever on Alan.

No chance for her to have her talk with Dennis to-day. He had hardly spoken to her at all. And already it was time to go.

She rose from her chair. Dennis, as if suddenly becoming aware of her presence, said: " You're off . . . .? I'll ring you up to-morrow morning."

She nodded without looking at him, and Alan got up and held out his hand. " Good-bye, Miss de Courcy, and in case we never meet again, which is more than probable, don't hate me too much, will you?"

" Why should I hate you?" she parried with ironic politeness. For a second their eyes met . . . surely thus might a victorious rival smile down into the eyes of one whom she had beaten off the field!

" I couldn't hate you if I tried," said Antoinette very softly. She had passed through the stage of incredulity, and through the stage of growing uneasiness; and through that of raging jealousy and hatred. And having got beyond all these, there was nothing left; no jealousy or hatred big enough to express what she felt for this intruder with the insolent smile, who with his every look and gesture could thrill Dennis, as she had never been able to thrill him. Hatred was quite inadequate.

" I couldn't hate you if I tried——" She had spoken the truth.

She felt mazed and bewildered by the traffic and

the raucous shouts of the paper-boys, as she began
to make her way to the Underground station. If at
least he had accompanied her, she would have had
him to herself for a few minutes. She would not
have had to say good-bye to him before all the
others, before . . . . Alan. Good-bye for always,
in that futile, unsatisfactory fashion. She did not
believe that he would ring her up, as he had said.
It was already the end—such a miserable, dribbled-
out ending. Once before he had given her this
nauseating sense of anticlimax : only it had not
really mattered then. . . . Perhaps he had not accompanied her to the station for fear that she should
make a scene. Once before, at that very station——
she shuddered back from pursuing that memory
any further. She must inevitably come to dwell
on that moment in the cab, when she had felt
the touch of his lips again. . . . But this time he
need not have feared that she would provoke a
scene : she was too fully conscious of defeat ; useless
to fight for what was already lost.

She had not gone very far when she came face
to face with Oswald Forsyth.

" Are they all down at the tea-shop, talking as
usual?" He spoke wearily and there were great
dark rings under his eyes.

Antoinette nodded. " Yes, much as usual."

Oswald gave an impatient laugh. " Much good
all their talking will do ! It can't prevent you from
being caught between the two mill-stones." He
went on rapidly as he turned and walked along beside her : " It's either the war or prison—you're
caught anyhow."

Antoinette said : " I thought you had made up
your mind . . . . ?"

" Made up my mind. . . . Oh, I've made it up and unmade it a thousand times ever since I met Barnaby and all his crew. Standing out with the C.O.s seemed to me the finest thing in the world, and—and it meant not going into the trenches. . . . You see, I'm a coward—the genuine article; not the magazine-type, who is really only a hero in disguise. I'm just an abject funk. The horror of pain—even when it's more or less humane—the dentist boring down to the exposed nerve—and then to think of pain inflicted purposely in a hundred different hideous ways. . . . When you know of all that can happen while you're still conscious of it happening, how *can* you go out and face it? How can all those others. . . .? It's marvellous, and it's beyond me, utterly. I can only think of what it feels like to have your inside torn open by a jagged bit of shrapnel, or to have a limb amputated without chloroform. . . ."

" Oh, stop !" Antoinette implored him, but overwrought as he was, he continued : " I thought I was getting away from all that and helping all the others to get away by fighting for pacifism. I've sent in my appeal, but Heaven knows if I'll be able to go through with it. It means—prison. . . . Doesn't the very word convey a nightmare of being confined in a small space, with light and air shut out, and you beating yourself to death against stone walls. . . .? You've heard them talk about prison down at Miss Mowbray's, haven't you?"

" They were talking about it to-day . . . ."

" And all the other days, when I've sat there listening—and imagining . . . I—I just can't go to prison any more than I can go to the Front. It drives you mad, slowly, day by day, while you feel

your reason slipping from you. I don't know which
I dread most! And there's the one lot of people
goading you to fight and the other lot goading you
not to fight, and I'm dead sick of it all."

"Then why don't you take Non-Combatant Service?" The others might well say that she was
being a traitor to the Cause, but Antoinette did not
care. She understood too well this boy's loathing
of the extremes of pacifism and militarism alike,
and a wave of thankfulness came over her for the
happy accident of having been born a woman. But
for this accident, and lacking all definite convictions,
she like the rest would have been placed between
those two equally dreaded alternatives.

"Why not take Non-Com.?" she urged again,
but Oswald shook his head. "That's no good.
They'd probably send me out to France just the
same—to pick up bits of the dead, perhaps. . . .
There's no real escape. You're not meant to escape.
There's something rapacious and cruel and inevitable waiting to torture your mind and your body
and twist them out of shape . . . . and whichever
way you take, it's bound to get you in the end!
And I thought—I thought life was going to be so
splendid. . . . Oh, I know I oughtn't to be talking
to you like this, but I've not slept for nights, and
I'm half crazy."

Antoinette cut him short. One did not need
apologies from a human soul *in extremis*.

"Are you going back to the tea-shop?" she said,
as they reached the station.

He looked up at her with his big, weary eyes.
"Yes, I suppose so—I don't know "—and hovered
indecisively in the entrance.

Antoinette asked with sudden irrelevance : " How old are you ?"

There was a whimsical twist to his smile as he answered : " Eighteen—just eighteen—it's waiting for you now, when you're eighteen . . . ."

She saw him wander off in the direction leading away from Miss Mowbray's. And all the way to Cadogan Gardens, one of his phrases rang in her ears : " And I thought life was going to be so splendid. . . ." She might have echoed it.

She arrived home only a few minutes before dinner-time and was met in the hall by a wrathful grandmother. Why had she chosen to be late just to-night ? Had she, then, forgotten that Monsieur Lefèvre, from Grenoble, was coming to dinner ? Antoinette had forgotten. . . . Would she as quickly as possible attire herself in the pink satin dress that Grand'mère had given her, and in which she looked a trifle less " *outrée* " than in some of the garments of her own choosing.

" Make yourself look nice, and above all, be amiable," were Madame de Courcy's final injunctions, as Antoinette vanished into her room, and reflected that she might have been spared the pink satin dress and Monsieur Lefèvre just to-night. She had never seen him before, but from Grand'mère's attitude it was safe to infer that he was coming in the capacity of a possible suitor. It might have been fun—if it hadn't been just to-night. . . .

She appeared in the drawing-room as the gong rang, and was presented by Grand'mère to a stout and middle-aged personage with shiny black hair, a waxed moustache, and a pince-nez. This engaging creature bowed low over Antoinette's hand and warmly congratulated Madame de Courcy on the possession of such a grand-daughter.

" She is our only one—our little treasure," said Henriette, and laid an arm caressingly about Antoinette's shoulders.

" Tableau—family-life . . . ." muttered Antoinette under her breath, and was almost grateful to her father for not taking part in the tableau, but grumbling in his usual irritable manner : " You are always late : will you never learn to be punctual ?"

They went in to dinner.

" *Eh bien,* Monsieur Lefèvre, you bring us news of our family in Grenoble ?"

Monsieur Lefèvre hastened to deliver the messages which seemed to consist mainly of : " *Saluts affectueux de la part de——*"

But he became more explicit when mentioning that in the near future an engagement was likely to be announced between Madame de Courcy's granddaughter Hélène, and the " lonely soldier," to whom since months she had acted as " *marraine.*"

" Letters has passed between them. Then the young man arrived *en permission.* The young people appeared to please each other. It seems that he is of good family. *Mais c'est tout de même un jeu bizarre. . . .*"

Grand'mère agreed that it was very bizarre, and announced her intention of sending a letter to her daughter and son-in-law in Grenoble, advising, or better, commanding the rupture of these highly irregular " *fiançailles.*"

. . . . If only she could have caught Dennis's eye now ! How he had laughed over that story of Sidonie's engagement. . . . How he would have

relished this feat on the part of Sidonie's youngest
sister.   Dennis—Dennis—would they never laugh
together again . . . . ?

M. Lefèvre was seeking to make excuses for
Hélène. One must not forget that it was war-time.
The glamour of the uniform—doubtless every patriotic daughter of France felt the same about the
glamour of the uniform.   Doubtless Mademoiselle
Antoinette also—" Et il y en a de très chics, parmi
les officiers anglais. . . ."

Grand'mère remarked curtly that Antoinette had
no interest in English officers, and M. Lefèvre
looked relieved. Since the outbreak of war, being
over military age, he had regretted his civilian
clothing; but to-day for the first time—with a beaming smile at Antoinette—he no longer found reason
to deplore it.

. . . . In the name of freedom and democracy—
ready to stand out till the last—rights of the people
—international federation— Broken phrases and
words shot through her mind. She would have
liked to throw M. Lefèvre into the tea-shop—a very
timorous Daniel into the lions' den—he was a war-
profiteer, manufacturing leather goods for the
French Government; they would make short work
of him down at Miss Mowbray's! She could hear
Alan——

Alan. . . . They were together to-night, she
supposed. Dennis would not leave him now till he
was arrested. She found no difficulty in picturing
what might pass between them. . . . Alan's provo-
cations . . . . Dennis's battles against desire that
might prove stronger than himself.   Only a few
days ago her imagination had halted, incredulous,
uncomprehending. It was amazing now, the ease

with which it swung forward and found its way
about in these forbidden regions. Because the taint
was in herself, too, it had needed but the slightest
touch to awaken her sleeping imagination. The
awakening had been complete. There was nothing
unfamiliar now in the thought that her man should
be passionately in love with another man.

"Mademoiselle is interested in music?"

"But yes, Monsieur. . . ."

Questions and answers . . . . and she knew that
M. Lefèvre's eyes rested appraisingly on her. Perhaps he was wondering if she would make a good
wife and mother to his children. . . . What a pity
he could not have read her thoughts of two minutes
ago! She had a great longing to speak them aloud,
to watch the effect, the stunned consternation, incredulity and disgust spreading upon his bland, fat
face. That *she,* a *jeune fille* of good family . . .
And very likely her own mother would not understand what she was talking about; and Grand'mère
would scream and rave, whether she understood or
not; and her father would turn her out of the house.
It was a pity that she could not allow herself the
luxury of giving a dramatic climax, a super-climax,
to the dinner-party. . . .

"Yes . . . ." said Henriette, "there were two
hundred persons present, I think. It was too much.
The whole audience was so *ému* by my first recitation that their feelings reacted upon me. *J'étais
toute bouleversée.* . . ."

"Madame is so sensitive."

"*Hélas,* yes."

"And so generous, to give so much of her time
and of her talent."

Henriette endorsed this. "But I give them gladly

in the great cause. Would that I could give more, and that with impassioned rhetoric I could fire the blood of every coward who lags behind and does not avail himself of the glorious privilege of dying for his country!" (. . . And a terrified boy had said only that afternoon : " It's waiting for you now, when you're eighteen!")

" ' *En avant, Belgique, pays martyrisée mais tojours glorieuse* '—when I said those words my voice was strangled with sobs; and there were many ladies in the front row who also sobbed. I noticed especially the wife of the Spanish Secretary of State . . . ."

M. Lefèvre made sympathetic sounds in his throat. " A well-merited tribute to your powers, Madame. And has Mademoiselle inherited her mother's great gift?"

Mademoiselle replied : " Unhappily not, Monsieur."

Henriette looked at her daughter through her lorgnon. " She lacks the temperament."

. . . . Yes, but whence or from whom had she inherited the particular temperament that was hers? The idea that it might have been the bequest of either of her parents or her grandmother, filled her with the hysterical desire to laugh. She was an anomaly and a freak in her family, just as Dennis was an anomaly and a freak in his.

Grand'mère was enquiring after the welfare of her grand-daughter Sidonie; and M. Lefèvre, by dint of arch smiles and hesitations, managed to convey the interesting news that Sidonie was once again in a delicate state of health. Antoinette smiled. Out of consideration for her youth and virginity, M. Lefèvre could not mention in a natural manner, one of the natural facts of life . . . . but he would probably regale her father with stories of the usual dubious French type once they were alone in the smoking-room. Dennis had not been so careful of her sheltered, girlish innocence and ignorance, but suddenly M. Lefévre, normal, typical man that he was, struck her as being much more perverse than Dennis! Again she longed to say so aloud. And to have Dennis here to watch M. Lefèvre's face. . . . How was she to go on living in a world turned upside down, world in which what was usually accepted as natural seemed to her inverted, and only the unnatural seemed natural? Certainly, she had exulted in being led by Dennis into this inverted world—she saw it as a kind of maze—but she had not anticipated being left alone in it. And she would never be able to find her way out again. Perhaps there was no way out for people like her.

And her mother would continue to calculate the dramatic effect of strangled sobs at fashionable charity concerts; and her father would continue to be fretful and irritable; and her grandmother would continue to attempt periodically to get her married to suitable people, until she was too old, and they gave her up as a hopeless case.

"Mademoiselle looks a trifle pale. Perhaps the air of London does not agree with her."

"Oh, I'm quite well, thank you . . . " with a false sprightliness of manner.

"She does not eat enough," grumbled Anatole.

"She runs about too much," supplemented her grandmother.

"The air of Grenoble is said to be famed for giving appetite. May I express the hope that soon Mademoiselle will prove it for herself?"

CHAPTER IX

WOULD he telephone this morning? Even if it were only to make final and absolute the severance between them? She felt that she must at all costs speak to him once again, and then unquestioningly she would accept her dismissal. She vowed that she would not in any way attempt to clutch at him, but he could not expect her to be superhuman . . . . and it would be superhuman to be content to drop out of his life, with never a word of farewell.

All that morning she was on the alert to catch the sound of the telephone, ready to run and answer it immediately, so as not to waste the precious moments he might have set aside for her. Other sounds there were; deceptive sounds that jerked at her taut nerves; bicycle-bells in the streets; the whirr of the telephone in the house next door; jingle of bells on a passing cart; bells that existed only in her imagination. The whole world seemed to be full of bell-sounds . . . . The telephone alone remained dumb, as if under an enchantment . . . . But later on it threw off this spell, and rang with persistent and diabolical frequency during the whole afternoon. And each time Antoinette was convinced that it must be Dennis, and with her heart beating wildly, flew to take off the receiver; and was told that she was the "wrong number," or else lured into chatty conversation with some friend of her mother's.

She raged impotently against these people who kept the line engaged, while Dennis was perhaps trying in vain to get on . . . . The exhausting day

wore to its finish; and after one more " Sorry
you're troubled," and a somewhat tactless enquiry
on the part of the Exchange as to whether the telephone was " in order," the instrument relapsed into
silence.

And no letter, no word from him next morning.

. . . . Scorching eyeballs and aching head; the
sick, hot swell of tears in the throat, and the unre-
mitting effort required to swallow them down, to
appear natural, to deny herself the luxury of unre-
strained emotion. If once she broke down, there
would be questions . . . . questions that she could
not answer. How much understanding could she
expect from her environment? They were strangers
to her, strangers all—her father, her mother, her
grandmother.

Even despite her really gallant efforts at self-
control, it was apparent to her relatives that she was
looking ill. Grand'mère, of course, took this to be
a piece of personal cussedness on Antoinette's part :
did not the presence of M. Lefèvre in London render
it eminently desirable that she should appear at her
best ?

" She is anæmic," said Henriette.

" She smokes too much," declared Anatole.

" We should have found her a husband when she
was younger," Grand'mère wagged her head
sagaciously.

" There is still time," muttered Anatole; " Jean
Lefèvre had quite a good impression of her, though
one must admit that she made very little effort to
please him."

Grand'mère brightened, and expressed the hope
that M. Lefèvre would soon come to pay his " *visite
de digestion.*"

"He will come soon enough," grumbled Anatole, who discouraged enthusiasm on principle.

Of course he would come. And more than probably he would propose to her. Antoinette knew that type from past experience. And the family would be indignant if she refused him—just as they had been indignant on previous occasions. Only this time the indignation would be greater, because, as Grand'mère had said, they should have married her off when she was younger; they were getting uneasy about her future; wanted to see her safely settled . . . . Perhaps they would make it difficult —impossible for her ˙to refuse him. Perhaps her own strength of resistance would give way. She felt as if she were being slowly strangled to death.

There was no one in whom she could confide, except, perhaps, Pegeen. Pegeen might not understand, but she would be good to her, and that, for the moment, was all that she asked : someone to be good to her, and before whom she could relax her wearisome pretence. She was to go to supper at the studio that evening; and the thought of it somehow helped her through the first part of the third day without news of Dennis.

But when she reached the studio, Pegeen was not there. The side-entrance had been left open, and on the table she found a scrawled note from Pegeen, saying that she had gone out to tea with Conn and would be back soon, and in the meantime would Antoinette help herself to the cigarettes . . . . Antoinette was bitterly disappointed, her nerves already fretted with over-much waiting. She had no idea of the time. The hands of the three clocks —an antique bronze, a little painted Bavarian one, and a cuckoo-clock—all pointed to different hours and ticked at variance with one another; through the window that stood open to the garden, a flood of orange sunset-light poured in, and lit up the colours in the gorgeous brocades and fabrics that lay strewn about. From the vicarage-garden next door came the sound of voices, and the smart dry crack of croquet balls in collision. Antoinette wondered if Pegeen and Conn were at Miss Mowbray's, and if Dennis and Alan were there too. Perhaps Pegeen would bring her some news, some message. But why was she so late? Perhaps, with characteristic absent-mindedness, while she listened to the usual vehement sort of talk in the tea-shop, she had forgotten that Antoinette was waiting for her.

Already the sunset had faded, and the skylight showed a square of dull grey. Restlessly she went to the window and looked out. The garden with its unkempt lawn and tangled shrubbery, had a sinister appearance : effect heightened by a yellow-eyed cat, crouching motionless among the bushes.

She returned to her armchair by the fireplace; selected at random a book from one of the shelves; discovered after five minutes that she had not taken in a single word that she had read. Why didn't Pegeen come? Yet, even if she came, Antoinette realised again that it would not be possible to tell her anything. How could she tell without implicating Dennis? Pegeen might turn away in shuddering disgust, or she might repeat Antoinette's story to Conn . . . . No, one could not tell that sort of thing. That was law that could not be infringed, even though infringement might bring such relief.

Terror and loneliness of the Ishmaelite, outcast among men and women . . . . She was coming to know by her own experience every stage of the

suffering he had foreshadowed for her, suffering that
she was not big enough, not strong enough to bear
alone.

Still the noise of the croquet balls persisted.
Idly she wondered how the players could see in this
dim light.   It was getting cold, but she dared not
go to close the door leading into the garden.   To do
so she would have to cross the whole length of the
studio . . . . and shadows were beginning to lurk
in the corners now, shadows that it would be horrible
to know behind one.   As long as one faced them,
it was bearable.   Just bearable . . . .   The square
of the skylight was changing from grey to dark blue.
The primroses that Conn had brought Pegeen the
other day still filled the green bowl, but they had
faded to a hideous shrivelled mass of brown.   The
sounds from the next door garden had ceased
entirely, but the studio was full of strange little
sounds—creakings, whisperings, mutterings . . . .
From the walls, the figures in the cartoons leered
grotesquely down at her.   There was something
sinister about the designs and the crude, brutal
colouring of the brocades, just as there was something sinister in that neglected garden with the weed-
grown paths and the crouching cat.   She could not
switch on the electric lamp at her elbow; in accord-
ance with the Lighting Regulations, the blind had
to be drawn over the skylight before the lamp could
be lit . . . . and she knew that she could never get
even as far as the skylight.   Those shapes in the
corners would creep up behind her, padding soft-
footed at her heels . . . .   Soon it would be quite
dark, and she would be alone with her terrible
thoughts, alone with the shadows and the mutterings
and creakings.

" Pegeen, come—please—please—please . . . ."
No possibility of getting a sane grip of herself
now.   If Pegeen came she would confess to her
everything—everything—not caring if she infringed
the law.   Only to have sight and sound of a human
being among these inanimate things imbued suddenly with a mysterious spirit of evil.

Footsteps at last, coming down the path towards
the entrance . . . . With a sob of relief, she rushed
to the door.

" *Dennis!*"

She was clinging to him, laughing and crying
hysterically.   " I—I didn't know you were coming
here."

" And I didn't know I'd find you here—I came
for a book that Alan lent Conn—' *Towards Democracy* '—he wants it," he spoke in rapid, jerky
sentences.

" Conn's out.   Pegeen too.   I've been waiting for
her for hours and hours . . . . Dennis, it was
dreadful!"   Still she clung to his hand, trembling.

" Poor child . . . . Antoinette, I know you expected me to ring up—I've behaved despicably, oh,
worse than that, but what's the use of piling on
adjectives?   I couldn't ring up because there was
nothing to say.   You see how it is with me, my
dear."

" I see, Dennis . . . ."

" And doesn't it make you hate me?"

" Could anything do that?"

He took her by the shoulders and kissed her again
and again.

With a horrible flash of insight, she cried :
" You're kissing me—and thinking of Alan."

He answered " Yes " . . . . determined that at

least there should be no deception between them.
" You shouldn't let me do this, Antoinette."

" I love you . . . ."

"I'm a cad and a beast to let you let me."

She laughed a little as the pressure of his hands
tightened around her. " I love you, Dennis."

She was aware that her self-respect, her sense of
moral degradation should have risen in revolt against
his treatment of her. Yet she knew no shame in
taking and returning his kisses, would have known
no shame in giving herself to him entirely, if by so
doing she could have brought him an instant's
fleeting delight, appeased the hunger of his senses.

" The waste, the utter futile waste of you . . . .
Oh, God, why can't I care for you more?"

It might have been the cry of a person drowning,
and it filled her with immense pity and despair—
pity and despair beyond all consciousness of her
own suffering.

" What is it that he can give you, and that I
can't?"

" You mustn't want to give me anything. I'm
not worth it. To-morrow I'm seeing Alan for the
last time. He's pledged his word to be ready when
the police come for him next morning. I'm . . . .
spending the last evening with him, Antoinette . ."

A sound of pain broke from her lips as he drew
her closer to him. " I've done my best to make you
hate me. I'm doing it now . . . . I shall be with
Alan to-morrow, I tell you! Don't you hate me
now, Antoinette, and now?"

Thus might a different man, the phantom lover
of her schoolgirl dreams, have sought to wring from
her the admission that she loved him. " Don't
you love me now, Antoinette, and now . . . .?"

Yet in this inverted world it could still seem natural that he should try to wring from her the assurance of her hatred, using the most cruel weapon in his power—the name of Alan.

" Don't you hate me, Antoinette ? It would be so much better if you could !"

Through her torture she cried, " No !"

He kissed her roughly and passionately then, in a sort of fury at her inability to satisfy him. And she, perceiving this, was yet happy after a distorted fashion ; happy despite her sad knowledge and lack of all illusions. While she was in his arms her terrors could still be kept at bay ; she could laugh at the menace of M. Lefèvre or of continued existence at Cadogan Gardens. It might be the last time that she would feel secure . . . . Sudden conviction came upon her, that this *was* the last time that his arms would be around her ; and now as once before, she knew that the moment must be held and held—even though past experience had proved that the memory of it would be powerless to soften the inevitable pain that was to come.

" Dennis—it's no good, you can't make me hate you. And I can't make myself hate you—I've tried . . . . And I can't do without you. I've tried that too. Seeing what it felt like . . . . Yes, I know you're in love with Alan, and that I'm nothing to you and that you'd rather be rid of me altogether— Oh, don't interrupt me—let me say all I have to say, for once . . . . I know if I had any pride or decent feeling I shouldn't be saying anything at all. You called me an immoral woman once, in fun. Perhaps you were right. I'd rather kiss you like this, knowing everything, than be respectably married to a respectable man. I suppose I'm not good enough to be able to care for a respectable man. But is it immoral to care for one man only, and for him so much, that nothing he is or does, and nothing he can make you be or do, can ever make you hate him?"

"And all this wasted on a wretched freak who can't take it—but who'd give his soul to be able to take it—bear that in mind, Antoinette, perhaps it'll help just a little."

"It's undignified of me to ask you not to cut me off entirely, but I do ask you, all the same. Dignity and pride don't seem to convey very much to me now. They're just words. But I know that I can't do without you. That's real."

He bent over her and murmured: "Forgive me, dear, for hurting you so much . . . ."

She answered with a half smile: "Forgive me, Dennis, for loving you so much . . . ." and added in a whisper: "As I forgive you for loving me so little . . . ."

He said after a while: "Perhaps it's just as well that Alan came when he did; otherwise you might not have believed me. Seeing was believing, wasn't it?"

"No," she said softly, "feeling was believing."

"It's monstrous that I should have had to drag you through all this!"

"I went gladly, Dennis—at first, anyway. So it was just as much my fault. And I'm still willing to go wherever you'll lead, if only you *will* lead, and not leave me stranded and alone. So it's still my fault now."

He said sorrowfully: "It's not your fault—and it's not my fault—we're both unfortunates . . . ."

As they left the studio, they heard footsteps scurrying down the walled passage between the gardens, and almost collided with Pegeen. " I'm so sorry to have kept you waiting," she whispered breathlessly, " but I couldn't help it. We had to arrange things—we're off to-morrow, Conn and I— so good-bye to the two of you, and all the best luck in the world !"

CHAPTER X

" SUCH decent chaps they were," said Alan reflectively, " we had a most delightful conversation. They don't really want to arrest me in the least. Not with any conviction. Still, they're coming to discharge their painful duty at 8 a.m. to-morrow morning. Don't look so wretched, Dennis. I'm glad to be really up against it at last."

Dennis made no answer. He was mentally calculating how many hours of freedom still remained to Alan. It was 2 a.m. now. Not many hours more.

"And they're mistaken if they think that imprisonment can make me forswear my creed, or declare that I believe in war as a means of regeneration of nations, or that the duties of citizenship lie in taking the lives of other citizens, rather than in trying to promote pacific relations between them. Benny was complaining the other day that we're so few, and I know some of us have ratted on that score alone, given up the battle because they think it's no use against such odds. Being in the minority doesn't imply being in the wrong. But capitulating means admitting that we believe that black is white, just because the majority says so. Poor devils all over Europe are being told that black *is* white, and are dying in proof of it. Dying gallantly and splendidly and wastefully for the sake of a lie."

"And when we try to assert our truth, we're condemned to the death-in-life of prison."

"I wouldn't call it so much death-in-life, as so

many years that a benighted State unlawfully robs
out of our lives, and it's our business to prove that
even that theft can't daunt us."

"You needn't be afraid that I shall let it daunt
me." To logic and commonsense and humanity;
to every argument, reason and motive that had
hitherto impelled Dennis to take up his stand as a
pacifist, was now added the greatest of all these—
love. "A couple of weeks hence I expect I shall be
safely under lock and key too."

Alan grinned. "Locked up because we're considered a danger to humanity. . . . Almost
humorous, isn't it?"

"Well, at least we shall both be going through
the same hell, Alan."

"The same hell, and the same good fight; I
think we fought side by side before now. In ancient
Greece, perhaps, or Rome. Sometimes I have
dreams. . . . . and in those dreams you are always
my comrade in battle, my comrade in love."

"And always will be, Alan, always. . . ."

"You're sure, Dennis—sure that it will be, when
we come out on the other side of this infernal
tunnel?" There was a note of anxious pleading in
the boy's voice. For all his keen determination and
courage, he looked suddenly even younger than he
was—as young as he had looked that night at Crannack.

"Alan. . ." Dennis dug the nails into the palms
of his hands as he tried to master the choking sob
that rose in his throat. But at that note in Alan's
voice all his laboriously built-up self-control and
restraint gave way. . . .

.   .   .   .

The Square was very still, flooded in the cold
K

bluish light of the moon. The two stood a moment in silence on Dennis's door-step.

Then Alan smiled up at his friend. "Good-night, Dennis. . . ."

"Good-night, boy. . . ." He tightened the pressure of his hand round Alan's arm. "If only I could keep you safe. . . ."

"Nothing matters now," murmured Alan, "I'm glad it's been like this—the last time. . . ."

PART III

CHAPTER I

"AND do you mean to tell me," Mrs. Ryan said severely, "that Dennis is appealing for exemption *again ?*"

Mrs. Blackwood looked troubled. "You see, the local tribunal passed him for General Service, so he's appealing against that at the House of Commons."

"I should have thought that being refused once would have brought him to his senses," persisted Mrs. Ryan. Mrs. Blackwood glanced helplessly across at Antoinette. They had met at Dennis's tribunal, for which Mrs. Blackwood and Doreen had come up to London; and they had invited Antoinette to England for the following week-end. Dennis had remained in town pending his new appeal.

In answer to Mrs. Blackwood's look, Antoinette rose in his defence. "Naturally he's appealing again. The local tribunal scarcely listened to what he had to say."

"I should think not," snorted Mrs. Ryan.

"But surely the object of a tribunal *is* to listen to what people have to say. . . .?"

Momentarily routed, Mrs. Ryan occupied herself with the sleeve of the pyjama she was sewing. All the ladies present were either sewing or knitting, and Doreen was busy with the tea. Antoinette found it both amusing and stimulating to be championing Dennis's views in his own home-circle. Mrs. Blackwood was too worried, and also a little shamefaced before her visitors to do much in the championing line; and Doreen apparently shared this attitude. It therefore devolved upon Antoinette alone to defend the conscientious objector against these female militarists—Mrs. Ryan and Mrs. Hallard the most rabid ones; Mrs. Griggs merely woolly and futile; little Miss Simpkins torn between admiration of "our gallant boys," and a reluctant personal admiration for Dennis. Unlike Mrs. Blackwood and Doreen, Antoinette had no regard whatever for the susceptibilities of the old ladies of Eastwold, and so felt quite equal to her task.

Mrs. Ryan returned to the offensive. "I suppose if he appeals long enough he will get himself put into that Non-Combatant Corps. A shame, I call it, for a healthy young man."

"Oh, he wouldn't dream of accepting Non-Com," Antoinette replied loftily, "that's only a compromise." She was glad that she had picked up enough at Miss Mowbray's to enable her to carry on the argument—carry it on clumsily, perhaps, but with Dennis's own weapons.

Mrs. Hallard, biting off the end of her cotton, said with brisk cheerfulness : "Well, there's always Work of National Importance for him to undertake if he won't fight. Plenty of that going, isn't there?"

"Dennis won't undertake anything that means releasing another man to be killed in his place," said Antoinette, and Mrs. Blackwood supported her weakly with : "You see, Dennis is a socialist."

"One of those horrid people who wear red ties and are always having riots. . . ." quavered Mrs. Griggs.

"Dennis doesn't wear a red tie!" declared his mother.

"As he doesn't believe in war himself, he won't help others to wage it," Antoinette ignored the asides.

"So selfish. . . ." murmured Mrs. Griggs.

"He might at least make munitions," was Mrs. Hallard's next bright suggestion.

"Isn't that helping to kill people, just as much as going to the Front? It's doing it at home in comfort, instead of out there in danger."

"But—but the Germans *have got* to be killed," expostulated Mrs. Ryan, "how else are we to win the war?"

Antoinette plunged round for some of the remembered arguments. "Pacifists don't see why we should win it, any more than the Germans. They think a decisive victory for either side wouldn't mean lasting peace, but would only be the foundation for future wars. Nothing will move Dennis from that belief!" she added proudly.

"It's quite a wrong-headed belief and someone ought to talk it out of him," said Mrs. Ryan, "I hope you've used all your influence, Mrs. Blackwood?"

"Oh, I can't argue with him," the mother shook her head, "his brains are so much better than mine . . . . and of course he must do as he thinks right."

"But do you realise that if he persists in upholding such nonsense, he runs the risk of being put in prison?"

Mrs. Blackwood did realise. To anyone observing under her eyes the dark hollows that told of many sleepless nights, the fact would have been obvious.

"Think of the disgrace!" said Mrs. Ryan in sepulchral tones.

"Yes, the disgrace that a man *should* be put in prison for standing by his convictions!!" Antoinette blazed out.

Mrs. Ryan glared at her. "Well, really . . . . these people are put in prison for being cowards, and quite right too."

"But the C.O.s who stand out aren't cowards: cowards take the easy way—they commit suicide." She was thinking of young Oswald Forsyth, who, maddened by fear of that which awaited him no matter in which direction he turned, had found a solution by taking his own life. "They're not all cowards—there are some exceptions to the rule."

"I always distrust the exception to the rule."

"But you can't have a world with everyone in it absolutely true to type, and built upon the same model by the dozen. Think how dull and tidy it would be—how German, in fact."

"I trust that my ideas do not in any respect savour of the Kultur of that despicable country," said Mrs. Ryan with dignity; "but I maintain that anything that puts itself outside the general rule and diverges too widely from the ordinary type, is an undesirable element, and should be barred out."

"That means that you'd bar out genius too, and lots of other fine qualities that only exist in the brains of people who are exceptions to the rule."

". . . . Such a very gifted young man," sighed Miss Simpkins, smoothing her buttonhole with her thimble, "it seems such a pity . . . ."

"In times like these," pronounced Mrs. Ryan, "if he can find nothing else to do, he should at least devote his gifts solely to composing Battle-Hymns for our men . . . ."

. . . . "And she won't be budged from her

opinion any more than Dennis will be from his,"
reflected Antoinette.   It suddenly made her feel
tired to think of the perpetual clash and battle of
opposing belief and opposing opinion going on all
over the world now—and no party ever coming
round to see the point of view of the other.

Mrs. Ryan, by way of intimating that the discussion was at an end, pointedly asked Doreen if
she had news from Hugh, who was in the trenches.

"I haven't heard for some days, Mrs. Ryan.   He
was all right when he wrote last, but the post comes
so irregularly now . . . ."   Doreen also was paler
and thinner with the strain of waiting for letters,
and dreading a certain kind of telegram from the
War Office.

There was a sympathetic murmur from all the
ladies; then Mrs. Hallard spoke with her habitual
brightness : " Never mind, dear.   Just think how
you and Lily will value the boys when they do come
home to you for good.   I expect we shall have a
double wedding, sha'n't we, Mrs. Blackwood?   Clive
and Lily, and Doreen and Hugh."

"There's nothing so pretty as a really pretty
wedding, I always think," came Miss Simpkins'
gentle voice.

"Arthur was the first man to enter Combles,"
said Mrs. Griggs for the tenth time that afternoon.
"He entered it at the head of his men, although
he was badly wounded in the knee, which I am sure
was very painful indeed, though he made light of it
at the time."

"Yes, he's quite a hero, isn't he?" said Mr.
Blackwood, and Mrs. Ryan put in : "He sent the
girls a letter the other day; it had been opened by
the censor, and they were ever so proud of it."

In imagination Antoinette could hear Amy's excited lisp : " Fanthy the thenthor reading all our thecreth—doethn't it make one feel important ?"

Later on Lily Hallard made her appearance. Hands plunged deep in the pockets of her khaki coat, she greeted the assembled company with : " Afternoon, everybody !" and helping herself to the sandwiches sat down between her mother and Doreen.

" I've had a letter from Clive, so I thought I'd better toddle round with it at once and show you. Says he's feeling awfully fit. Killed three Huns all on his own—sniped 'em. Good man !"

" Oh, well done, well *done!* cried Mrs. Hallard, " that ought to mean a decoration of some sort. " Well, if he gets it or not, he'll have deserved it. Your boy has given you something to be proud of, Mrs. Blackwood."

" Yes—yes, indeed . . . ." But Mrs. Blackwood's mind was troubled by an echo of something her other boy had once said to her : " Do you think because they're Germans they love their sons less ?"

" Oh, by the way, Lily continued with her mouth full, " Tom Sanderson's been rather badly smashed up. I met his mother this morning. They had to amputate both legs—the one only as far as the knee, though. They say he's wonderfully cheerful—learning to knit and make himself useful with his hands, now he'll never be able to ride or walk again. I won't tell Clive when I write ; he'd be so cut up. He's awfully fond of Tom. Rotten shame, isn't it ?"

" The brutes !" exclaimed Mrs. Ryan.

. . . . Those who had maimed Tom were brutes ; but Clive, who had sniped three of the

enemy, was a hero. And to the other side Clive
was the brute, and Tom's assailants were heroes.
Antoinette marvelled that the one-sided absurdity
of it all should be apparent to no one save herself.
But she recognised that it would not even have been
apparent to her were she not seeing the world
through Dennis's eyes. And had he been a soldier
she would have collected his badges and buttons,
and listened to his stories from the Front with just
as much zest as Doreen or Lily. But while she
utterly lacked convictions of her own, there was a
certain pride in taking up the attitude which she
knew would have been his if he had been here.

Mrs. Blackwood's invitation to Eastwold had been
a god-send. Ever since Alan's arrest, two months
ago, she had felt strangely shy of Dennis; had
feared that he might think she was taking an unfair
advantage over Alan. He might hate her and recoil
from her, just because she was there, and he did
not want her; and Alan, whom he did want, was
inaccessible. All she prayed for now was not that
Dennis should love her, but that he should not hate
her.

And at Eastwold, surrounded by people and
things that belonged to him, she was continually
being reminded of his personality. There were the
old photographs of him as a baby, as a boy . . . .
such a serious-eyed little boy. There were his
books which she was invited to borrow if she liked.
There was in Doreen that faint family likeness to
Dennis; an expression in the big light-brown eyes;
the curve of the lips. There was the fascination of
listening to Mrs. Blackwood's stories of him as a
child . . . . Antoinette felt nearer to him here
than when she was actually with him in London.

300 DESPISED AND REJECTED

After the sewing-party had broken up, Lily, Antoinette and Doreen sat talking in the latter's bedroom.

Doreen appealed to Antoinette: "Can't you do anything to make Dennis give up his dreadful ideas?"

Antoinette smiled inwardly at the assumption that she had some influence over Dennis; but thought it just as well to keep up the illusion before Dennis's sister. "Why should I, Doreen? Surely every man has a right to his opinions, and I think it's splendid of Dennis to stand by his, as he's doing."

"Splendid!" cried Lily, "sheer theatricality, I call it. They should never have had the chance of making such an exhibition of themselves. I'd shoot 'em all if I had my way."

"When so many are being shot already—and some are shooting themselves for fear of being shot —and some are shooting themselves rather than shoot others?"

"Oh, I like your so-called humanitarian who is so squeamish that he won't take the lives of his country's enemies, and yet doesn't scruple to take his own, rather than let it be of service to the State."

"Rather than use it for a purpose which he considers vile!" Antoinette broke in. "There's some heroism in that too, even if there isn't in the suicide of the person who's just afraid. That's only pitiful. . . ." she added softly.

"Why concern yourself with such riff-raff? The C.O.s and all their like are just a lot of contemptible weaklings."

"You're not very complimentary to your future brother-in-law, are you?"

"Doreen knows well enough what I think of

Dennis's behaviour; there is no need for compliments. People of his sort are no good to the
nation. Cut 'em out I say!"

" You can't call a man who's ready to go to prison
for his convictions a weakling or a coward."

" Prison's safe. What's prison compared with
the trenches?"

" They do queer things to the C.O.s in prison—
forcing food through tubes up their noses if they
won't eat, putting them in chains and painful irons
—yes, you *shall* listen, Doreen . . . . The
officials have more or less got a free hand with
them, and backed up by public opinion they can
wreak their spite upon them as they please, giving
them ghastly punishments that may injure them for
life."

Lily shrugged her shoulders. " If a man
disobeys orders he's got to be punished. The men
in the trenches run other risks—real risks."

" The men in the trenches also stand a sporting
chance of escape. Those in prison don't. They
have to undergo deliberate, cold-blooded torture.
It—it's like atrocities!"

Lily snorted. " Well, it would be a nice thing
if these precious pacifists of yours were allowed to
run loose and enjoy themselves while all the really
decent people have to suffer."

" No, you'd like to see them punished just for
having ideas that are different from other people's.
You rampant militarists at home can't endure the
thought of any joy or freedom being left in the
world. You seem to take a ghoulish pleasure in
crushing it all out. It galls you to think of anyone
escaping with a lesser share of the general misery."

" Frankly I don't see why the C.O.s should

escape. Why should men enjoy the freedom and
the rights of citizenship that they won't fight for?"

"They're not given their rights of citizenship as
a free gift or a charity; they pay for them in rates
and taxes : that's fair. But why should they also
be expected to pay in flesh and blood?"

"You've a very lofty idea of patriotism, I must
say!"

"I hate all the talk about 'a man's duty to the
State.' Why should the State have the right to
claim a man's life when it can't *give* him life—when
it can't give him back as much as a finger-nail that
he may lose in the war? Why has the State the
right to take more than it can give?"

"You're mad," said Lily; and having thus
clinched the argument, departed.

Doreen sighed. "Dennis can't stop the war by
keeping out of it, so I do wish he'd join in like
everybody else, and help to win it."

"Of course one man can't stop the war by
standing out, any more than one man by joining in
can win it. Each man can only answer for himself,
and do what he thinks right."

Doreen cried impulsively, "I love you for sticking
up for Denny like that, but only because I love him
too—not because I think he's right. I think it's
right to do what Hugh's doing, even though I
sometimes feel I just can't bear it a second longer
—the waiting for news—and knowing he's in
danger always—and hating the sight of a telegraph-
boy."

"Yet you wouldn't want him not to be at the
Front, would you?"

Doreen shook her head.

" And I don't want Dennis not to stand by his views, either."

" Oh, that's different," said Doreen childishly.

Antoinette smiled. "Is it . . . .? And supposing Hugh had been a pacifist, Doreen?"

" Oh, he never could have been . . . . but if he had," Doreen softened, " if he had, I suppose I should have tried to find excuses for him." She added after a moment : " But how I should have hated having to!"

CHAPTER II

HE was adrift again now, while he waited for his tribunal, perilously adrift : wandering down to Miss Mowbray's and half-heartedly joining in the talk, with his thoughts elsewhere; wandering into theatres when the performance was nearly over, seeking in vain that which might distract and hold him. Hold him. . . . Was there anything on earth that could hold him, now that Alan had gone? And now that Alan had gone, his life was one stupendous aching regret that what had happened that last night had not happened sooner. The senselessness of all his repression and self-denial stood revealed to him. Seeing at last with Alan's eyes, and in the light of his own experience, he recognised that herein had lain the real perversion : in the continuous struggle between brain and body, the continuous struggle to suppress his instincts and force them into ways not natural to them. It had not lain in his passion for Alan. That, and that alone, given the peculiarities of his nature, had been right, had been beautiful, because it was truthful. He could curse himself now for the short-sightedness, for the principle of imagined æstheticism that had made him for so long resist his own impulses.

If only. . . . And now it was too late. Alan was behind the bars, and Dennis left with the burning knowledge of all that he had missed. What, indeed, was there that could hold him now? Yet despite his desire to be held, at times he longed with weary irritability, to be able to sever all ties; to break from his family; from Antoinette; perhaps,

like O'Farrell, to escape to Ireland; to live in truth
the life of the outlaw and outcast that he was.

Perpetual argument, achieving no result, and ending always in the same inevitable deadlock, was
carried on between the two conflicting strains of his
nature.

" It would break your mother's heart."

" She's got the three others, and they are more
satisfactory than I am."

" She loves you more than the others—and differently."

Dennis groaned, impatient of this wealth of affection to which he could make no adequate return.
He loved his mother—but she was not the pivot of
his existence, as he was of hers.

There was Antoinette, too, with her useless gifts,
with her useless pleading that he might accept them.
Sometimes he hated her for his very inability to accept them; and sometimes he could laugh at the futility, the grotesque, ludicrous futility of these ties
that held him—and held him—and did not hold him.
But if he broke them, he asked himself, what then?
What then?

Doubtless the Central Appeal Tribunal would in
some measure furnish the reply.

CHAPTER III

" CLEAR the court !"

The people were hustled out into one of the long stone corridors of the House of Commons, and the door closed upon them. Behind that door the fate of two of the applicants for exemption was being decided. Antoinette groaned at the delay. Dennis had been called for 2.30 that afternoon, but it was nearly 4 o'clock now, and so far only five out of the twelve cases had been heard. The fact that one did not know in what order they were to be heard, added to the suspense of waiting. In the first case there had only been a brief interval between the applicant's statement and the delivery of judgment. The spectacled, obviously highly-strung young man had appealed on socialistic grounds. His speech was both virile and vehement, and he quoted Tolstoy and Wells and Karl Marx and Philip Gibbs in a breathless Cockney voice that told of self-education and the night-school. When he had finished, he still stood tense and rigid, although he had the Board's permission to be seated. And when the blow fell—" Appeal dismissed. Applicant passed for Foreign Service "—he crumpled up quite suddenly into his chair in a way that made Antoinette's throat feel tight.

The two next appeals had been decided in much the same manner; but the last two had evidently presented greater difficulties and were now being considered behind the closed doors.

In the corridor a crowd of men and women, friends and supporters of the applicants, were

huddled together, talking in low voices. Amongst
them there were representatives of both pacifist and
militarist newspapers, a plain-clothes detective, and
two policemen. There was only one bench, and
that was occupied by a youth in khaki and three
white-faced women in black. The others had to
stand, shifting restlessly to and fro, yet not daring
to move too far from those doors that might open
again at any moment. People who had never met
before drifted into whispered conversation with each
other, linked together by an outlook and an anxiety
common to them all.

An elderly woman was talking to Dennis, and
Antoinette was glad that his attention was engaged.
His behaviour to her had been entirely aloof and
impersonal ever since Alan's arrest. Perhaps he
thought—thus she interpreted his mood—that if he
were less aloof and impersonal he would be guilty
of treachery towards Alan. Even now, though she
had accompanied him here, and was outwardly quite
in the picture—" the woman at his side "—there
was no intimacy of thought between them. She
knew well enough who it was who really " stood by"
him.

She heard the woman say to Dennis : " I shall
will you to get total exemption. I am a great be-
liever in will-power, aren't you? If they offer you
Non-Combatant Service, I do hope you won't take
it! Yes, I've been to prison three times—look!"
She lowered her voice to a whisper and pointed to
the suffragette badge she wore inside her jacket.
Then, turning to Antoinette : " I shall will him to
get off for both your sakes, my dear. . . ."

Antoinette thanked her gravely.

The doors were flung open again, and the people

pressed back into the court, struggling to regain their old places on the benches that ran, three deep, along the walls. Would it be Dennis's turn now to face those twenty-five men upon whom his fate depended?

Judgment was delivered upon the previous applicants. Then a name was called: not Dennis's. The young man in khaki stepped forward and took his place at the desk, and a murmur of astonishment went through the crowd at the sight of his uniform. He stated that when the military authorities had come to remove him, he had told them that he had an appeal pending, but they had taken no notice. . .

There were groans of " Shame. . . ." " A disgrace!" which were instantly quelled. The Chairman declared that the man must be put back into civilian ranks before his case could be heard.

The next applicant claimed exemption on the grounds that he was the sole support of his mother, his grandmother and a paralysed sister. His father was dead, and his brother had been killed in the war. While the Chairman enquired into the details of the circumstances, Antoinette looked at the woman who had accompanied the applicant; the mother, probably. Her hands were clenched in her lap, her eyes fixed imploringly upon the Chairman's face. Impossible to tell from the perfect impartiality of his manner in which direction he was biassed, if at all. Antoinette found herself following this case, as she had followed most of the others: not impersonally, but as if all her own hopes and longings were centred in the desire that the man should get his exemption. She shared the breathless painful suspense of the mother, and the feeling that the agony was being unnecessarily prolonged, when judgment was for the moment deferred, and the next man called.

This one stated that he had religious scruples against the taking of life. In proof of this he had reliquished his post with a firm of motor-tyre manufacturers on discovering that they were working for the Government. He put his case badly, halting and stammering; but his underlying determination seemed to be inflexible.

" The Lord said : ' *Thou shalt not kill.*' "

Here the Military Representative, to whose smooth fat face and sneering expression Antoinette had taken an instantaneous dislike, rose to his feet and asked the applicant with affected politeness if he were aware that one or two of the Germans—yes, let us say one or two of them—had already broken that commandment, and that it was his duty to his country to retaliate?

" If the Germans do wrong, sir, I can't help it. I can't get beyond the words of God."

" You wish to interpret them in the manner most convenient to yourself. Since you are so well up in the Bible, what about the passage that demands ' *An eye for an eye* ' ?"

" The God of vengeance may have demanded that, sir—never the God of love."

" Ask the Germans how much the God of love enters into their calculations !" sneered the Military Representative; " it must be obvious to every normal intellect that we were never meant to love hordes of barbarians like those we have at present to combat."

The man hesitated; fumbled for words; opened his mouth once or twice; then : " But the laws of the Almighty weren't meant to hold good only in times of peace, sir !"

A ripple of laughter and applause ran through the crowd and was severely repressed. The applicant was told that exemption would be granted him if he returned to his employment with the Government-firm, or took up other work of national importance. He shook his head in answer to both suggestions, and his appeal was dismissed.

And then Dennis's name was called. . . . They were both actually to go through it now, he and she; no longer mere spectators of other people's anguish and suspense. She would have liked to touch his hand and whisper " Good luck . . . ." as the other women did to their men, but he did not even glance down at her as he passed by, with sombre, preoccupied gaze and furrowed brow. He took his place. She could see him in profile—if she looked. But at first she could not bear to look, knowing him there before the twenty-five, defenceless and at bay. Nor did she take in the meaning of his words, when he began to speak.

With all her faculties and thoughts concentrated upon the final issue, she sat tense and rigid—as Dennis must have sat through Alan's tribunal. Alan had been in prison for three months already. If they offered him release now, at the price of abandonment of his principles, she wondered if he would accept it. Gladly, perhaps how gladly. . . Always at Miss Mowbray's one heard tales of the things that were being done to the conscientious objectors in prison. Could those fat, bald-headed old gentlemen who sat there in judgment really be callous enough to condemn Dennis to things of that sort?

The Chairman was saying : " So you think all

warfare is wrong : I daresay a good many people
share that view, but most of them are fighting all
the same, realising that that is the only way to end
this particular war."

Dennis replied : " It is my firm belief that I
should not in any way be benefiting humanity by
taking part in this war, as I am convinced that there
is no such thing as a ' war to end war,' and that
victory would only lead to successive wars, each
more terrible than the last ; also that the solution of
international disputes should be sought in arbitra-
tion and diplomacy, rather than in bloodshed."

The old gentleman sitting nearest to Dennis trucu-
lently demanded if he had held these views previous
to August, 1914.

" Certainly," he answered.

" How can you prove that ? Have you ever
written or stated in public anything of the sort before 1914 ?"

" No ; but most of my friends were acquainted
with my views. I'm afraid I can't offer you any
more definite proof. You must take my word for it."

The old gentleman grunted, and relapsed into
silence. Antoinette hoped and thought that this
was the end, but immediately another interlocutor
rose in place of the first.

" Does the applicant not differentiate between a
righteous war, a war of self-defence—and one waged
for gain and greed, with the sole object of crushing
smaller nations ?"

" I'm afraid I can't think of any war as a
righteous war—war in all its essentials being so pro-
foundly unrighteous. And as to the comparison of
the respective war-aims of the Allies and of Germany—who can say at this stage that England is

only fighting to avenge Belgium, and with no view
to the conquest of enemy territory or the extension of
power? What about the conquest of German colonies
in East Africa? The French say they won't make
peace till they've got Alsace-Lorraine back. Have
they the right to it? Alsace-Lorraine was German
territory before ever it became French—before they
got it back again in 1870."

"Yes, yes, young man, you're not here to teach
us history," the first speaker cut him short, and
the second rejoined : "Nor to give us your highly
unpatriotic views of your country's war-aims. It's
your business to fight for your country, not to criti-
cise it."

"If I am sent out to kill, surely I have the right
to question the cause that requires me to convert
myself into a murderer."

"'Right or wrong, my country'—that's the line
for every true Briton to take up."

"I am a humanitarian before I am a 'true
Briton,' then, if either the 'right' or the 'wrong'
of my country involves the deliberate slaughter of
human beings."

The suffragette who had spoken to them in the
passage signified her approval of this by nodding
and smiling across at Antoinette. The girl flushed.
Her man was making a good fight, and she was
proud of him, even while she knew that she had no
right to think of him as her man, and hence no right
to her pride. But she could almost have wished
that he were being just a little less vehement : it
was obvious that the general attitude was hostile
towards him ; only the Chairman still appeared impartial, as he said : "You categorically refuse in
any way to help to carry on the war?"

" I do. I want to help to stop the war, and all possibility of future wars. My justification for being here is my confirmed belief that I am doing more towards that end by adhering to my refusal to fight than by unthinkingly and unquestioningly going out to kill."

Again there was a murmur of applause; and a moment's silence followed. Antoinette glanced from one to the other of the men's faces; she longed to tackle each of the twenty-five separately, to beseech and implore him to be merciful. She tried to pick out at least one, whose physiognomy held a promise of tolerance or understanding; but there seemed to be an absurd family-likeness between them : they all looked pompous, comfortable, overfed; and at the present moment, righteously indignant. These old men had lived their lives; they would neither be called upon to shed their blood for their country, nor to go to prison, if they upheld opposing views; they had probably sent their sons to the war, but of themselves no personal sacrifice would be demanded. They were old—they were safe—and what right had they to send out the young men to kill each other? What right to sit in judgment upon one with all the potentialities of life still before him? To decree whether he was to be allowed to act according to his principles, or faced with the alternative of being forced to violate them or cast into prison?

Like the suffragette, Antoinette tried to " will " them into the required frame of mind. Perhaps some of her " willing " was having its effect. That moment's silence could surely be taken as a good sign?

But already the unctuous tones of the Military Representative had terminated the silence.

"The applicant is so very anxious to end the war at all costs : does he realise that there are not two ways but only one way in which he can help to do so?"

"I've declared the reasons for my unwillingness to take that one way," returned Dennis.

Another endless-seeming pause; looks and inaudible remarks exchanged between the old gentlemen.

Antoinette held her breath.

"*Total exemption granted*"—could not all her wishing or "willing" force the Chairman to speak those words? He was about to speak now :

"Clear the court!"

With sighs of exasperation at the renewed delay, the people rose and crowded into the passage again. The young man's mother was crying. The reporters scribbled ceaselessly in their notebooks.

The suffragette was congratulating Dennis. "You made a splendid stand, splendid, but they're prejudiced against the ' conscience ' men; it's easy to see that."

Yes, he had made a splendid stand, but Antoinette would have liked him to come to her for reassurance . . . . to whisper to her in the crowd : "I was all right, wasn't I?"

He evidently had no need of her reassurance. With an abstracted smile, he thanked the suffragette for her congratulations, and stood gazing out of the window, as if determined to keep unshared whatever turmoil of fear and hope might be passing in his mind. But perhaps if the words were spoken, that they both longed to hear, and the appalling strain snapped, he would turn to her. . . .

The bank-clerk's mother was moaning : " If only they'd be quick and tell us—can't they see we need him more than the army does?"

But at present the Board showed no signs of " being quick." A man carrying a tray laden with tea-things had just unceremoniously jostled aside the crowd and entered the court. He was followed by a boy with a very large cherry cake. The old gentlemen were going to have tea. . . . Antoinette suddenly understood some of the feelings that had given rise to the French Revolution! Soon the sound of hearty laughter mingled with the rattle of cups. The old gentlemen were apparently telling each other funny stories, while the people waited outside in suspense and agony of mind.

For a weary half-hour they were still kept in the passage. Then at last the doors were flung open again.

The Chairman stated that in the case of the bank-clerk who was the sole support of his family, the Board had decided to grant three months' exemption, with leave to appeal again. The decision was cheered, and the mother cried hysterically : " Oh, thank you—thank you so much . . . ." and was led out on her son's arm.

" In the case of Mr. Dennis Blackwood—Non-Combatant Service."

In dead silence they walked to the Charing Cross Tube station, the strain between them almost intolerable. If only he were to break down, so that she might comfort him. . . .

Non-Combatant Service—that, as far as Dennis was concerned, amounted to a sentence to penal servitude. Quite shamelessly she wished that he would compromise now; hated with all her might the principles and convictions that would not allow him to do so.

He said at last : " Good girl, to have stood by me."

" I'd stand by you through worse than that," she cried, " if only you wanted me to."

Another long silence. Then : " I'll let you know when I get my notice to join up—I suppose it'll be in a day or two. I won't go without saying good-bye to you."

" Dennis."

" Well?"

" Dennis . . . . must you—are you really going to . . . .?"

He laughed drearily. " You ask that now? Why, what would Alan say, if I ratted at the eleventh hour?"

" Alan wouldn't know . . . ." was her thought. But she was glad that she cared enough for Dennis to keep it to herself.

.   .   .   .   .   .

From day to day he waited now, expecting his call. Alan's had come within four days of the rejection of his appeal, but there seemed to be no definite rule as to the length of time that might elapse. He might be left in peace for a week, or the call might come to-morrow. The uncertainty seemed an additional and superfluous refinement of cruelty, a veritable sword of Damocles, the presence of which sometimes preyed on his nerves to such an extent that he felt inclined to precipitate its fall by giving himself up to the police without further delay. . . .

Abysmal terror dogged his heels by day and by

night; terror of being held, actually held to one place, when he had longed to throw off all bonds, tangible and intangible; terror of monotony and brutality, and the depths to which his own mind, thrust back upon itself, might sink. Day after day went by, and still the call did not come. But he was too heavily oppressed to be able to appreciate this added span of freedom. It might be ended at any moment. The uncertainty precluded all possibility of enjoyment.

Day after day he waited; and waited. . . .

And then the creative impulse which had temporarily lain dormant stirred in him anew. At first he struggled against it, knowing the futility of starting upon any great composition now; but as usual the power within him proved stronger than himself. He was its slave, and he had to obey.

His opera, " Karen and the Red Shoes," was still unfinished, but he recognised that the ideas which crowded his brain now could not be used to complete it; they were too big, too heavy for the subject. Almost independent of his own volition, they began to build themselves into a great symphonic poem : " War."

A chaos of conflicting motives bewildered him; he could hear each instrument clamouring at cross-purposes with all the others in the orchestra; clashing rhythms and counter-rhythms battled for supremacy. It seemed at first a labour for giants to bring order into this chaos, to select and reject wisely among the dissonant themes. Then he began to perceive that he must eliminate none, reject none; each must have its place in the scheme, for each stood for one of the innumerable beliefs and reasons, ideals and madnesses that had led the peoples into

war . . . . all must be woven in until, in the final
solution and climax, he had succeeded in showing
their fundamental unity, converting strife and turmoil and the sorrows of all the nations into the tran-
scendent harmony of peace.

And throughout, the image of Alan stood to him
for inspiration. Into his work he poured all the love
and the tenderness and the passion that the boy had
kindled in him. Feverishly he worked now, fearing
that in the space of time that remained—and it could
not possibly be long—he would not be able to accomplish his task. It was of necessity written for a very
large orchestra, and many months, if not years,
might go to the scoring of it.

He perceived his goal ahead, knowing that he
would not be able to reach it in time ; not before that
steadily-approaching shadow entirely blotted out the
light. . . . He could have prayed for more days,
and more in which to work : and awoke every morning to the knowledge that this might be his last day
of freedom.

And for Antoinette, also, this knowledge.

CHAPTER IV

"HALLO, Dennis, still at large? That's one's
habitual form of greeting nowadays, isn't it?"
Benny Joseph joined Dennis and Antoinette at their
table in the tea-shop.

"Still at large, thanks for kind enquiries. I
think they must have forgotten all about me. It's
nearly two months now . . . . what about you?"

"I've just had my appeal dismissed by the local
tribunal," replied Benny with an affectation of
indifference.

"We all share the same fate, apparently. What
happened, Benny?"

"I started off, of course, by telling them that
I was a Jew, but that I wasn't claiming exemption
on religious, but on socialistic grounds. I really
didn't get much further than that. The Chairman
said he didn't think my case worthy of a moment's
consideration as I had admitted myself to be an
atheist, and could therefore scarcely lay claim to
have a conscience!"

"Well, if that isn't the limit!" cried Dennis,
and Antoinette asked : "Are you going to appeal
again?"

"Oh, yes. Same old programme of delights for
all of us. Local tribunal—Central Court of Appeal
—arrival of police—prison! By the way, they
refused to renew Harry Hope's exemption when he
appealed the second time."

"What—has his widowed mother died in the
meantime?"

"No, I don't think so, but the Board seemed to

think that he had supported her long enough,
and that it was time he devoted his efforts to work
of greater importance than keeping a harmless
old lady in Chiswick from starvation. He'll look
simply fantastic in uniform, like poor Everard, do
you remember?"

The impersonator of many cardinals had been
killed during his first month at the Front. Antoinette could not but help wondering in what
manner he had died. She was haunted by memory
of a languid voice, saying: "This is all—so—
stupid. . . ." Haunted by memory of other voices,
too; Alan's vigorous speech; the youthful bombast
with which Oswald used to mask his terror; the
heavy lilt of Pegeen's and Conn's tones. And Conn
had been shot down in the streets of Dublin during
Easter week, proclaiming with his last breath, that
Ireland would never bend the knee "to England's
bloody red " . . . . And of Pegeen, no one had
heard; perhaps she had shared her man's fate—
but no one knew for certain.

"Our ranks are getting sadly depleted," said
Benny, "I see your friend Crispin has deserted
us."

Dennis laughed and Antoinette exclaimed: "Has
Crispin ratted, then? I didn't know." She saw
Dennis so rarely now, that it was small wonder that
she was not quite *au courant*.

"Crispin, yes, he ratted some time ago. Of
course, not a word of his appeal at the local tribunal
was audible, only a wild gurgling and spluttering.
But they thought it quite safe to dismiss the appeal
though they hadn't heard it; and he didn't like the
idea of going through it all again, so he just drifted
into the army, and now guards railway-bridges or

stands drearily at the end of a pier, reciting long Beethoven symphonies to himself."

Benny murmured : " ' *Lieb Vaterland, kannst ruhig sein* '—while Crispin guards our coasts."

" You're right. All the Zeppelins and submarines in the world wouldn't disturb him when he's listening to classical music played inside his own head."

" Poor Crispin," said Antoinette, " I suppose he never gets anywhere near a piano now." She had a quite absurd sentimental regard for Crispin : Crispin had played the Waldstein Sonata during her first talk with Dennis at Amberhurst; Crispin had figured throughout those letters from Devonshire. . . . .

Dennis replied : " Oh, don't make any mistake, he's amply provided for in that respect. He spends all his time getting himself adopted by old ladies possessing pianos—grand pianos only, of course, he won't touch an upright. . . . . And each of the old ladies thinks that this marvellously gifted Tommy is her own special discovery, and cherishes him accordingly. Crispin led them cherish. It gives them pleasure, and doesn't hurt him. He merely walks into the room, sits down at the piano, and plays for the full extent of his leave, with intervals for meals."

Antoinette glanced surreptitiously at Dennis. Whence arose this rather hectic animation on his part? There was about his whole manner to-day an air of suppressed excitement for which she was at a loss to account. A few minutes later, it was explained to her.

Benny said : " Mansfield's doing hard labour; he shared the common lot at his tribunal. I really

L'

don't know why they go through the farce of offering a man Non-Com., they might just as well arrest
him straight away. . . .   What about Rutherford,
Dennis : have you heard anything of him?"

"He's coming out for a few days next week,"
said Dennis, "I shall see him then. . . ."

.   .   .   .   .   .

Four weeks had elapsed for Antoinette without
sign or sound from Dennis. She scarcely thought
that he had been arrested, as he had promised to
let her know when he received his call; but she
dared not attempt to make sure by writing or
telephoning, lest he should think her importunate.
On the rare occasions when she was with him, he
seemed to keep her both mentally and physically at
a distance. She chafed at the waste of the days
drifting by.

If he had cared for her the least bit in the world;
if he had shared with her his terrors, how good those
days might have been, even while they knew that
each day might be his last.   But he would not share
with her, terrors that were for another as much as
for himself.   Dennis had kept staunch faith with
Alan, as far as Antoinette was concerned.

But though she might have Dennis perpetually
before an imaginary tribunal of her own; though
she might hurl the bitterest accusations at him—
"You've ruined my life . . . . you've made it
impossible for me to care about ordinary people
. . . . you've forced me to live in a crazy inverted
world that I didn't know existed, till you led me
into it—" neither these accusations, nor his confessed love for Alan, nor his aloof treatment of her,
could call forth the least flicker of hatred or condemnation. His defence was always ready to hand :

how could she hate or condemn the only man for
whom, with her peculiar temperament, she was
capable of feeling love? Love without any of its
usual corollaries; without faith, without glamour,
without illusion; without the slenderest hope of
fulfilment; just love alone, all the stronger, perhaps, for being stripped to its barest essentials.

She was surprised one day by a telephone-call
from Doreen Blackwood—Doreen agitated and in-
coherent. Clive was at Denmark Hill Hospital,
seriously wounded, and had Antoinette any idea
where Dennis was?

"Mummy and I came up yesterday to be with
Clive, and we wired Dennis that we were staying
at the Grosvenor Hotel, and he never turned up
there, so Mummy went to his lodgings this morning, and the landlady said he hadn't been there for
nearly three weeks. We thought perhaps you
might know something about him."

"I don't, Doreen, I've not seen him for ages."

"Oh, you don't think he's been put in prison,
do you? Surely he'd have had time to let us know.
He hasn't written home for ever so long, but then
he often does that. Antoinette, what *can* have
happened to him. . . .? As if it wasn't bad
enough, having Clive like this. . . . ."

They arranged finally that whichever of them
first succeeded in discovering Dennis's whereabouts,
should inform the other. When she had rung off,
it struck Antoinette that Barnaby might know; she
therefore dashed off to Fleet Street, glad that she
had at last a valid excuse for trying to ascertain
what had become of Dennis. But on arriving at
the office of "The Dove," she was told that Mr.

Barnaby had gone to Manchester to attend a socialist meeting, and would not be back for a few days. Antoinette determined to try Miss Mowbray's next; perhaps Miss Mowbray herself, or one of the *habitués* could shed some light upon the mystery. It was three o'clock, the hour at which the tea-shop was usually empty. If Miss Mowbray could tell her nothing, she would have to wait till the others began to straggle in.

As she had anticipated, the tea-room was deserted save for one man who sat at a table with his back to the door, head buried in his hands.

" Dennis !"

At her cry, he slowly raised his head, looked at her with a dazed stupefied expression.

Involuntarily she drew back from him. " Dennis —what's the matter?"

Still he sat looking at her.

" Is it—have you had your call?" But even while she asked, she knew that it was not that—not that alone.

" I've seen him," Dennis said at last, " in the prison hospital. They moved him there from the cells because he had a bad attack of fever. And when he's better, he's got to go back again—back to that hell. . . ."

He went on, as if unable to stop, now that he had begun : " He's been in solitary confinement—think what that means to an active brain like his ! The gnawing everlasting boredom and terror, the helpless exasperation at it all. . . He tries to draw on the walls of his cell with his finger-nails—or counts the flies crawling up the bars of the windows— invents foolish games just to keep his mind from giving way—talks aloud to himself for fear of losing

the use of his voice.   Then there are senseless cruel
punishments—sleep made impossible by having his
bed removed; nothing but bread and water to eat;
hours in a dark underground cell infested by rats—
this in a country that calls itself civilised!   Sometimes they ask him if he'll join the army if he's
let out—rather like using thumb-screws to force a
man into confession.   He kicked one of the men
who asked him, and was given twenty-four hours
in the strait-jacket.   The militarist papers declare
that the strait-jacket doesn't injure the man, and
is merely good discipline.   Good discipline, Oh,
God. . . . .   Do you know what it's like, Antoinette?   It's a narrow strip of canvas as long as
a man's body, but not as wide, and it's laced tightly
round him with cords, usually with one of the
warders digging a knee into his back, so as to
prevent him from holding his breath and so gain-
ing an extra inch of space.   Then he's left, trussed
up like that, alone on the floor of his cell, gasping
for breath, the cords cutting into his flesh, all the
organs of his body being squeezed and tortured——"

" Dennis, Dennis, don't—I can't bear it. . . ."

" Alan's had to bear it—more than once.   The
governor of the prison seems to have a special spite
against him.   There's no escape unless he promises
to give in.   And he won't do that.   He's an emaci-
ated wreck, but he's determined that they sha'n't
crush him, even though he's going through things
more devilish than any your imagination could have
devised for him, Antoinette, when you hated him
most !"

She was stung to reply : " I never hated him like
that.   You're unjust and cruel to think that I
should."

" Yes, I daresay I am . . . . I'm sorry. . . .
But I'm at the end, just at the end of everything,
and I hardly know what I'm saying."

And at the utter misery of him, she knew only one
longing : to break down all the artificial barriers
that had arisen between them, and to take his head
between her hands. . . . " Say what you like, my
dear, go on telling me, if it helps at all."

" I'd heard some weeks ago that he'd got special
permission to go and see his mother, who was ill, and
I'd arranged to meet him and spend all his spare
time with him. He never turned up, and I discovered that his permission had been withdrawn—
for goodness' knows what petty breach of the regulations—and that he was in the punishment-cells.
The next thing I heard was that he and nine others
were being removed to Princetown. Through miles
and miles of red tape I tried to get permission to
see him. I stayed down there waiting and waiting
for it. Well, it came at last . . . ." his voice sank
almost to a whisper; " I can't sleep at night, for
thinking of the look in his eyes, and knowing that
when his brief respite is over, they'll send him back
to go through all their vile indignities and privations
and cruelties again. It's the idea of his going back,
Antoinette—— !"

" Oh, don't—don't . . . ." she was sobbing outright now, in an agony of pity for that vivid, brilliant boy, in an agony of fear for the man before
her. Helplessly she cast about in her mind for
something that might bring comfort to Dennis.

" Even if they make him endure all that, they're
not winning really—not succeeding in making him
give himself to the army. So he's winning in the
end, Dennis, he's beating them,"

He gave her a look of gratitude. " But what a price to pay for victory. . . . And he'll have to go on paying as long as this cursed war lasts. We shall all have to go on paying. I've had my call, too, you know, for the day after to-morrow. I ought to see mother."

She told him then the reason that had sent her to look for him here.

" Clive wounded? What's happened, did they say?"

" Doreen wasn't very explicit over the telephone. He's got a poisoned arm, I think, and a wound in the face."

" Poor mother—I'm sorry for her. . . . But Clive will have his family and his girl at his bedside, and every possible care and attention. . . . He fell into brooding silence, thinking of a bare prison hospital, and an unsympathetic prison doctor. " Well, as they're in town I'll spend to-morrow with them. And I'll say good-bye to you now, Antoinette."

" Yes . . . ."

He looked at her with great unhappy eyes. " There's nothing we can either of us say, is there?"

" Nothing . . . ."

Of all that she longed to say to him—nothing, now that this moment of parting had been thrust upon her with such suddenness. Useless to make any attempt to say anything. But because it was the last time, she wondered, would he at least leave her memory of his lips on hers—just for the last time?

Already his thoughts had rushed many miles away from her. " It's as if some particularly terrible fate were always reserved for the people I love most. There was Eric—he had his hell to go through. And now Alan . . . ." Almost inaudibly he added : " And he's such a kid . . . ."

His voice held the pain and tenderness of a mother whose child has been stricken to death.

" Good-bye, Dennis . . . ." She turned quickly away so that he might not see the tears that blinded her, and left him standing there, gazing fixedly at the walls that had once echoed with Alan's rhetoric.

And at the top of the stairs she was met by an insolent smiling wraith.

" In case we never meet again. . . . don't hate me too much . . . ."

She acknowledged the completeness of her rival's victory. Alan could triumph over her still.

CHAPTER V

"*Chérie*, it is most inconsiderate of you always to go out without telling anyone where you are going. Madame la Comtesse de Froment rang you up on the telephone—doubtless she wished to invite you to her big concert in aid of the French Red Cross—and I could not tell her where you were, nor when you would be in, because I did not know. I agree for once with your father and your grandmother, that it is not *convenable* for a *jeune fille* to run about London as you do."

"You allow yourself more freedom than I as a young man was allowed at your age."

"It is that young Blackwood who has taught you these Bohemian manners."

"After all, we never knew his family."

"As I have always said, you cultivate the wrong people."

"Yes, if you would try to make yourself a little more amiable to my friends . . . ."

"Your behaviour towards M. Lefèvre was disgraceful. No wonder he did not press his suit more ardently. You are spoiling your life. It will be your own fault if you remain an old maid."

"Till now one has let you do as you pleased. But it is agreed that in future one will have to be more severe."

CHAPTER VI

IT was pouring with rain when Antoinette reached
Haywards Heath, where she had to change for
Eastwold. She had had considerable difficulty with
her people before being allowed to undertake this
journey. They were by now quite convinced that
the Blackwoods were a bad influence for her, and
that sooner or later she would contrive to become
engaged to that very eccentric young man . . . .

Antoinette did not think it necessary to mention
that the very eccentric young man was in prison,
but pleaded her friendship with Doreen, and her
need of a change of air . . . . pleaded very gently,
for these were not the days when she felt capable of
facing a hard conflict of wills.

In the old days she had relished a good up-hill
fight; the harder the battle the more valuable the
victory. So she had thought years ago when she
had met Hester. Hester . . . .

" Sing before breakfast—cry before night "—
Hester had been wise. Those early years had held
enough song and laughter and sunshine. But now
the years seemed drained for her of all song and
laughter and sunshine, just as she herself felt
drained of all the exuberant vitality that had once
led her to rejoice in battle. She was tired now, and
there was nothing left in all the world worth fighting
for.

The train for Eastwold drew up at the platform,
its windows so blurred with the rain that it was
impossible to see into the compartments. Gripping
her suit-case with one hand, Antoinette struggled

to open the door nearest to her, and immediately a soldier from the far end of the compartment sprang forward, helped her to lift the suit-case on to the rack, and then resumed his seat beside the girl who sat huddled by the window. Antoinette wished that she could have drawn back and chosen a different compartment. It was a shame that she should have obtruded herself upon their solitude. But already the guard was blowing his whistle, and several other Tommies had entered the compartment too, so that in any case the couple in the corner would not have remained undisturbed. They sat without speaking, arms interlaced, occasionally looking at each other. And the girl had a pretty, pasty, tear-sodden face under a gaudy hat with red roses on it; and he had round boyish eyes and a rather stupid expression . . . .

The other Tommies had disposed themselves and their kit about the compartment. Above the rattle of the wheels Antoinette caught scraps of their conversation.

" When we were way over home, we thought this war was a grand fine thing, and not one of us wanted to be left out of it," a dapper young Canadian spoke, running his fingers through his upstanding brush of hair, " but now I've been out there a year, I tell you straight, *next* time my King and Country call, I'm going to be lame, blind, dumb, *and deaf.* Yes, when you've bin out and seen some of the sights and smelt some of the smells, and lived in a trench full of ver-*mine,* you find war isn't the gala garden-party you thought it was, with the band and the music and the flags flying."

One of his companions, a long-limbed Irishman, grunted assent. " I've lost an eye in this bloody war, but do you think they'd be afther givin' me my discharge? 'Ho,' sez the docthor, 'you're still plenty of use to your counthry'" . . . .

"Guess they won't be satisfied till you've lost the other eye to match," remarked the Canadian cheerfully.

"And fwhat's ut all for, that's fwhat I'm askin', fwhat's ut all for? I'm no revolutionist; I'm only askin' fwhy . . . . Divil a bit did we care about the *Sinn Féin* rebellion out there in the thrinches as long as we had enough cigarettes to smoke. Which we had not . . . ." The melancholy cadence of his voice reminded Antoinette poignantly of Pegeen and Conn.

The third man, a little Cockney chap, tilted his cap to a rakish angle. "They say as it'll all be over in the spring."

"*Which* spring?" demanded the Canadian, and the Cockney embarked irrelevantly upon a personal reminiscence: "It was near Am-an-tears, we got to a village that the 'Uns 'ad evacuated. Leastways, they'd evacuated wot was left of it, and that's not sayin' much. Bin up to some o' their usual tricks, they 'ad, with wimmen and kids and wotnot . . . . One o' their snipers got left be'ind—swarmed up a tree, and four of us yanked 'im dahn; and first we said a few things to 'im . . . . and then we did a few things to 'im, just for luck, as you might say, and because of wot 'e and 'is pals 'ad bin up to in that village. War's a funny thing . . . ." he continued musing, "you could 'ave knocked me dahn with a feather two years ago if you'd told me I'd 'elp to cut aht that bloomin' 'Un's' 'eart with my bloomin' jack-knife!"

"Yes, war's a funny thing," the Irishman broke

out again, " and they don't want ut to end—them
that make the war. ' Your pals in the thrinches
are callin' to you '—'tis a lie! Your pals in the
thrinches would say : ' Keep out of this if you can,
we'd never have gone into it if we'd known.' We
know well enough *who* calls to us and *who* sends
us out to ut. 'Tis the Government sitting at home,
and never your pals out there. . . . And 'tis the
same on the other side. I took a prisoner once.
The man was wounded and I looked after him a
bit; got quite fond of him, too. I was sorry when
he died . . . . He said that their men are as dead
fed-up with it as we are."

The couple in the corner seemed quite oblivious
of the conversation. They might have been deaf to
it. Only the silent fervour with which they gazed
into each other's eyes increased. . . .

At the next station the man opened the door of
the compartment and helped the girl out; then he
kissed her, and got into the train again.

She said : " Good-bye, Gawd bless you, Dickie,"
and he answered : " So long! See you again when
the war's over—perhaps . . . ."

The train moved on. Alone in his corner the man
sat staring straight before him, inarticulate misery
incarnate. " When the war's over—perhaps ". . .

Antoinette choked, and wished again that he and
the girl who had been left on the platform could
have had this last journey to themselves. In the
circumstances he might have been forgiven for
showing less willingness to help her in with her
suit-case.

.   .   .   .

Arthur Griggs, home on leave, had come with
his *fiancée*, Millie Ryan, to call upon the Black-

woods; and Antoinette, on her arrival, fell straight
into the tea party, as she had once fallen into the
nursery party held in Reggie's honour the day of
the dance. Reggie was home from school now, and
sat at the foot of the couch on which Clive was
reclining . . . . Clive with one empty sleeve and
a badly scarred face and mouth.

"Well, well, you've at least got plenty to show
for it, plenty to show for it," Griggs rallied him.
"I'm often sorry that my honourable scars aren't
—ah—on exhibition."

"I'm sure Millie isn't sorry," smiled Mrs. Blackwood.

Millie looked coy, and Lily who was sitting at
Clive's side, and helping him to manipulate his tea-
cup, exclaimed : "What does it matter what they
look like when they come back to us, as long as we
know they've done their bit? I'd rather have Clive
as he is than the greatest Adonis in the world."

Clive smiled wryly up at her with his twisted
lip. "I could do with the other arm all the same,
you know, Lil."

"Never mind, my boy," cried Mr. Blackwood,
"when your children ask you what you did in the
great war, they won't have far to look."

"And one can really say here that your wife will
be your right hand," said Griggs, "I can only hope
that you and Miss Hallard will be as happy as
Millie and I intend to be."

"And we hope you'll be as happy as *we're* jolly
well going to be !" returned Lily, boisterously.

"Quite a competithion of happineth, ithn't it?"
giggled Amy.

"I think there can be no doubt that where there is
sympathy there is happiness," mused Griggs;

"sympathy is a beautiful thing, don't you agree?"
His audience assented collectively, and he went on:
"Millie, of course, calls forth sympathy as naturally as the sun draws out the scent of the
flowers. . . ."

There was a murmur of approval, and Millie said:
"Why, Arthur, you're quite a poet this afternoon."

"Not a poet, Millie, not a poet. Just an ordinary
man. But might not even an ordinary man turn
poet for your sake?"

Millie blushed. "Oh, you're flattering me."

"You doubt my sincerity?" exclaimed Griggs,
very injured. "I assure you that I place sincerity
on the same high level as sympathy. Sincerity and
sympathy—my twin ideals . . . ."

Millie, quite embarrassed by now, turned to ask
Clive how he had received his wounds, but Reggie
interrupted with: "Clive hates talking about them
—it looks like swank."

"Clive doesn't need to swank," said Lily, "we
all know what he's done. Those three Huns—not
bad, that, not bad!"

Griggs beamed upon the assembled company.
"Who would have thought two years ago when we
were getting ready for the fancy dress dance that
we should all come together again like this? Seeing
you here, Miss Antoinette, reminded me of that
happy occasion. Little Miss Ottilie was there too—
but I suppose the least said about her the better;
Reggie's looking at me so fiercely . . . ."

"Her *fiancée* has been killed," said Doreen, "I
got such a sad, funny letter from her through
Switzerland. She said that her 'truest-loved
Joachim for his Fatherland has died, and that her
heart broken was' . . . ."

"Poor little Britannia," cried Antoinette, "I wonder if he was one of the three whom Clive sniped?"

"Good job," muttered Reggie.

"War's war," said Lily tersely, shrugging her shoulders.

"All I can hope is," the irrepressible Griggs continued, "that two years hence we shall be as complete as we are now."

Clive grunted, and Griggs strove to cheer him. "Come—come—come—we all know you don't really mind having lost your arm. Not a bit. Proud of it. And quite right too! When I said ' complete,' I meant as far as numbers go. Here we all are—" Suddenly he recollected himself; floundered; coughed behind his hand, and repeated rather feebly : " I mean here we are . . . ."

"Yes, of course, we are, Mr. Griggs." With admirable tact Mrs. Blackwood came to his assistance . . . . and Antoinette wondered if it could bring Dennis's mother the slightest degree of comfort to know that her thoughts also were with the one who was not included in the " all."

She could not rid herself of the impression that Dennis might be expected at any moment to enter with dramatic suddenness, as he had entered the night of the dance. It seemed as if they were all laughing and talking here, just to mark time in anticipation of his arrival. And when, sharply, the drawing-room door was flung open, her heart gave a great leap.

"The maid from Dr. Clavering's would like to speak to you, please, sir . . . ." The parlourmaid addressed Mr. Blackwood in an undertone, but already Doreen was on her feet.

"What is it?   Where is she?   Is there any news?" She freed herself from her father's detaining hand, and rushed to the door.   "Oh, what is it? What is it?"

The little servant who had been told to "break it gently" to Mr. Blackwood, completely lost her head on seeing Doreen, and sobbed out: "It's Mr. Hugh, Miss—killed in action Oh, the poor young master . . . ."

It seemed to be the general impulse to rush towards Doreen, as if by actual contact, by stroking, patting, embracing, to draw nearer to her in her isolation of grief. But there was something in the way she stood there, her back to the door, her eyes dead, mouth and hands twitching, that forbade further approach . . . . and Antoinette remembered on whose face she had seen just that same baffling expression. For a second, but it might have been an eternity, the group stood poised, alert, watching the rigid, dry-eyed little figure in the doorway.

Then at last Doreen's voice, a woman's voice and yet piteously childish, cut into the stillness.

"And I—I loved him so . . . ."

She turned and broke from the room.

Mr. and Mrs. Blackwood followed her.   The others remained as they were, talking in low voices.

"Thall I go and thee if they want anything?"

"No, better leave them alone together now."

"A good cry, you know, will do her all the world of good . . . ." this from Griggs.

"Ithn't thith war dreadful? You never know from one minute to the other, do you?"

"Poor old Hugh, I wonder how it happened. I expect some of his men will be able to give details.

I think I ought to go to Doreen. Mrs. Blackwood
will only encourage her to give way." Thus the
sternly practical Lily.

Clive muttered : " Poor little kid . . . ." and
Reggie, still sitting motionless on the end of the
couch, looked at his boots and scowled heavily.

" And to think that only two years ago—what a
handsome couple at your dance, eh, Millie? The
Black Knight and the Dresden Shepherdess. . . ."

Millie collapsed into tears.   " I can't bear it,
Arthur, I can't bear it. . . ."

Arthur patted her hand. " There, there, little
woman, there, there."

" Doreen's got plenty of grit," said Lily, " she'll
pull round all right. I'm sure he died game and
she'll be able to be proud of him. That'll stiffen
her backbone right enough."

But Clive only repeated : " Poor little kid " . . .

Griggs said : " Well, I suppose we'd better be
going," and followed by Amy, led his weeping bride
away. Reggie, even at this juncture mindful of
" good form," went to see them to the gate.

As Antoinette turned to go up to her room, she
heard Clive say : " Lily . . . ." and saw him put
out his remaining hand to draw her down to his
level.

" Dear old man. . . ."

Late that evening Antoinette sat at the window of
her room, and watched the last of the sunset fading
behind the dark ridge of the Downs. The crimson
light still stained the white walls, and danced upon
the gay flowered chintz . . . . a room in which to
feel very girlish and happy, so she had reflected on
her first arrival here, so she had reflected as she
donned her " Bacchante " costume. . . .

She shuddered and turned from the window to face Mrs. Blackwood.

"My dear child, I am so sorry that it should have happened just during your visit." Still obedient to the instincts of the good hostess, she was apologising to her guest for an unfortunate *contretemps* that had marred her stay. . . .

Antoinette said : " Oh, don't . . . ." and got no further.

Mrs. Blackwood sat down and wiped her eyes.

" Poor little Doreen—and they were to have been married next time he got leave—we'd begun to get one or two things together, though I always thought that was wrong, my family were always inclined to be superstitious—but of course Daddy laughed me out of it. . . . . Poor Hugh, he would have made her so happy—I feel is if I'd lost a son, too." She paused a moment, then went on in a lower voice : " Antoinette, do you think he'll be all right ? He's in solitary confinement now, but that's better than being together with a lot of other horrid people, isn't it ?"

" Much better," Antoinette assented without looking at her.

" I can talk to you about him, because you were always such good friends, and of course I daren't mention him before Clive or Daddy. Dennis was a great disappointment to his father, even as a little chap, when he wouldn't go out shooting with him, because he couldn't bear to see the animals hurt. . . . And now—it's dreadful, my dear : Daddy has struck his name out of the Family Bible, where we've got all the children's names and the date of their birth written down. . . ."

" Oh, what does that matter ?" cried Antoinette,

" that can't make him your boy any the less, can it?"

Mrs. Blackwood shook her head. " Nothing could ever do that. Denny would just be my boy, whatever he'd done, but his father has such high principles . . . . Lily keeps on saying that the people in prison are safe. You do think he's safe, don't you, Antoinette, although I lie awake some· times wondering if they give them enough blankets on their beds."

Safe . . . . in solitary confinement!

Oh, well, it was fortunate at least that Dennis's mother did not seem quite to realise. Did she suffer, perhaps, from a providential lack of imagination?

Antoinette gave the assurance required of her. " Yes, of course he's safe—quite safe."

But Mrs. Blackwood was uneasy. " If one knew for certain—how they are treated. . . ."

Antoinette was grateful to the increasing darkness that hid her face.

Mrs. Blackwood repeated : " If only one knew. . . ."

" He'll be quite safe," she could only trust herself to speak in a very low voice.

" Of course Daddy says they're well treated, and you do think so, too, don't you—really?"

Antoinette made a final effort. " He'll come out all right . . . . when the war's over——"

Her voice snapped.

CHAPTER VII

At the table in the alcove at Miss Mowbray's, Antoinette sat with Barnaby a few weeks later. He had let her know that he had heard from Dennis, and would pass on the news if she cared to meet him at the usual haunt.

"He's doing hard labour now, breaking stones in a quarry, but he says even that's a relief after solitary confinement. They put them into that at first, as if they were wild animals that had to be tamed."

"Does he—say anything else?" she asked tentatively, hoping that Dennis might have sent her some word or message.

Barnaby shook his head. "No, he doesn't say much, except that his hands will never be fit to play the piano again, and that one of the greatest torments is not being able to write down his music. You know what he was like over that—directly he'd got an idea, down it had to go, or he was afraid of losing it. He must be losing a good many now. Rather a waste." He pulled at his pipe, and continued more vehemently: "The silly waste of it all. . . . That boy Alan—hot-headed young devil he was, but he had the right stuff in him, and the personality and the understanding to make him a good leader of the people. Only instead of utilising his brains they have to let them rot!"

Antoinette sighed. "The utter futility of hoping that anyone from the other side will ever see our point of view. . . . When I was in the country with Dennis's people, I did try to make them see,

but I couldn't budge one of them; not an inch.
And then his little sister's *fiancé* was killed at the
Front—gassed—such a good-looking, golden-haired
boy—and it was too ghastly . . . . and suddenly
I felt—I mean, I understood how they might feel
towards pacifists. They don't seem to realise that
going to prison isn't fun. . . . ' Prison's safe,'
that's their argument. Or ' What are their sufferings compared with what the men in the trenches
have to go through?' They almost made one feel
—as if one hadn't the right. . . ."

Barnaby broke in : " It's not a case of measuring
the sufferings of the men in the trenches with those
of the men in prison. No one can be childish
enough to pretend that shrapnel-wounds and poison-
gas aren't a hundred times worse than whatever the
conscientious objectors may have to endure in
prison. The point is, that men who genuinely ob-
jected to take part in warfare, because they could
see no possible good that would result therefrom ;
men who refused to shelter themselves by enabling
others to go in their place, and who exposed themselves to ridicule and vilification, loss of friends and
loss of financial position, rather than be faithless to
their principles, should be flung into prison, and in
some cases treated worse than ordinary criminals.
This, mark you, in spite of the assertion that they
would be given a fair hearing ! The Government
regretted that clause relating to the conscience-men
in the Military Service Act, as soon as it was out.
They realised the folly of giving a loophole of
escape to any man, when the need of cannon-fodder
was so great. So the whole business became a
mockery—mock trials at which the men, having
been invited to state their views, stood condemned

before their cases were heard. How many of them were given the total exemption to which they had the right, according to the clause? And England is said to be fighting to uphold justice . . . .! Look at the uproar created by the so-called murder of Edith Cavell : the woman was a spy, and they were strictly within their military rights to shoot her. But it doesn't seem to strike people that shutting up some of these C.O.s in prison is deliberate, wilful murder of brains that were fine, sensitive instruments which might have brought some lasting beauty, some lasting wonder into the world. These men might be rendering far greater service to their country by following their natural bent than by doing navvies' work or performing silly brutalising tasks in prison.

" Of course the press is eager enough to make the public believe that prison is a sort of slacker's paradise, where they have quite a delightful time of it. . . . We know differently. Alan's isn't the only case of systematic brutality wreaked upon a defenceless victim. Only that kind of thing is carefully kept out of the papers. However magnificently England may think to figure in the world's history after the war, the gross stupidity and cruelty of the way she has treated the genuine pacifists should stand as an eternal blot upon her honour."

Antoinette did not interrupt him. She sat watching the bodiless legs that passed and passed in front of the blurred window, remembering the many different moods in which she had watched them. The tea-room was empty, save for the ghosts that sat grouped at the tables; almost she could have expected them to take part in the conversation. . . .

Dennis; Alan; Everard, with his languid drawl; Crispin's stammer; O'Farrell's Irish phrasing; the whole chorus of familiar voices. But the chorus was silent now.

"And the war goes on, and day by day the torture of those at the Front and those in the prisons goes on; and the schoolboys, the striplings of sixteen and seventeen, are growing up to face the choice of the two alternatives—children cherished and carefully reared, so that when they are still little more than children they may be ready for this. . . ."

"Oh, I know, I know," cried Antoinette, "there was poor little Oswald. . . . He talked to me once in a queer burst of confidence, and he said almost the same thing: 'It's waiting for you now, when you're eighteen. . . .' And I'm glad he's dead," she passed her hand over her eyes, as if to shut out some horror. "He took the cowards' way out, if you like, but I'd rather know him dead than think of him like the others, going on, and on . . . ."

Suddenly the door to the street was opened and banged. Footsteps came pelting down the crooked stairs, and Benny Joseph hurled himself into the tea-room.

"I've been turned down!" he cried incoherently, "turned down by the doctor after I was arrested. I'm a free man, Barnaby, do you hear? Totally exempt. . . . And I've got a part—this is my lucky day—I just walked into it—I'm going on tour in musical comedy for eighteen weeks!"

Benny was radiant and breathless, but he spoke to an audience of ghosts; ghost of Everard, long dead on the field in Flanders; ghost of Harry Hope, drilling drearily on Salisbury Plain; ghosts of the

many professionals of all grades who had once frequented Miss Mowbray's, and been gradually
sucked into the army, and who would have overwhelmed him with a flood of questions. Which
towns was he doing? Who was in the company?
Did he want addresses of rooms?

"I'm so awfully glad, Benny" . . . . Antoinette said warmly; she could not bear that he
should shout his joyful tidings into unresponsive
space; "do let me know if you're anywhere near
London; I'd love to see you in your show."

"Thanks ever so much. Yes, I'll let you know.
I say, I wish the others could have been as lucky.
. . . Well, I must be off now—millions of things
to do—letters to write—we start rehearsing next
week. Lord, it's a queer sensation not to have it
hanging over you any more. . . . And when the
war's over, I'll be able to go to Vienna and Paris
and Berlin and Budapest again, without feeling
I've helped to muck up any of the countries I'm
staying in. I *must* be off. Good-bye. . . ."

He was gone.

Barnaby smiled. "So Benny's aunts in the
various parts of Europe will at least be safe from
Benny's ridiculously inadequate shooting."

But Antoinette was not thinking of Benny's
aunts: she was thinking of the girl whose existence she had once heard rumoured—the little Jewish
girl, somewhere in Hampstead, to whom he would
ultimately turn. Antoinette envied that girl the
moment when she heard Benny's news.

"So they've all found their destiny," mused
Barnaby; then he bent his shaggy brows to a kind-
lier scrutiny of Antoinette herself. "And what
about you . . . .?"

She did not answer. Her thoughts were with the
couples, the many couples who had the right to each
other : Lily, who had the right to cherish her battered, broken Clive; Doreen, who through all her
pain, still had the right to cling to her memory of
Hugh; Millie, who could actually cling to Griggs;
Pegeen, who had probably died at her man's side;
little Mrs. Mansfield, staunchly awaiting her husband's release from prison; even the pasty-faced
girl in the train . . . . her man would write her
illiterate love-letters from the Front, for a little
while, perhaps . . . .

And all these women had the right to stand by
their men, in prison or at the Front; in the cause
of rebellion or in the cause of stamping out rebellion; wounded or even after death, they had this
right because their men loved or had loved them.

Doreen, by virtue of being on the popular, the
militarist side, had had the right to an official joy
and an official sorrow; to official congratulation and
official condolence. Antoinette's joy and sorrow had
alike been " unofficial." Not that she minded being
on the unpopular side. She could have enjoyed
being an Ishmaelite outside the gates of Eastwold,
enjoyed the rebel-sense of her unofficial right to
stand by him, if only he had loved her. But—by
his lack of love, he debarred her from this right,
just as she had been debarred from official congratulation and condolence. She was an outcast in
a double sense; an Ishmaelite twice over.

" Well?" said Barnaby.

" I? Oh, I don't know where I come in. I think
I don't come in at all. . . ."

He nodded. " I understand. May I say I'm
sorry for you? You know I don't mean it as an

insult. . . . What is to become of you, though?"

She smiled wearily. " I suppose I too—just go
on. . . ."

" Yes. I'm afraid you're the symbol of what has
to be sacrificed to the love between man and man."

" He couldn't have done otherwise "—loyally she
was prepared to defend Dennis against anything
that even his friend might have to say about him.
" He was made like that, and he made things more
difficult for himself by bottling up all his thoughts
and feelings, and being terribly afraid of them, and
never telling anyone about them—till he told me."

" He never told me," said Barnaby, " at least not
in so many words. But I could see for myself.
He's got a queer strain of the maternal in him. It's
obvious in the way he looks upon his work, and in
the way he looks upon that boy. . . . It's
a woman's passion as well as a man's that he feels
for Alan ; virile and yet tender ; stronger even than
death or madness ; a wonderful motive-force that
might accomplish much . . . . only the world
would condemn it as an evil, vicious growth that
should be stamped out ! We want more light, more
breathing-space, more tolerance and understanding : not this narrow-minded wholesale condemnation and covering-up ; this instinctive shuddering
and turning away from a side of nature that, like
every other side, has its right to a hearing, its right
to open discussion."

" Everybody seems to imagine that you're abnormal because you *like* being abnormal," Antoinette burst out, " just as they imagine that men go
to prison because they like it better than going to
the Front. As if being different from normal
people weren't curse enough in itself, without hav-

ing them think it's your own choice, and that you
enjoy being different!"

"Of course there are those who enjoy it—who
wallow in the perverted sensations of their abnormality, as normal sensualists wallow in their own
' permissible' lusts. And by these, the worst
types—or perhaps the most to be pitied—the multitude judges them all, just as they judge the whole
class of conscientious objectors by those actuated
only by fear for their own skins. They don't attempt to separate the grain from the chaff : the
innocent have to suffer with the guilty."

"It's a pity no one thinks of saving the guilty
for the sake of the innocent!" she cried.

"Christ thought of it, my dear girl, many long
years ago; and look what a mess they're making of
His teachings now. . . . But perhaps these men
who stand mid-way between the extremes of the
two sexes are the advance-guard of a more en-
lightened civilisation. They're despised and rejected of their fellow-men to-day. What they suffer
in a world not yet ready to admit their right to
existence, their right to love, no normal person can
realise; but I believe that the time is not so far
distant when we shall recognise in the best of our
intermediate types the leaders and masters of the
race."

He paused, and went on : "They *do* wander
through dark ways at present, there's no denying
it; and some of them understand themselves and
the eternal conflicts of their nature as little as others
understand them. The normal person cries :
' Don't encourage them—stamp them out—imprison
them—crush them——' You can't crush them;
you can't stamp them out; they've got to be

reckoned with. From them a new humanity is being evolved, and in the process of evolution Nature produces all sorts of poor little deformities and abnormalities as samples. They're necessary to the production of the higher type, though, the bad specimens put out from every factory or work-shop. Bad specimens—and yet forerunners! For out of their suffering, out of pain and confusion and darkness, will arise something great—something God-given : the human soul complete in itself, per-fectly balanced, not limited by the psychological bounds of one sex, but combining the power and the intellect of the one with the subtlety and intuition of the other ; a dual nature, possessing the extended range, the attributes of both sides, and therefore loving and beloved of both alike."

With brimming eyes she listened to him; and then she put the question that Mrs. Blackwood had so often put to her :

" Do you . . . . think Dennis will be all right?"

" I think he'll keep his reason, if that's what you mean, even if he's never able to write a note of music again. But even so—one can't say that it is all for nothing : those train-loads and boat-loads of cheery boys taken from the land, the workshops, the universities, who go out singing and joking to their death; who never did anything remarkable in their life before, and yet who do incredibly plucky things on the battlefield ; the patient heroes on both sides who do their bit and much more than their bit, because it's been instilled into their faithful hearts that it's right that they should do it—it is for love of these, and to save these and such as these in the generations to come that Alan and Dennis and others like them are making their sacrifice!

And then to label the lot of them cowards——" He broke off, and sat a while silently brooding. Then he shrugged his shoulders. " Oh, well : people don't think. . . ."

THE END.

HOMOSEXUALITY

**Lesbians and Gay Men
in Society, History and Literature**

Acosta, Mercedes de. **Here Lies The Heart.** 1960

Bannon, Ann. **I Am a Woman.** 1959

Bannon, Ann. **Journey To a Woman.** 1960

Bannon, Ann. **Odd Girl Out.** 1957

Bannon, Ann. **Women in The Shadows.** 1959

Barney, Natalie Clifford. **Aventures de L'Esprit.** 1929

Barney, Natalie Clifford. **Traits et Portraits.** 1963

Brooks, Romaine. **Portraits, Tableaux, Dessins.** 1952

Carpenter, Edward. **Intermediate Types Among Primitive Folk.** 1919

Casal, Mary. **The Stone Wall.** 1930

Cory, Donald Webster. **The Homosexual in America.** 1951

Craigin, Elisabeth. **Either Is Love.** 1937

Daughters of Bilitis. **The Ladder.** Volumes I - XVI. Including an **Index To The Ladder** by Gene Damon. 1956 - 1972. Nine vols.

Documents of the Homosexual Rights Movement in Germany, 1836 - 1927. 1975

Ellis, Havelock and John Addington Symonds. **Sexual Inversion.** 1897

Fitzroy, A. T. **Despised and Rejected.** 1917

Ford, Charles and Parker Tyler. **The Young and Evil.** 1933

Frederics, Diana. **Diana: A Strange Autobiography.** 1939

Friedlaender, Benedict. **Renaissance des Eros Uranios.** 1904

A Gay Bibliography. 1975

A Gay News Chronology, 1969 - May, 1975. 1975

Gordon, Mary. **Chase of the Wild Goose.** 1936

Government Versus Homosexuals. 1975

Grosskurth, Phyllis. **John Addington Symonds.** 1964

Gunn, Peter. **Vernon Lee: Violet Paget, 1856 - 1935.** 1964

A Homosexual Emancipation Miscellany, c. 1835 - 1952. 1975

Karsch-Haack, F[erdinand]. **Das Gleichgeschlechtliche Leben der Naturvölker.** 1911

Katz, Jonathan. **Coming Out!** 1975

Lesbianism and Feminism in Germany, 1895 - 1910. 1975

Lind, Earl. **Autobiography of an Androgyne.** 1918

Lind, Earl. **The Female-Impersonators.** 1922

Loeffler, Donald L. **An Analysis of the Treatment of the Homosexual Character in Dramas Produced in the New York Theatre From 1950 to 1968.** 1975

Mallet, Françoise. **The Illusionist.** 1952

Miss Marianne Woods and Miss Jane Pirie Against Dame Helen Cumming Gordon. 1811 - 1819

Mattachine Society. **Mattachine Review.** Volumes I - XIII. 1955 - 1966. Six vols.

Mayne, Xavier. **Imre: A Memorandum.** 1908

Mayne, Xavier. **The Intersexes.** 1908

Morgan, Claire. **The Price of Salt.** 1952

Niles, Blair. **Strange Brother.** 1931

Olivia. **Olivia.** 1949

Rule, Jane. **The Desert of the Heart.** 1964

Sagarin, Edward. **Structure and Ideology in an Association of Deviants.** 1975

Steakley, James D. **The Homosexual Emancipation Movement in Germany.** 1975

Sturgeon, Mary C. **Michael Field.** 1921

Sutherland, Alistair and Patrick Anderson. **Eros: An Anthology of Friendship.** 1961

Sweet, Roxanna Thayer. **Political and Social Action in Homophile Organizations.** 1975

Tobin, Kay and Randy Wicker. **The Gay Crusaders.** 1972

Ulrichs, Carl Heinrich. **Forschungen Über Das Rätsel Der Mannmännlichen Liebe.** 1898

Underwood, Reginald. **Bachelor's Hall.** 1937

[Vincenzo], Una, Lady Troubridge. **The Life of Radclyffe Hall.** 1963

Vivien, Renée **Poèmes de Renée Vivien.** Two vols. in one. 1923/24

Weirauch, Anna Elisabet. **The Outcast.** 1933

Weirauch, Anna Elisabet. **The Scorpion.** 1932

Wilhelm, Gale. **Torchlight to Valhalla.** 1938

Wilhelm, Gale. **We Too Are Drifting.** 1935

Winsloe, Christa. **The Child Manuela.** 1933